SPECIAL POWERS

Civil War internment at
Newbridge Barracks and Tintown Camp, 1922–24

Sure 'twas for this Lord Edward died and Wolfe Tone sunk serene

Because they could not bear to see the Red above the Green

And 'twas for this that Owen fought and Sarsfield nobly bled

Because their eyes were hot to see the Green above the Red

LIAM DUFFY

No. 3 CAMP TINTOWN CURRAGH, 7 JULY 1923

SPECIAL POWERS

*Civil War internment at
Newbridge Barracks and Tintown Camp,
1922–24*

JAMES DURNEY

MERCIER PRESS

Dedicated to my children Brian and Tara, whose names evoke legends of Ireland

—∞◇∞—

MERCIER PRESS
Cork
www.mercierpress.ie

© James Durney, 2025

ISBN: 978-1-80690-010-7

eBook: 978-1-80690-011-4

Cover design: Sarah O'Flaherty

CONTENTS

ACKNOWLEDGEMENTS

Thanks to: Uachtarán na hÉireann Michael D. Higgins, Claire Power, Art and Aisling McCoy, Dr Rory O'Hanlon, Michael Smyth, Tony McCarthy, Sinead Brennan, Fergal Browne, Regina Dunne, Mick Healy, Dr Gerri O'Neill, Mario Corrigan, Kildare County Archivist Karel Kiely, Mark A. McLaughlin, Brendan Berry, Mike Rafter, Liam Kenny, John Evernan, Aaron Ó Maonaigh and Con Cummins.

Thanks also to Mario Corrigan and Cill Dara Historical Society, Don McAlistar, Hugh McGinn and the Slevin Family for sourcing and use of photos. Special thanks to my wife, Caroline, for her patience. Thanks to County Kildare Archives & Local Studies and Cork Public Museum for use of photos from their collections.

A huge thanks to the Mercier Press team, Dee Collins, Carina McNally and Mary Feehan, who believed in this work and who continue the great tradition of Irish publishing, and to Sarah O'Flaherty for the cover design.

INTRODUCTION

The final battles of the Irish Civil War were fought in the jails and internment camps. Confronted with an armed insurrection that threatened to destabilise the emerging Free State and wreck the local economy, the Provisional Government resorted to Special Powers to defeat the IRA. As the convening of the new Dáil had been deferred because of the disturbed state of the country, this left few forums where public concerns about the treatment of prisoners could be raised.

On the Curragh plains, over 4,000 Republicans languished in dire conditions, while in nearby Newbridge Barracks, another 1,500 men were interned. Captured Republicans soon discovered that their former comrades in arms showed less concern for prisoners than their British predecessors. Faced with general neglect, trigger-happy guards and no release date, the prisoners maintained their defiance of the Free State regime with escapes, protests and hunger strikes. The camp regimes replied with executions, harsh punishments, random shootings, careless medical treatment, and a murder that went to the top of the Irish government.

Public Safety (Emergency Powers) Act, 1923.

Public Safety (Emergency Powers) No. 2 Act, 1923.

302

ORDER BY THE MINISTER FOR DEFENCE.

WHEREAS *Michael Sheehan Newbridge Kildare* (hereinafter referred to as the prisoner) was at the date of the passing of the PUBLIC SAFETY (EMERGENCY POWERS) ACT, 1923, detained in Military Custody,

AND WHEREAS the prisoner was not before the passing of the said Act sentenced to any term of imprisonment or penal servitude by any tribunal established by the Military Authorities,

AND WHEREAS I am of opinion that the public safety would be endangered by the prisoner being set at liberty,

NOW I RISTEARD UA MAOLCHATHA an Executive Minister within the meaning of the said Act do hereby order and direct that the prisoner be detained in custody under the said Act until further order but not after the expiration of the said Act.

Dated this 9th day of August, 1923.

Signed **RISTÉARD UA MAOLCÁTA,**

Minister for Defence.

Member of the Executive Council of Saorstat Eireann.

Internment order for Michael Sheehan, Henry Street, Newbridge. He was held at the Military Detention Barracks, Curragh Camp.
Photo: Kildare County Archives & Local Studies.

1

EMERGENCY POWERS

The signing of the Anglo-Irish Treaty, on 6 December 1921, between the Irish plenipotentiaries and representatives of the British government was the best possible compromise at the time. There was, nevertheless, opposition to the Anglo-Irish Treaty from many in the Republican Movement who thought it did not go far enough. Under the Treaty, Ireland was to have dominion status and to be known as 'the Irish Free State' while six north-eastern counties would form 'Northern Ireland' and remain in the United Kingdom. Recognition of the crown and Irish membership of the British commonwealth was asserted. The British amended the wording of the oath of allegiance to the crown, but it was still, in the eyes of Republicans, an oath to a foreign king. Public reaction to the Treaty in the twenty-six counties, which would form the Free State, was favourable.[1]

A vote on 7 January 1922 returning sixty-five pro-Treaty candidates, against fifty-seven anti-Treaty, saw the Anglo-Irish Treaty narrowly accepted by Dáil Éireann, but it sealed the political split. The 'Provisional Government' provided for under the Treaty was established on 14 January, and opponents immediately rejected it as illegitimate.[2] The Provisional Government took office on 16 January 1922 and began the formal transfer of power from Britain with the handover of Dublin Castle.[3] Nevertheless, as soon as it came into power, the Provisional Government of the Irish Free State began exploring options for the imprisonment of government opponents. On 27 January, General Prisons Board chairman, Max Green, wrote to the Provisional Government out-lining how certain prisons could be administered militarily and that there was accommodation 'for 647 women and 2,038 men'.[4]

Across the country, police and military barracks were vacated and occupied by both pro- and anti-Treaty forces. On 26 March 1922 anti-Treaty IRA units held a convention in Dublin where they reasserted their allegiance to the Republic, repudiating the authority of Dáil Éireann and the Provisional Government. Delegates confirmed the appointment of a new General Headquarters (GHQ) Staff, headed by Gen. Liam Lynch, commander of the 1st Southern Division. On 15 April, anti-Treaty forces commandeered the Four Courts in Dublin for their new headquarters.[5]

However, a general election called by the Provisional Government for 16 June could potentially provide a clear indication of public support for the Treaty. The Provisional Government hoped that if the pro-Treaty faction won a majority in the election, democracy would prevail and the anti-Treaty IRA would leave the Four Courts and other buildings they had occupied in Dublin. While the general election returned a majority for the Treaty, it hardened the hearts of the anti-Treaty minority. A breakdown of the votes is revealing; of the 620,000 votes cast, pro-Treaty Sinn Féin won 239,195 (58 seats), anti-Treaty Sinn Féin 135,310 (36), and the combination of Labour (17), Independents (10), Unionists (10), and Farmers (7) won 247,082 votes. Overall, there was a resounding vote for peace and normality.[6]

Another IRA Convention was held in Dublin's Mansion House on 18 June. Gen. Lynch made proposals for unity, which were rejected. Cork IRA leader Tom Barry then proposed that, unless all British troops left Dublin in seventy-two hours, they should be attacked. When this was vigorously opposed and rejected, about half of the delegates left to join the Four Courts garrison. Lynch was considered too moderate by Liam Mellows and Rory O'Connor and was excluded from the Four Courts. He established his headquarters at the Clarence Hotel, while in the Four Courts, Joseph McKelvey was elected as the new chief of staff in Lynch's place.[7] The likelihood of a clash of arms was almost certain.

On 22 June, Field Marshal Sir Henry Wilson, security advisor to Sir James Craig, prime minister of the newly created Northern Ireland state, was assassinated outside his home in London. Two members of the London Battalion, IRA, Reginald Dunne and Joseph O'Sullivan, were later hanged for his killing. Secretary of State for the Colonies, Winston Churchill, assumed, incorrectly, that the anti-Treaty Four Courts garrison was responsible, and warned the Provisional Government that if they did not act against them, British troops would be used to retake the Four Courts When Republicans from the Four Courts garrison arrested Gen. J. J. 'Ginger' O'Connell, deputy chief of staff of the National Army, the Provisional Government was left with little choice. A decision was made to clear the Four Courts.[8] Civil war was inevitable.

At 4.07 a.m. on Wednesday, 28 June 1922, Dublin awoke to the boom of a field gun as the National Army began its bombardment of the Republican garrison in the Four Courts. Two 18-pounders, borrowed from the British, were positioned at Winetavern Street and Lower Bridge Street, and barely scratched the stone of the huge building. As well as artillery fire, the National Army used rifle fire, Lewis guns, Hotchkiss machine guns and Thompson sub-machine guns to batter the building. The Republicans had machine guns and rifles on the roof of the courts, but they were no match for the National Army's arsenal. The garrison held out until 4 p.m. on Friday, 30 June, when they surrendered to the pro-Treaty forces. Republicans suffered relatively few casualties in the battle for the Four Courts: three volunteers were killed and eight wounded. National Army forces, however, suffered at least seven killed and upwards of seventy wounded. Most of the National Army wounded occurred when mines laid by the Republicans exploded – the cause of the explosions has never been verified – which destroyed the central hall and priceless historical records dating back hundreds of years. The surrendered garrison was marched off to captivity in Jameson's Distillery, at Bow Street. From there, they were taken to jails around the city.[9]

The Provisional Government had hoped that this would be the end of the conflict, but fighting spread to the centre of Dublin and then throughout the rest of the country. Prisoners captured in Dublin during the week-long fighting were held in Mountjoy Jail, Kilmainham Gaol and Wellington Barracks, one of the first military installations taken over by the National Army. Rank-and-file anti-Treaty prisoners who undertook not to take up arms were subsequently released from custody. Around the second week of July, huts at Hare Park Camp, at the Curragh Camp, in Co. Kildare, were once again put into use as troops from the National Army arrested local Republicans and brought them to the military base.[10] Comdt Michael Love was appointed Military Governor, Hare Park Camp. Only weeks before, Hare Park Camp had housed an advance party of National Army troops who had arrived for the handover from the British army of the Curragh Camp on 16 May.[11]

One problem the British authorities faced during the War of Independence was identifying those who were involved with both the IRA and Sinn Féin. Often, sympathisers who were not involved with the Republican movement were arrested and interned. Many innocent people ended up in jails or internment camps because of mistaken identity. At the outbreak of the Civil War, the Free State authorities knew exactly who their enemies were and arrested many Republicans in countrywide sweeps before they had a chance to organise resistance.

Paddy Mullaney, the officer commanding the 3rd Battalion,

North Kildare, was stopped at a military roadblock outside Kilcock on 28 June 1922. With him in a car was Michael O'Neill, his vice-OC, and Domhnall Ua Buachalla, the former TD for North Kildare. Manning the barricade was Comdt Michael Flynn, a former member of Mullaney's unit, who was now a National Army officer. He knew that all three men were anti-Treaty and by arresting them, deprived the area of effective leadership. O'Neill and Ua Buachalla were sent to Millmount Barracks in Drogheda for detention, while the most dangerous of the trio, Paddy Mullaney, a very capable and active leader, was sent to Hare Park Camp.[12] On 20 August, Mullaney escaped from Hare Park by concealing himself in a Board of Works laundry lorry. He returned to command the 1st Meath Brigade, of the 1st Eastern Division, anti-Treaty IRA, and became a thorn in the side of the National Army until his Active Service Unit (ASU) was captured after a battle at Grangewilliam, Leixlip, in December 1922.[13]

By 1 August 1922, there were 1,986 people in military custody throughout the country.[14] Prisoners taken after the outbreak of hostilities were referred to as 'military prisoners'. In Dublin, the number of prisoners held exceeded 1,000 men, and space was becoming limited. Prisoners were initially taken to Wellington Barracks for processing and questioning, then transferred in batches to prisons at Mountjoy and Kilmainham in Dublin, Maryborough (Portlaoise) Jail, Hare Park Camp and Keane Barracks at the Curragh, where 100 men were detained.[15] The pro-Treaty authorities were less than sympathetic in the matter of prison conditions. Wellington Barracks had such an unsavoury reputation for brutality against prisoners that many men were relieved to be sent to the relative safety of a jail or an internment camp.[16]

On 24 July, Count George Plunkett, father of the executed Easter Week leader Joseph Plunkett, wrote to the Catholic archbishop, Dr Edward J. Byrne, to complain about the conditions in which prisoners, including two of his sons, George and Jack, were being kept. Count Plunkett also singled out Catholic priests who were giving absolution and the sacraments only to prisoners who undertook never to take up arms again against the Provisional Government, a significant grievance at a time when people took religious observance seriously.[17] Former Kildare TD, Art O'Connor, captured in the city centre fighting, wrote to Archbishop Byrne on this issue, too:

> We prisoners are soldiers of the I.R.A. ... We do not complain of the discomforts which are part of a prisoner's lot, but we feel that one comfort at least should not be denied us; that is the consolation of the Sacraments. For almost seven weeks we have been deprived of this consolation, because the chaplains with-hold absolution, unless, in defiance of our reason, and conscience, we admit that the recent action was wrong, and promise not to do the same in future.
>
> In common with hundreds of thousands of Irish people and many of the people's elected representatives, we deny the authority of the Provisional Government, and we respectfully submit that if a priest holds an opposite view in this matter he is not entitled to force his view as an article of the church's teaching.[18]

At the start of the fighting, the Provisional Government took several steps which covered areas dealt with or touched upon by the British under the Restoration of Order in Ireland Act (ROIA) and under martial law powers. In Dublin, the court system established under British rule was still functioning, but so also were the Dáil courts. During the first month of the civil war, issues relating to the arrest of Republican combatants seemed relatively clear to the Provisional Government in that conditions approximated conventional warfare.[19] However, Count Plunkett brought an application for a writ of *habeas corpus* before a Dáil court for the release of his son George, captured in the Four Courts.[20] On 19 July, Michael Comyn, King's Council (KC), instructed by solicitor Seán Ó hUadhaigh, met Supreme Court

Judge Diarmaid Crowley at his home to make the application, which was grounded by an affidavit sworn by Count Plunkett. After a legal argument which deemed Plunkett's arrest illegal, a writ was issued by Judge Crowley against Minister of Defence, General Richard Mulcahy and Colm Ó Murchadha, governor of Mountjoy Jail, where Plunkett was incarcerated. Mulcahy and Ó Murchadha were ordered to appear at the court at 18 Parnell Square with the prisoner George Plunkett to explain why he should be detained.[21]

The hearing was set for 26 July and Crowley also wrote to three other judges – Cahir Davitt, Arthur Cleary and James Creed Meredith – asking them to attend the court. Ó Murchadha refused to obey the writ and passed it to National Army Headquarters at Portobello Barracks, Dublin. The cabinet spent a week considering what to do in the case of Plunkett, who was a military prisoner and, as such, was viewed by the Provisional Government as falling outside any civil jurisdiction. If taken to its logical conclusion, the release of Plunkett would also have led to the release of all other Republican prisoners. Finally, the cabinet decided to use the provisional order decree to rescind the original order of 29 June 1920, which had created the Dáil courts. The provisional order decree had been passed by Dáil Éireann to allow the president and cabinet of Dáil Éireann to make provisional orders that had the same effect as if passed by the Dáil itself. That cabinet decision was taken on the night of 25 July, as the case was to be tried the following morning. Some within the Provisional Government viewed the order rescinding as illegal, and Minister for External Affairs, George Gavan Duffy, immediately resigned from the cabinet in protest.[22]

On 26 July, Crowley declared the orders invalid and ordered the arrest of Mulcahy and Ó Murchadha for their failure to appear before him to justify Plunkett's imprisonment, which he regarded as illegal. Nine days later, Crowley granted a conditional order to Kathleen Clarke, TD, to have the speaker of the Dáil, Eoin MacNeill, convene the Dáil on 11 August so that the Republican Legislature, according to Crowley, 'might be in a position to take steps to suppress the rebellion against the Republic'. At the same sitting, a *habeas corpus* order was granted for the release of Seán T. O'Kelly from Kilmainham Gaol.

Mulcahy's response to Crowley's arrest order was to have him arrested, and on 31 August, Judge Crowley was detained by what he described as 'two gunmen', as he walked along a Dublin street with a companion. He was held in a cell at Wellington Barracks, while the Provisional Government immediately abolished all the Dáil courts, except for the parish and district courts in the provinces, until an alternative form of summary justice was devised, but retained the British court system in Dublin.[23]

Judge Crowley shared a small cell with nine other Republican prisoners, one of whom was dragged out and beaten severely. The prisoner was then brought before a mock firing squad, who loaded their rifles and marched him away out of earshot. The men in the cell thought the prisoner was shot until, sometime later, he was brought back and thrown into the cell. His face was swollen, and he was missing some teeth. 'My soul sickened at the thought that I belonged to a country where such abominations were committed and paid for by the people,' Crowley said.[24] He was held in Wellington Barracks for ten days without charge, and at one stage, Crowley threatened to go on hunger strike unless he was released.[25] After his arrest and release, Crowley said the people were afraid to take any business to the Dáil courts.[26]

In mid-September 1922, three judges sitting at the King's Inn (School of Law) refused an application on behalf of Seán Beaumont, Clare Street, Dublin and James R. White (ex-captain, Gordon Highlanders), Cushendall, Co. Antrim, for writs of *habeas corpus* directing their release from custody in Wellington Barracks. The two had been arrested in a raid at Beaumont's flat on 22 August and taken to Wellington Barracks.[27] Mrs Olive Rowe, sister of Seán Beaumont, received a communication from James White, who informed her that no charge of any description had been made against him and that he believed he was illegally detained. White further instructed her to institute legal proceedings with a view to obtaining his release. Mrs Rowe believed the arrests and detention were without legal authority or warranty of any kind.[28]

In defence of their detention, an affidavit showing that a state of war existed and filed by Adjutant-General Gearóid O'Sullivan, stated:

> In suppressing these disturbances and protecting the lives and property of the people, the Army Command has found it absolutely necessary to arrest and hold in custody a large number of persons. Many of these have actually been taken in armed action. Others assist Irregular forces, or have come under grave suspicion of aiding and abetting. In the greater part of the country up to the present, there are no civil tribunals before which such persons could be brought and the charges investigated.

While admitting that Seán Beaumont had not been taken in arms and was not charged with any offence, the affidavit said he was arrested under grave suspicion of close association with Republican forces.[29]

Beaumont was subsequently taken to the Curragh Military Hospital with eleven other prisoners, from where he then escaped. His escape further complicated the matter, but the writ was refused. James White's application for release was also denied. The sitting judges agreed that the country was in a state of war and that justified the application of martial law. The Restoration of Order in Ireland Act was still on the statute book as an existing law, and as it was a standing law, it could be put in force by the Provisional Government, and the courts could not interfere with its application. This would be enough to detain many Republicans over the coming years.[30]

The Provisional Government was technically unconstitutional since the Second Dáil Éireann had officially ended with the general election of 16 June 1922. It was initially scheduled to meet on 1 July but was prorogued five times, with its first meeting postponed successively to 15 July, then to 29 July, and again to 12 August. Later, when it failed to convene, the Labour Party demanded that the Dáil reconvene by 26 August or their seventeen deputies would resign *en masse*. Ultimately, Dáil Éireann reconvened at Leinster House on 9 September, with the formation of a new Ministry by the Third Dáil. Opponents of the Treaty were absent, except for Laurence Ginnell, TD, Westmeath-Longford, who was ejected from the chamber for repeatedly interrupting proceedings. The post of president of Dáil Éireann was continued and was conferred on William T. Cosgrave, who, on 25 August, had been elected chairman of the Provisional Government at a meeting of that body.[31]

As the convening of the new Dáil had been deferred because of the disturbed state of the country, this left few forums where public concerns about the treatment of prisoners could be raised. The prisoners' plight provoked concerns and led to the formation of the Women's Prisoners' Defence League. It began, informally outside the gates of Mountjoy Jail, in August 1922, by the mothers, wives and sisters of Republican prisoners. Crowds of women were outside the gates attempting to obtain news of their missing sons, husbands and daughters, or to bring food and clothing to those whose location they had discovered. No visits were allowed and no information was supplied by the authorities. Terrifying stories circulated of beatings and torture of prisoners for information. The constant sound of firing in the jails and wounding of prisoners made the need for a Prisoners' Defence League obvious and urgent. The Women's Prisoners' Defence League (WPDL) was formally confirmed at a mass meeting of women in the Round Room of the Mansion House, and a committee was appointed with Charlotte Despard, president, and Maud Gonne MacBride, appointed secretary. They were affectionately dubbed 'The Mothers' by the prisoners and their supporters.[32]

The objectives of the WPDL were to obtain the release of Republican prisoners, gain prisoner-of-war treatment for those jailed, and help families to get news of their relatives in jails. In furtherance of these goals, the League held weekly meetings in the ruins of the Gresham Hotel, O'Connell Street, where all prison news was pooled and distributed. The League organised meetings, parades and demonstrations in support of the 'boys and girls', visited hospitals and places of confinement, sought legal aid, sent bulletins to the press and helped billet prisoners' families. The only qualification for membership was a family relationship to some prisoner and payment of one half-penny a week. Maud Gonne MacBride had a son, Seán MacBride and her son-in-law, Francis Stuart, in jail, and the welfare of the prisoners began to take up all of her waking hours. Charlotte Despard, who had hoped their protests would soften the government's approach, said, 'possibly if we had held our tongues, things would have been worse than they were. But we know the agitation has kept up the courage of our boys and girls in prison'.

On 20 September, the three women most closely identified with the prisoners' issue – Charlotte Despard, Maud Gonne MacBride and Hanna Sheehy-Skeffington – interrupted the debate in the Mansion House on a clause of the new Free State constitution. According to a newspaper report, 'Mrs Despard, standing at the rails overlooking the floor of the House, shouted out a protest against the alleged barbarous treatment inflicted on untried prisoners.' The trio were hissed at by members of the public in the visitors' gallery, while the speaker ordered her removed. 'I do not like this,' Charlotte replied, 'but I feel it is my duty.' She was escorted from the room, but Maud Gonne and Sheehy-Skeffington had to be forcibly removed, with Maud Gonne valiantly, but vainly, holding onto the front rail.[33]

In January 1923, the government banned the Women's Prisoners' Defence League as an illegal organisation. Ignoring the ban, the women continued to protest and parade and to hold regular Sunday meetings in O'Connell Street. Neither the police nor the odd stray army bullet prevented them from broadcasting news about the prisoners. When the internees were regularly released, the women of the League were there on hand to meet and greet them from the trains arriving in Dublin, while their headquarters became a rendezvous and information centre for prisoners' families.[34]

2

THE FORMER JAILED

The six weeks that followed the fall of the Four Courts saw the capture of Dublin and the Republican strongholds of Cork, Limerick, Waterford and Tipperary. Meanwhile, the National Army had swollen to 38,000 men and was well-equipped, if ill-trained. Republican numbers were far lower, with estimates of 6,000 men under arms, although they were not as well equipped as their opponents.[1] After the fall, that summer, of the self-styled 'Munster Republic' – Cork, Waterford and Limerick – the war had reached a stalemate. The anti-Treaty IRA abandoned conventional warfare and reverted to guerilla tactics. The death of Michael Collins on 22 August, in an ambush in West Cork, transformed the political climate in the country. Collins' death hardened the hearts of his fellow members of the government and the National Army. However, the search for a peaceful resolution continued throughout the autumn. A meeting between Richard Mulcahy, Minister of Defence, and former Dáil Éireann president Éamon de Valera, on 6 September, convinced Mulcahy that there were no grounds for compromise and that extraordinary methods were needed to end the conflict.[2]

On 15 September, Mulcahy sought the introduction of military courts from the Provisional Government and within ten days, the Army (Emergency Powers) Resolution was drafted and approved in the Dáil. It called for the establishment of military courts, with power to arrest, detain and sentence to death citizens found guilty of a range of offences, including 'taking part in or aiding or abetting any attack upon or using force against

National Forces'. These courts could deal with cases of looting, arson, destruction or seizure of public or private property, and unlawful possession of weapons or ammunition. It made any breach of general orders or regulations introduced by the 'Army Authorities' an offence punishable by death, penal servitude or a fine. The resolution also permitted the imprisonment 'of all or any person taken prisoner, arrested or detained by the National forces', setting the scene for a long battle between Republican detainees and the Provisional Government, one that would lead to dire prison conditions, executions and a mass hunger strike.

Despite the opposition of the Labour Party, the Emergency Powers Bill (commonly and mistakenly known as the Public Safety Act) was passed the next day by forty-eight votes to eighteen. Introducing the bill, W. T. Cosgrave denounced 'murderous attacks' by Republicans who 'must learn that they have got to pay the penalty for them'. He assured TDs that prisoners would be treated well, but 'we are not going to treat rebels as prisoners-of-war'.[3]

As the Civil War entered a new phase, more space was needed to house the growing number of Republican prisoners. The prison services were unable to cope. Jails were full and cramped, with up to six people confined to one cell in some cases. There were constant complaints about diet, disease and overcrowding. Over the following months, as the number of prisoners grew, so did controversy over how they should be treated, providing one of the few issues for which Republicans opposed to the Treaty were able to mobilise public support. In a Dáil debate, Labour deputy Cathal O'Shannon asked if the government intended to send prisoners to the African Congo. Dr Pat McCartan, a pro-Treaty deputy, countered: 'Have some respect for the nation, if you have none for yourselves.' In fact, the government was actively considering both Lambay Island and the British Territorial Island of St Helena as internment centres.

The 617-acre Lambay Island, off the coast of north County Dublin, was contemplated as it could accommodate 10,000 men, but cost, an inadequate water supply and the determined opposition of the owner, the English banker Cecil Baring, ruled it out. St Helena in the South Atlantic was also considered, but the British government would not oblige. Predictably, the measure led to accusations that Irish government methods were more draconian than any legislation introduced by the British government during the earlier War of Independence.[4]

Instead, it was decided that Gormanstown Camp in Co. Meath, formerly a training ground for auxiliary police and British military, could be converted to an internment camp.[5] Gormanstown Camp eventually housed up to 1,000 Republican prisoners, among them Tom Barry, who escaped as soon as he arrived there on 7 September 1922.[6] Preparations were also made to use parts of the Curragh Camp for the internment of up to 12,000 men.[7]

The former British cavalry barracks at Newbridge, Co. Kildare, was additionally earmarked as an internment centre. The *Kildare Observer* of 12 August 1922 announced that Newbridge Military Barracks was to be evacuated by the Civic Guard as it was to be used as an internment camp.[8] Newbridge Barracks was designed by the British army to accommodate up to 1,000 horses and 900 men. However, it was soon overcrowded with Republican prisoners and their guards.[9] Captured anti-Treaty Republicans soon discovered that their former comrades in arms showed even less concern for prisoners than their British predecessors. What was particularly frustrating was that in many cases, these former comrades were now their jailers.

Newbridge Barracks, completed in 1819, was surrounded by a twelve-foot-high wall with the main entrance off the main street. It stretched from Liffey Bridge on the Naas Road to Moorefield Road, bounded to the east and south by Kilcullen

Road. The barrack blocks stood three storeys high and were built of stone, some of which was salvaged from the nearby derelict Abbey of Great Connell. A road led from the stables at the southern (Moorefield) end through the archway of the central tower, surmounted by its water tank and cupola, eastward between the parade ground (later forming the playing fields) to the river Liffey, where the cavalry horses were formerly led to drink at what are still known as the 'watering gates' on the riverbank.[10] It was in the main centre barrack blocks, beneath the cupola, along with some huts, that the new internees were housed. The men were kept in a three-storey building with dormitories containing 30–40 beds and another three-storey building with 3–4 beds in each room. Former stables were transformed into dormitories with fifty beds, and eleven wooden huts also provided additional accommodation. Each prisoner was provided with an iron bed, pillow, mattress, sheets and two blankets. Three kitchens provided food to mess halls containing tables and benches. Toilets were situated in all buildings and in the centre of the main yard. The former recreation hall was used as an infirmary. Prisoners were allowed one letter each week, and parcels received had to be opened under supervision.[11]

The evacuation of the British Army from Newbridge led to widespread unemployment and financial hardship. Thus, another person's hardship was a source of advantage for others, with the *Leinster Leader* gleefully reporting that 150 members of the Irish Transport and General Workers Union (ITGWU) were employed at Newbridge Military Barracks, preparing the facilities for new inhabitants – the National Army – after the Civic Guards moved to Dublin. Fifty additional men were given employment at Newbridge Barracks, preparing part of it as an internment centre. Many more union members were employed at the Curragh Camp constructing prisoners' holding centres, with newspapers reporting that practically every man who was a member of the ITGWU in the Newbridge and Kildare area was now in employment.[12]

On 2 September, the *Kildare Observer* reported that the 'spacious military barracks' at Newbridge had been converted into a prison and had received its first prisoners. Seán Hayes, a pro-Treaty TD from Cork, was appointed military governor of Newbridge internment camp, with Comdt Seán Kavanagh as deputy military governor. On 5 September, sixteen prisoners who had been detained for several days at Naas Military Barracks were transported by military escort to the new internment centre at Newbridge Barracks.[13]

All new arrivals received a lecture from Governor Hayes, who welcomed them by saying, 'you will each get one knife, fork, spoon, mug and plate – three blankets and you better not try to escape and we have taken very good care that you won't, so that's that.'[14]

A special train carrying 250 prisoners from the SS *Arvonia* arrived at Newbridge railway station on the evening of 7 September. The prisoners were marched to the military barracks under a heavy escort.[15] Another 870 men arrived by rail by 15 September, while more came from the Curragh, bringing the total to 1,100 prisoners at Newbridge Barracks, according to the *Leinster Leader*.[16] The governor, Seán Hayes, wrote in his notebook on 7 October: 'we cannot take any more prisoners … we have actually 963 and 12 in hospital making a total of 977'.[17]

The SS *Arvonia* was commandeered by Gen. Emmet Dalton from the London & North Western Railway's (LNWR) Holyhead-Dublin service on 7 August 1922.[18] Subsequently, having been used as a troop transport during the capture of Cork, the steamship was sent on 30 August to Limerick to collect 550 Republican prisoners and transport them to Dublin. Among the prisoners were about fifty Fianna Éireann youths, whose ages ranged from twelve upwards. The only food consisted of tea and bread doled out twice daily. The *Arvonia* lay in Dublin Bay until 9 September, discharging prisoners in batches at the North Wall, where special trains took them to the internment camps.[19]

Having successfully escaped from Dundalk Jail, on 15 August 1922, brothers Patrick and Jim O'Keefe (Kilcock, Co. Kildare) were recaptured and detained in a school off Main Street, in Drogheda, Co. Louth. Both brothers were subsequently transferred to the *Arvonia*. Patrick O'Keefe said:

> when we arrived it was full of prisoners from Cork, Limerick and Kerry. When we got on board there was hardly any room (it was like Hell on Earth) on top and bottom decks. Jim [O'Keefe] and myself stayed on the top deck, to go below you would be suffocated with stench and foul air.
>
> We had to sleep where we were standing, some got under seats to sleep only to find that all the urine went down a channel underneath. We were like a lot of 'wicked dogs'. Bread was fired in, the best catcher getting the most. In a short time most of the prisoners got the itch or scabies. A doctor came on board and ordered their transfer to the mainland. Jim scratched his arms, went to the doctor and was put on the transfer list.
>
> On the day the relief ship came all the sick were put on board. I was very depressed over parting with Jim. Then the officer-in-charge said, 'There is room for two or three more, who will volunteer to come?' I accepted immediately, along with Kitt Lynam [Ballyfore, Co. Offaly]. I was glad to get off the ship. Jim told me, that on a few days previous, they were thinking of 'scuttling' her, with all on board.
>
> The relief ship sailed over to the North Wall, where we disembarked and went by rail to Newbridge Detention Camp (or Barracks). The rooms were big, holding about ten or twelve prisoners. The ground outside was quite large, having plenty of room to move around. A lot of the leaders were interned there. Tom Harris T.D. was their recognised leader, and I was in the same room as him.[20]

Tom Harris had mobilised for the 1916 Rising and fought in the General Post Office (GPO) and the Parliament Street area. He had served terms of imprisonment in London's Brixton Prison, Frongoch Internment Camp, in Wales, and Ballykinlar

Internment Camp, Co. Down. Harris was appointed Kildare Brigade Officer Commanding (OC) during the Truce period. Although an opponent of the Anglo-Irish Treaty he worked hard for peace in the early days of 1922. During the visit of Michael Collins to Naas in April 1922, Harris took vigorous action to prevent interference by those who held opposite views. He was arrested on 28 June 1922 by National troops on his way to attend a meeting of Kildare Co. Council.[21]

Among the prisoners from the south was Seamus O'Connor (Knocknagaoshel, Co. Kerry), a captain attached to GHQ. O'Connor was assigned to intelligence work in Munster when he was captured at a checkpoint outside the village of Pallas, on the Limerick/Tipperary border. He spent two weeks imprisoned on the *Arvonia*. O'Connor said:

> The air was unbelievably foul. After a while, we fell into a stupor … Over a hundred got covered with a revolting growth of black ulcers. The food was scarce which was just as well. Some prisoners' legs swelled up, and on leaving they were unable to walk off the ship.

O'Connor, too, was destined for Newbridge:

> Conditions were quite good, except perhaps for the food which never seemed to be enough. There were about twenty prisoners to each room; each of us had a bed and sufficient blankets. Besides the *Arvonia* contingent, there were many prisoners from the Dublin Brigade. These were well away, because they were able to get food parcels from home. We from the south were unable to get any, but the fact that they were getting parcels helped us because we filled up with cuts of bread and cold porridge which they did not need. We had brought our tools [for escaping], as such as they were, concealed on us.[22]

One of those from the Dublin Brigade was nineteen-year-old Denis O'Dea, who was arrested on 17 September 1922 near St Stephen's Green, after a civilian bystander was killed during a shoot-out. O'Dea, from 52 South Richmond Street, Dublin, was interned at Newbridge Barracks, where he began to organise plays on a temporary stage in the dining hall. It was his first time acting, and his interest developed. Following his release, O'Dea and other former Republican internees staged plays in Dublin to help raise funds for the dependents of prisoners. In the 1920s, O'Dea became a professional actor and forged a successful career, leading from the Abbey Theatre to Hollywood, USA.[23]

In the barracks, a camp council was formed and operated along military lines, with a camp OC and staff, for two battalions. Each block had an OC, and each room had a section leader. Prisoners could move freely around all day from 7 a.m. until 8 p.m. The compound was enclosed with barbed wire about twelve feet high, with an armed sentry every forty yards. It was also floodlit at night, and the sentries were often heard warning prisoners after 9 p.m. to 'put out that light'. Failure to do so could result in the sentries firing shots at the huts.[24]

Republican prisoners were also held at the Curragh military base, at Hare Park Camp and in Keane Barracks. Hare Park had been a British army overflow camp in the Great War and then a centre for internees during the Easter Rising and the War of Independence. The following letter appeared in the *Irish Independent* on 22 September:

> Sir. — As officer in charge of the Republican prisoners in the Curragh Camp, I wish to bring to the notice of the public the following: There are at present in the general hospital here two boys. J. Smith, of Dunlavin and T. Driver, of Ballymore-Eustace, aged 14 and 16 years' respectively. They were arrested by patrols of the Free State troops on the roads near their homes more than weeks ago. No reason was given for their arrest, neither of them carried arms, and no charge has been made against them. They were both kept in close custody in Hare Park prison where they were allowed no visits from their relatives. Both boys adopted the only form of protest available. They had started a hunger strike with the object of gaining unconditional release. After four days the medical officer attending them gave them his word of honour that they would be released if they stopped the hunger strike. They did so, and were removed to the General Hospital. During their convalescence they were brought before the senior medical officer not the doctor who had promised their release, and asked if they

would sign the form. They refused and claimed unconditional release, according to the promise made to them. This was refused and they immediately recommenced their hunger strike. These facts are in glaring disagreement with the accounts of prisoners' treatment given by members of the Government in the recent debate. Would the Minister for Home Affairs claim that these two boys have not been treated with cruel vindictiveness unsurpassed in the disgraceful story of English prisons in Ireland during the last six years? I leave it to the public to form their own opinion.

T. Boyle, O/C Prisoners, Keane Barracks, Curragh.[25]

The letter to the newspaper did not give the full names of T. Boyle, T. Driver or J. Smith, but it was wrong in some respects. Frank Driver was arrested on 5 July 1922 and held for ten weeks at Keane Barracks, the Curragh, being one of the youngest internees at fourteen years of age. Along with James Smyth (16), of Grangebeg, Gilltown, Co. Kildare, he went on hunger strike for release. Following promises of release, the two ended their hunger strike and were transferred to the Curragh Military Hospital. The deal collapsed when Driver and Smyth refused to sign an undertaking that they would not engage in activities against the Provisional Government. Driver was not released from custody until 11 January 1923. Smyth was transferred to Newbridge Barracks on 6 October 1922 and subsequently moved to Hare Park Camp, the Curragh. He was released from custody on 18 January 1923. His brother, John Smyth, escaped from Newbridge Barracks in a mass breakout on 14–15 October 1922; he was recaptured and interned at the Curragh Camp.[26]

On 10 October 1922, twenty prisoners from throughout the country were released from Newbridge Barracks. Thirteen of them were from 'Northern Ireland', which had remained in the United Kingdom under the terms of the Anglo-Irish Treaty. The prisoners left by train during the evening and according to the *Leinster Leader* 'had a hearty send off'.[27]

For those remaining prisoners, the future looked bleak. An entry in an autograph book from P. Smith, Hut 55, Newbridge

Barracks, recorded the boredom and routine of internment:

> A prisoner's routine
> We are up every morning for breakfast at eight
> With knife, fork, and spoon and a big mug and plate
> We march to the cookhouse and sit down in our mess
> And breakfast is ours in five minutes or less
> When breakfast is finished, we stroll round and stare
> At the house tops in Newbridge, in Co. Kildare.[28]

Sports were one way to relieve boredom. The final of a series of inter-county football matches amongst the Republican prisoners at the internment camp was played on Sunday evening, 8 October, between Kildare and Dublin. Dr Paddy MacCarvill, TD, refereed the match.[29] Paddy MacCarvill had been arrested by National troops on his way home, having attended the removal of Lt Tom Gillanders to St Joseph's chapel, Monaghan. Gillanders had been shot dead during a bank raid by anti-Treaty forces in the town. MacCarvill's arrest caused a 'great sensation' in Monaghan. He was brought under heavy escort to Dundalk Jail and subsequently transferred to Newbridge Barracks.[30]

There was a large gathering on the sidelines, and much enthusiasm occurred as county men and neutrals cheered on the two teams. The *Leinster Leader* reported that: 'A very interesting and hard fought contest found the "Short Grass" representatives proving superior to their opponents who put up a much better display then the final scores would indicate.' The final whistle left Kildare the winners with three goals and six points to Dublin's one goal and five points. The match reporter was very thorough and recorded that Kildare had twenty-one wides and Dublin, nine. Frees for Kildare stood at five, with one for Dublin. Kildare registered three 50s, while Dublin had none. The Kildare team was captained by Jer Dooley, with Michael Byrne in goal. The rest of the team was made up of Bill Gannon, Michael Breslin, Tom Lynam, Francis Lynam, Stephen Gorey, Paddy Kavanagh, Maurice Lambe, Tom Gaffney, Jim Brady, Joe Smith, Joe Martin, Peter Lambe and Jim Dempsey.[31]

A then relatively unknown Kildare player, Bill 'Squires' Gannon, subsequently became the first captain to raise the Sam Maguire Cup, presented for the first time in 1928 when Kildare beat Cavan. A veteran of the War of Independence, Gannon played for Kildare for the first time in February 1922 in a charity match against Tipperary for the Republican Prisoners' Dependents Fund.[32] Within a week of this game being played in the camp, Squires Gannon had fled from Newbridge Barracks via an escape tunnel.

As in the War of Independence, Dublin city and county accounted for more men imprisoned than anywhere else in the country. Visitors from Dublin would arrive at Newbridge Barracks by rail or bicycle. It was about twenty-seven miles by bicycle from Dublin to Newbridge, not an easy cycle in the inclement weather of an Irish winter or spring. Joe Carey, writing to Charlie O'Neill who was detained in Newbridge Barracks, said, '… I intended going down to Newbridge with a parcel for Joe [Joseph Carey, Jnr, his son] some Saturday but we have had such bad weather lately that I do not like to travel on my bike so far, you may tell him he may expect me down the first fine Saturday we get, I will hand in the parcel myself at the gate. I will also send something nice for you when I get the chance.' The letter writer also mentioned that he would bring down a football for his son 'as it is not safe to send parcels by rail at present'. Charlie O'Neill was captured in Dublin by National Army forces on what was termed 'The Night of the Bridges' in August 1922. His brother, Paddy, was also arrested and both were interned in Newbridge Barracks.[33]

Journalist Con Casey, from Tralee, was captured in December

1922. He was the organiser of the 1st Southern Division and had been adjutant to Andy Cooney, OC 1st Eastern Division. Casey was sentenced to death in Tralee, but was later imprisoned in Mountjoy Jail before being moved to Newbridge Barracks, where he would later undergo thirty-seven days on hunger strike. He worked in *The Kerryman* newspaper and resumed his post following his release from Hare Park in 1924. Casey ultimately became the paper's editor for fifteen years. He died in 1996.[34]

There were prisoners from other counties, too. Denis Barry, from Riverstick, Co. Cork, wrote to his sister Nora, from L Block, Newbridge Barracks: 'All the boys from Cork are here now, in fact any person who did work for the Country for the past 7 years are as yet together here so I am wondering who is in Cork.' L Block consisted of old wooden army huts without beds or heating.[35]

To try to end the conflict the government offered full amnesty and pardon to all Republicans who, on or before 15 October, delivered up their arms and ammunition, restored seized property, including all lands and buildings of which they were in occupation, and ceased to take part in, or aid, armed opposition to the government. Anyone granted amnesty on these terms would be permitted to return unmolested to their homes. The offer was also open to those held as prisoners by the authorities. Since the outbreak of the conflict, there had been a method of releasing the people from jails or places of internment on their giving a specific undertaking not to take part again in the insurgency.

From issuing the proclamation on 4 October to 15 October, the powers of trial and punishment were suspended. After the specified date, the government would, without any hesitation, allow the army to use the rigorous powers conferred upon it.[36] Many of the jailers had experience of being prisoners and their knowledge of the strategies that their former comrades employed was instrumental in dealing with the new circumstances. With the deadline's passing, military courts authorised to impose the death penalty were set up. The prison struggle now entered a newer, deadlier phase.

3

DOWN AND OUT IN NEWBRIDGE BARRACKS

Many of the prisoners held in Newbridge Barracks had no intention of remaining in their new 'prison', and as soon as some of them arrived, they began plotting to escape by any means possible. Brothers Patrick and Jim O'Keefe arrived in Newbridge from the SS *Arvonia* in September Patrick said, 'An escape plan got under way, to tunnel from the room to the sewer. It took a few weeks to complete, from the old Barracks into the sewer and then under the field to the Liffey.'[1] It was not that simple – there was a sequence of tunnels in progress at the one time.

The Kildaremen were not the only prisoners planning to escape. Neil Plunkett O'Boyle, from Leac Eineach, Burtonport, Co. Donegal, began work on a tunnel from R Block. He had some experience, having worked in Scottish coal mines and assisting his father, a civil engineer. It was decided to dig several tunnels, starting with G Block, then R Block, and V Block. The G Block project was halted when a lorry ran over the tunnel roof, causing the front wheel to fall in. Veteran escape artists had noticed that the sewer traps ran in a line across the quadrangle by the married quarters in the direction of the Liffey, which flowed near the barracks. A disused sawmill on the bank of the Liffey in a direct line with the sewer traps was noted as likely to afford cover to potential escapees. The prisoners were housed in two three-storey buildings in the centre of the barracks beneath the clock tower, known as the 'Cupola' building. It was about 500 yards to the river, so the magnitude of the task undertaken can be realised.

A Board of Works map of the sewerage system provided by Nellie Kearns (Eyre Street, Newbridge), Officer Commanding of the Newbridge branch of Cumann na mBan, made the tunnel escape possible. Kearns said, 'I had Free State soldiers taking messages to and from prisoners in Newbridge barracks. Dr Liam Clark and Dr Bracken from Dublin and T. J. Williams, Naas, received messages from me and sent a request for a plan of the sewage system of the barracks which I obtained from Dublin and which they received. On this plan was marked the man holes which were no longer used for sewage and through which they could and did escape several days after.'[2]

Plunkett O'Boyle and Séamus O'Donovan (Castleview, Roscommon) were the main diggers on their tunnel from R Block into the sewerage drain. A start was made by the O'Boyle group in the ground floor of a block near the clock tower. Direct descent into the sewer was not possible, and it was found that a tunnel of around thirty feet in length would have to be cut to connect with an unused sewage pipe approximately two feet high and 150 yards long, which ran under a road in the barracks and came out at the River Liffey.

With a saw manufactured from a dinner knife, a square of flooring was cut from beneath one of the trestle beds. Carefully trimmed and with the marks of cutting erased, the square fitted into place and defied detection. Using a pointed poker as a pick and a fire shovel, the work was quickly underway, as lookouts carefully watched the guards' movements. It was a tough job, and when they came across a brick wall, it took five days to get through.[3] As the work progressed, it was rendered less liable to detection as the square piece of flooring was replaced during tunnelling. The loose earth was disposed of beneath the room floor and on the top floor of another building in the camp. It was a good hiding place – the soil in this building would not be discovered until the structure was demolished in the 1960s. Day after day progress was made, with many narrow escapes from discovery when some of the guards arrived in the room, while the tunnellers were at work beneath the floor.[4]

At the same time another group led by Séamus O'Connor (Knocknagoshel, Co. Kerry) were working on their tunnel. O'Connor had made several escape bids since his capture and, with his comrades, smuggled tools into Newbridge – screwdrivers, knives and odd bits of iron – which they had used digging a tunnel in Limerick Jail before they were transferred. He said:

> We immediately set to work on a tunnel. Underneath the floor boards there was a high air space – perhaps two feet – an ideal place to hide the excavated earth. Everything had to be done neatly. There were periodic inspections for tunnels. All operations were kept as secret as possible for fear of spying.
>
> After a while, there were four separate tunnels being made by four different gangs. We came together and agreed that whichever tunnel came through first would be made available to the other teams, so that all could escape at the same time … There was a large manhole in the barrack square. This was the manhole of the main sewer, which ran right through the centre of the building into the Liffey, perhaps 300 yards away. The authorities had shown nervousness about the manhole previously, thus drawing attention to its possibilities. Now the gang in this centre block had only to sink a shaft in the appropriate room on the ground floor, and run a short tunnel to connect with the sewer which passed underneath.[5]

When the sewer was located and penetrated, the escapees' troubles were far from over. As the tunnellers entered the sewer, they found the air was so foul it was impossible to explore for a few days. One man who got into the sewer was violently ill for some time. Then there arose the difficulty of finding the correct route in a network of sewers, with one of the explorers getting lost for several hours in his attempt to find his way back. All these difficulties were overcome by the dedication of men intent on leaving their involuntary confinement. Not only was the correct route discovered, but a way out was cut from the sewer through the floor of the sawmill on the banks of the Liffey.[6]

On the night of Saturday, 14 October 1922, the men of R and V Blocks bid their farewells to each other as some were going to Kildare, Carlow and other parts of the country. There was a swift exodus as over seventy prisoners escaped. Thirty-four men from Co. Kildare, under the command of Tom Harris, made a successful escape. Patrick O'Keefe said, 'The night of the escape, Tom Harris allowed Jim O'Keefe [his brother] and Kitt Lynam to come with me. We went on the third batch and got free.'[7]

Neil Plunkett O'Boyle was among three Donegal men who escaped that night.[8] O'Boyle made his way to Dublin and was put up by Sheila Humphreys at her home in Ailesbury Road. He received a change of clothing and remained there until sometime later, Patrick Brennan brought him to Wicklow, where O'Boyle formed a flying column.[9]

At the point of entry, the sewer was large enough to enable the escapees to stand upright, but it gradually narrowed, and for the last 20–30 yards, they had to crawl with their mouths barely above the flowing sewage. The half-suffocated men emerged from the sewer in the centre of a carpenter's workshop at the sawmill on the riverbank.[10] They left it quietly in groups of threes and fours under the cover of darkness, dashed silently to the river, crossed it just as soundlessly and disappeared across the fields on the east side of the bridge out into the open country beyond.[11]

Following this successful escape, the men in V Block decided to go out on Sunday night as there was no rollcall that day and they would not be missed until Monday morning. Séamus O'Connor said:

> We were ready for escape that night [Saturday]… There were four rooms, twenty men in each room and each block was self-contained. At 8 o'clock each night the guards blew a whistle. This was the signal for all prisoners to get into their block for the night. Once you were in your own block you could not enter any other block, except by coming out in the square, which was all lit

up and under surveillance of the sentries, who were all around, in raised sentry posts. This meant that all those who were to escape should move into the four rooms of the escape block, instead of their own, when the whistle blew. After this, there was never any inspection of these rooms each night, because there was nowhere else the prisoners could go, once the square was vacated.

On Saturday night, O'Connor and his group prepared to move into the escape block, but a few minutes before the whistle blew, they received word that the escape was called off until the following night. The following morning, O'Connor was told that the escape had occurred and that over seventy men had escaped.[12] When Seamus McCann (Waterloo Street, Derry) learned of the early escape, he decided that the V Block group would go out on the Sunday night. All the block OCs arranged for as many as possible to go to Sunday mass, which effectively concealed the absence of the earlier escapees. For the rest of the day, men were assigned to come and go from R Block to create the impression that it remained inhabited. Later that day, McCann met with the other block OCs in G Block to coordinate for different groups of men to escape that night.[13]

Séamus O'Connor wrote:

> Ours were the only tunnel-diggers left. We moved into the escape block, which was mostly empty, and took over possession and control of the tunnel. The authorities knew nothing of the escape. It was in our favour that this day was Sunday … the prisoners here looked after themselves and on Sundays especially, the soldiers never made their appearance amongst us, except to man the sentry posts. As far as I know, the news spread inside, and everybody must have known of the escape.
>
> We knew nothing of the working of the tunnel or where it led – all who did were gone. A wiry diminutive lad – [William] Hussey from Killarney – was selected to go and make an inspection. He did so, and came back. He found that the Free Staters had blocked the entrance into the Liffey with inch-thick iron bars, but that the tunnellers had struck upwards and made their exit into the inside of a disused sawmill. They knew their geography because some were local fellows. The mill, however, was on the wrong side of the

river for us, and between the mill and the river any escape would be under view of the sentries; this made a successful day escape unlikely, so we decided to take the chance and wait until night.

According to O'Connor, a Dublin Brigade officer approached him and claimed that he was in command of the escape attempt because of his position. He insisted that some important Dublin men should escape first, and O'Connor's group would be in the second batch. The O'Connor group reluctantly agreed. When the whistle blew at 8 p.m. for all prisoners to go to their blocks, about 200 moved into the escape block. The key men from the Dublin Brigade were the first group to enter the tunnel. The cover of the shaft leading into the tunnel was under a bed, and the O'Connor group was gathered next to the bed. However, after the sighting of an armoured car on patrol duty outside the walls of the barracks, the escape was called off. Finally, after an anxious hour, O'Connor decided his group were going out. He said, 'I bent over and lifted the neat square board that covered the hole and placed it aside – the bed underneath which it was hidden had already been pushed aside. I signalled to Hussey, who jumped in first, and each of us who wished to come followed him. After about a dozen feet of tunnel, we got into the sewer proper. We were able to crawl without difficulty on our hands and knees. The distance seemed long. I think it took over half an hour. The noise made by crawling seemed very loud. We knew we had to pass under a sentry-box outside. It seemed incredible that the sentry could not hear us.'

The disused sawmill, underneath which the sewer passed, was on the bank of the river, and the tunnel architects knew the location well, for they bored right up into the mill house. The sewer entrance to the river was blocked, as already stated, with iron bars. When the first few escapees got out of the sewer into the mill room, they waited to give a helping hand until all those following were pulled up.

O'Connor said:

> About twenty-five had elected to follow us. Anyone who wished was free to follow or otherwise ... We decided that five of us should make the first attempt to leave the mill and cross the river; the others to wait until they were sure everything was all right and then come as they wished.

> We crawled out in single file. All was quiet. When outside we turned to the right, along the river bank for perhaps a hundred yards, in order to avoid going too close to where we knew there was an outpost on our left, and then struck straight across the river. The river was not deep and was quite fordable at the point, and helped to cleanse us after the sewer.

> On the other side of the river was a steep bank. We climbed it and into a large field. Then we were free. Never have I experienced such delight which that sense of freedom gave me when going up that field.

In the O'Connor group were: Kerrymen Pat Allman (Rockfield), William Hussey (Killarney), and William O'Sullivan, a fifteen-year-old Fianna scout from Tralee; Dubliners Jimmy Kenny and Tom O'Brien; and Joseph Nash, from Limerick City.

'I picked out the North Polar Star,' O'Connor said, 'and from it selected one bright star which I calculated should lie directly over Dublin, and we struck neither to right nor left but straight towards the star ... After about half an hour we heard continuous bursts of gunfire from the direction of the Camp. We knew then that the escape had been discovered. We learned later that a party of escapees – not the one which came with us – had been caught under fire ... One wounded man was swept down the river, got into a friendly house and escaped. Some went back through the sewer again. One going through went astray in a smaller offshoot and got stuck there.[14]

Jimmy Kenny had been in the GPO during Easter Week 1916, subsequently became OC Dublin 4th Battalion and was arrested trying to free Tom Barry from Mountjoy Jail in August 1922. Recalling the escape, he said, 'it was a hazardous operation and we were advised against it, even by our own O.C. But Séamus O'Connor was adamant. He led and we followed … And it was here I came to recognise Séamus O'Connor as a born leader. He brought us safely and astutely through dangerous territory, taking his initial guidance from the stars on a torturous journey that led across the Dublin mountains into Wicklow and on southwards, snatching rest whenever and wherever we could.'[15]

An un-named escapee interviewed in 1927, in the *Leinster Leader* newspaper (published in Naas, Co. Kildare), recalled:

The lifting of the flooring revealed a dark pit into which one dropped, 'Feet first', a voice whispered and guided one's foot to a hole in the side of the pit. Feet first and face upwards one wriggled along until his feet found an opening in the floor of the tunnel. 'Drop your feet and turn them backwards' whispered the same voice, and one found that the feet rested in about twelve inches of water, and having successfully wriggled the rest of the body through, found that further progress had to be made on hands and knees and that broken bottles, tins, etc. did not tend to make the journey easier. Holding the heel of the man in front and similarly held by the man following, progress was slow in the pitch darkness and the journey appeared well nigh interminable. The 'swish swish' of the water and the heavy breathing of the men broke the silence which was enjoined on all, save when some unlucky one made unexpected contact with some sharp obstacle.

'Talk about Lough Derg,' muttered a disgruntled voice in the rear, and a titter of laughter was sharply suppressed. And so on and on. 'Pass back word for silence. Passing under the grating' came from in front and was duly passed on. At last came an order, 'Up here', and one found the ground rising and the water was left behind. 'Through here', and still a further opening – this time through a floor. Then quickly came the orders:- 'You are in the house on the bank of the river. There is an armed guard on the bridge. When the door is opened don't walk but roll down the slope to the river and across. Don't make noise or you'll be under machine gun fire. Good luck. Make your way as best you can.' The door is opened. The lights from the bridge shine faintly on the river and one catches a fleeting glimpse of figures moving about there. Behind, the barracks we have left is outlined in electric lights. A quick roll down the slope and into the water which feels very cold. Dim figures are beside you, but no one speaks. To be caught in the river would be fatal. The opposite bank at last. Quickly way is made up the slope to a fence which you grasp and pull yourself

> over. The fence is barbed wire, but one does not discover the fact until later the condition of your hands reminds you of it. At last, filthy from contact with the sewer, wet from the immersion in the river, bleeding from hands and knees, but free, we make our way across the fields determined to increase the distance between ourselves and our late domicile. It is about half an hour later when an outburst of gun-fire tells us the escapes have been discovered and that soon the searchers will be on our track. But at last we are free and determined to remain so.[16]

The escapees climbed out of the sewer and up through the sawmill floor and out the back door. Rolling down a slope and moving noiselessly into the cold Liffey water, they waded to the other side, mindful of the sentries on the bridge, and then were out into open country through which they could flee towards Kilcullen. There was high tension the following day as those who knew of the escape endeavoured to cover the absence of their comrades. Many inquiries had been made about prisoners who were among the absentees and, by evening, it was evident that vague suspicions had been aroused by the camp authorities. With the arrival of darkness, it was decided to rush another batch for freedom.

The escape was discovered around midnight when sentries spotted movement on the bank and opened fire, wounding several prisoners. They had divided into three small parties, and it was when the first of these groups moved off from the shed on the riverbank that one of the sentries noticed. He saw their shadows passing across the fields and called on them to halt. There was no response, and the shadows moved faster. The sentry then sounded the alarm and opened fire on the moving figures, some of whom were seen to fall.

At the sound of the alarm, more garrison members turned out. The sawmill, where several prisoners were huddled, was surrounded. There were over thirty prisoners in the sewer, and when called on to come out, they refused, but when told they would be bombed out they exited the sewer quite rapidly. Thirty-seven men were caught inside the sawmill and the sewer and were returned to the barracks. A search of the surrounding fields was conducted, and a wounded man was found and brought to the barracks hospital.

The wounded prisoner stated that when he and another comrade were running along the bank of the river, they were caught in a volley of rifle fire, and both were hit. He lay on the grass for a few moments until he heard a splash and looking to where his comrade had fallen, he could see no trace of him. On the following day, troops were engaged in scouring the countryside, while others dragged the river Liffey for the body of the prisoner who was supposed to have fallen in when wounded, but they did not discover anyone. During the search of the countryside, several of the escaped prisoners were recaptured, including a railway porter who had been interned and was discovered in a hayloft in a nearby farm.[17]

In later years, Dr Joseph Roantree, residing at Moorefield Lodge, Newbridge, recalled his part in the aftermath of the escape. He said armed men called him out that night to attend to a wounded escapee. The revolvers they brandished were incidental, for he had never needed persuasion or enticement to offer his professional services to the sick. Dr Roantree gave aid to the escapee, but never mentioned who he was or his injuries.[18]

Séamus O'Connor and his group continued their freedom flight from Newbridge. He said, 'There were Free State posts at Naas and Blessington. It was important that we went between them. Our star carried us right through.' The seven escapees were treated to a breadcake at a friendly house where Tom O'Brien gave the 'poor woman' a half-crown for her hospitality. They then went on to Brittas, Co. Wicklow, where they bought a few bottles of stout at a pub, paid for by O'Brien's last half-crown, then proceeded to Rathfarnham, where they arrived on Tuesday morning, 17 October. Saying goodbye to their Dublin comrades, O'Connor and the remaining four escapees made their way back home to the south, travelling across country through Wicklow, Carlow and Tipperary.[19]

The breakout from Newbridge Barracks was the largest escape in Irish penal history. All told, 112 men escaped successfully, and a further thirty-seven were captured in the tunnel. In total thirty-five men from Co. Kildare escaped from Newbridge Barracks on the first night of the escape, including T. J. Williams, who had received the plans of the sewer from Nellie Kilbride. It was the largest group by county. Carlow county was next with twelve escapees, followed by Dublin with ten and Wicklow with nine. Three of the Kildare escapees, James Dempsey (Celbridge), Jimmy Whyte (Naas) and Patrick 'Paddy' Bagnall (Kildare Town) had been released from Dundalk Jail in August when Frank Aiken's men had captured the town from the National Army. They had been subsequently recaptured and interned in Newbridge Barracks. Having escaped from Newbridge, Paddy Bagnall joined the Rathbride Column and on 12 December was recaptured in a dugout at Mooresbridge, outside Kildare Town. Tragically, if he had not escaped, Paddy Bagnall would have cheated the firing squad on 19 December 1922.[20]

William Byrne, Ballysax, the Curragh, had been captured near Baltinglass, Co. Wicklow, in July 1922. He had commanded a column of around sixty anti-Treaty Kildare men and had taken part in the holding of Ballymore Eustace village and the takeover of Baltinglass Barracks. Byrne stated: 'I was captured with a few of my men, while covering the retreat of the main body. We were taken to Carlow and then to the Curragh and later to Newbridge Internment Camp. I made my escape through the sewer. I reported [back to duty] and took command of my Battalion …'[21]

Another escapee was James L. 'Séamus' O'Donovan, a native of Castleview, Co. Roscommon. O'Donovan was educated at Glasgow's prestigious St Aloysius' College, and at University College Dublin, where he earned a Master of Science degree

in Chemistry. He was the IRA Director of Chemicals during
the War of Independence and invented the explosive compound
'Irish War Flour' (named after its appearance: it was a nitrated
resin using the ingredients of resin, flour, acid and potassium
chlorate) and 'Irish Cheddar' (named after the explosive
cheddite). While experimenting with explosives in May 1922,
he blew off two fingers and part of a third finger on his right
hand. O'Donovan escaped from Newbridge on 14 October and
was sheltered by Kildare Brigade Adjutant Dick Harris in a hide
in the locality. He served as Acting Director of Munitions as
well as Director of Chemicals until his recapture on 15 March
1923. O'Donovan was imprisoned until 17 July 1924. 'It was the
second last day,' he said. 'Seán Russell was about the only one
that was left over until the following day.'[22]

Quartermaster, 3rd Battalion, North Wexford Brigade, Denis
Allen arrived at his home in Ratheenagurrin, Co. Wexford, on
the late evening of 17 October, having fled from Newbridge on
Saturday, 13 October. He was arrested the next morning, along
with three other local Republicans, by National Army troops as
they sat down to breakfast. The raiding party arrived, detained
the four men, and took away a rifle, two revolvers, ammunition,
and documents. All four men were transported to Enniscorthy
Castle.[23] Allen escaped again on 19 November 1922 from Wexford Gaol.[24] Another Wexford escapee was Patrick Whitty (17
William Street, Wexford), whose brother Joseph would die the
following year whilst interned in Newbridge Barracks.

Four men from Co. Cork escaped, including Capt. William Reynolds (24) of Ballinhassig. A veteran of the War of
Independence, Reynolds had arrived at Newbridge having
been held on the SS *Arvonia*.[25] Three escapees from Armagh
– Frank Hannaway (Castle Street, Armagh), Eugene Loughran
(Ballycranny) and Charlie McGlennan (Ballybrodden) – were
caught at Dublin's Amiens Street Station by National Army

troops and brought to Hare Park Camp, the Curragh. They were members of the Fourth Northern Division whom Free State troops had rounded up in September 1922. At the outbreak of the Civil War, the 4th Northern had dumped their arms and tried to remain neutral, making their camp near Ballybay, Co. Monaghan, an unarmed encampment. It was all to no avail, as they were surrounded by National forces, captured and they ended up interned in Newbridge Barracks.[26]

Escapee Joe Smyth was recaptured at an arms dump at Oghill, Monasterevin, Co. Kildare, along with Christopher Tracey and Thomas Melia, on 24 November 1922. He was imprisoned in Mountjoy Jail, took part in the mass hunger strike in October 1923 and was one of the last on the fast when it was called off. He was subsequently interned in Tintown No. 2, the Curragh.[27]

On 26 November, National Army troops surrounded Broughall's public house in Kill, Co. Kildare, and arrested John Rafferty and Jimmy Whyte (of Naas), both were escapees from Newbridge Barracks. Whyte had escaped from Dundalk Jail in August and had been recaptured and interned in Newbridge. They were unarmed at the time and were brought to Naas Military Barracks. They were subsequently held at Newbridge Barracks and Tintown Camp.[28]

The engineer of the successful tunnel, Neil Plunkett O'Boyle, led a group of escapees in the Wicklow mountains who became a thorn in the side of the National Army. They were responsible for several fatal attacks on National troops and the burning of Senator Bryan Mahon's mansion at Mulloboden, near Ballymore Eustace. On 8 May 1923, the column was finally cornered at a cottage at Knocknadruce, Valleymount, where Neil Plunkett O'Boyle was shot dead, having surrendered to overwhelming National forces to save the lives of the civilian occupants. It was alleged Col Roger McCorley shot O'Boyle twice in the face as he held his hands up in surrender. Neil Plunkett O'Boyle is remembered as the last man to die violently in the Civil War.[29]

Immediately after the great tunnel escape, Seamus O'Toole, Rathdangan, Co. Wicklow, fled from Newbridge Barracks by climbing onto a building's roof and gaining access to the outer wall, where he jumped down and slipped away unnoticed by the sentries. His freedom was short-lived. On 5 December 1922, Seamus O'Toole and Myles Carroll (Killedmond, Borris, Co. Carlow) were shot dead while crossing a field at Straduff, Shean, near Garryhill, Co. Carlow. They were on the run at the time with three others: Ned Kane (Castledermot), Hugh O'Rourke (Tinahely) and Charles Byrne (Myshall). Two men were captured, while Charles Byrne escaped.

They had stayed the previous night in the Shean area and were warned of an approaching raiding party, so they left the house where they had been sheltered. As they crossed the fields at the foot of Knockdrinagh Hill, they were spotted by National Army troops and told to halt. The IRA group opened fire, and the National troops returned fire. Both Carroll and O'Toole were hit. Carroll died instantly, and O'Toole shortly after. Kane and O'Rourke were captured. The two prisoners were taken to Tullow. The bodies of their fallen comrades were taken to the mortuary at Carlow Military Barracks. The remains of Myles Carroll were refused entry into St Fortchern's church, Rathanna. Subsequently, the priest who delivered the graveside prayers in Rathanna graveyard wore a dark suit, not the usual white vestments. This was in stark contrast to the reception given to the remains of Seamus O'Toole, who had the burial of a hero in his family grave at Cranerin, Rathdangan.

By the end of the year, prisoners faced a new weapon intro-duced into the Free State's arsenal – official executions. To prepare for the execution of more prominent prisoners, four young volunteers were shot by a firing squad on the morning of 17 November 1922 at Mountjoy Jail. Emergency legislation, the Public Safety Bill, was passed in the Dáil on 27 September 1922, granting the Provisional Government special powers of punishment for anyone 'taking part in or aiding and abetting attacks on the National Forces', possessing arms or explosives 'without the proper authority' or disobeying an Army General Order. Leading anti-Treaty figure Erskine Childers was executed on 24 November, while four more leaders – Rory O'Connor, Liam Mellows, Dick Barrett and Joe McKelvey – faced the firing squad on the morning of 8 December 1922. They were shot in reprisal for an attack on pro-Treaty TDs that resulted in Seán Hales being killed, and another, Padraic Ó Maille, seriously wounded. The four Republicans had been imprisoned since the summer and had not been charged with any offences. It was an act of vengeance and reprisal. Republicans regarded it as political murder.

In a message from the 'Camp Council to the men of the Irish Republican Army imprisoned at Newbridge Barracks on the occasion of ordering a signal mark of respect to be paid to the murdered Rory O'Connor, Liam Mellows, Joe McKelvey, and Dick Barrett,' the prisoners PRO, Thomas Boyle, wrote:

> Four of Ireland's Bravest have been done to death on yesterday morning by the Free State government as an official reprisal.

> You are hereby ordered to remain calm and disciplined under this and other great trials to which as Irishmen and soldiers of the I.R.A. you are being subjected.

> Determined to hold steadfast and look on the Republican cause as the finest and noblest that could be endorsed and to continue to be prepared to offer yourself if necessary, as those did, is the finest tribute that you can offer to their sacred Memories.

> May they rest in peace.[30]

The *Irish Independent*, 11 January 1923, reported on the arrival of

500 prisoners at Newbridge railway station, under heavy escort. The men were marched from there to the barracks. Among the prisoners was Daniel Cahalane (Ahakeera, Dunmanway, Co. Cork), arrested in October 1922 when he was seventeen. As a group of prisoners was being transported from Dublin by train to Newbridge station, an unnamed prisoner jumped out of a carriage onto the line and escaped. When the train stopped at the station, several soldiers pursued, but they found no trace of the escapee. There was a heavy fall of snow at the time.[31]

4

BACK IN THE CURRAGH AGAIN

By late 1922, most anti-Treatyites were imprisoned in internment camps. The Curragh Camp was the main place of
detention for male prisoners, while all women detainees were
held in Dublin. Republican prisoners were held in the old huts
at Hare Park, the Military Detention Barracks, known as the
Glasshouse, and in Keane Barracks (now Pearse Barracks). Hare
Park Camp, which was utilised as an internment camp during
the War of Independence, was again put to the same use in
1922. Over 300 prisoners arrived there on the evening of 27
November. Around 200 prisoners were removed that afternoon
on military lorries from Dublin's Wellington Barracks – 100
prisoners had been removed previously – and brought in convoy
to the Curragh.[1]

Visits to prisoners were not allowed except by special permit
from the adjutant general, which was only granted in exceptional
circumstances.[2] A scathing letter on the conditions of Hare
Park Camp from T. McCarthy (North Kensington, London),
published in the *Cork Examiner*, stated:

> At Hare Park, Curragh no parcels of food, tobacco, books, or toilet
> requisites are allowed. It is a great pity the authorities cannot grant
> even the same privileges which Irish prisoners enjoyed under
> British rule. To deprive the men of reading matter might have a
> serious effect on the mental condition of many of the prisoners. The
> deprivation of tobacco also is an unnecessary hardship. Clothing
> may be sent to the prisoners, but surely the Irish Government,
> like the Governments of all civilised peoples, clothes its prisoners
> properly. It seems that Christmas is to bring no amelioration in
> the condition of the prisoners. Lack of Christian feeling at this
> festive season is not a pleasing testimony to the Irish Catholic
> spirit. It is certainly not a good omen for peace.[3]

In reply, the following telegram was received from Hare Park Camp, and printed in the *Freeman's Journal*, which stated: 'Inform prisoners' friends parcels allowed here for Christmas.' C. Murphy, Supervisor, Hare Park.

'Suggestions having been made that the restrictions on the delivery of parcels to Irregular prisoners might be relaxed during the Christmas season, a *Freeman's Journal* representative made inquiries on the subject in Government circles yesterday. Mr Kevin O'Higgins, Minister for Home Affairs, had nothing to say except that he understood that the adjutant-general at Portobello Barracks was giving his consideration to the matter. At Army Headquarters, it was stated that there was no general official routine in regard to the granting of privileges to prisoners, and that the position in each prison was being considered separately. There were cases where privileges could not be increased, and others where they had been withdrawn owing to the conduct of the prisoners. In the latter cases, it was being considered whether the privileges, or part of them, formerly enjoyed by the prisoners, be restored. Anything relating to the matter would be announced by the military authorities in the way they thought fit. It is understood, however, that parcels may be sent to Mountjoy, but only one to each prisoner.'[4]

A letter addressed to Hare Park Camp from Phylis Ryan of the Irish Republican Prisoners Dependents Fund asked if the authorities supplied clothes as they 'repeatedly got request from dependents of prisoners for clothes – boots, underclothes, suits, overcoats, etc. …' Furthermore Ms Ryan stated: 'Are we not right in understanding that you – or any body of men – who undertake to keep prisoners in confinement make yourselves responsible for all their needs as long as they are in your charge? Such needs must reasonably include clothing as well as food and shelter.' The letter writer said that she had received a satisfactory answer from the deputy governor of Newbridge Barracks in this matter.[5]

In reply, the camp commandant, Seán Ó Caomhanaigh, said, 'Precisely the same conditions prevail here as obtain in Newbridge. Prisoners are allowed underclothes, boots, outside clothes, but we are not instructed to supply them with overcoats. Our supplies on hand may not have been equal to the demand, so that only the more urgent cases were taken into consideration in the first rush …' Blaming the prisoners' distribution methods he continued, 'When clothing is distributed it is given to the gentleman inside whom the prisoners call their "Quartermaster." The immediate distribution is in his hands … I believe our scheme is not only complete but, believe me, very generous and I think there is very little room for complaint.'[6]

Relatives often wrote to the different prisons and internment camps enquiring if their family member was held there. A letter of reply sent from Hare Park Camp to Miss Myra Lucey, Jervis Street Hospital, Dublin, who was enquiring of the whereabouts of William Barrett, of Newmarket, Co. Cork, who was arrested several months before, stated, 'Your enquiry of 20th inst., re William Barrett to hand. There has never been a prisoner of that name in any camp on the Curragh. We also made enquiries in Newbridge and find he is not there.' Ms Lucey had enclosed a stamped addressed envelope for her reply.[7]

On 29 August 1922, a Republican prisoner, Richard Monks (Barrack Street, Kilkenny), was shot dead as he allegedly tried to escape from custody. An inquest was later held by Dr J. O'Neill, deputy coroner for South Kildare, and the jury found that the deceased had died from the effects of a bullet wound, fired by a sentry 'in the discharge of his duty.' The provost marshal, Comdt Peter O'Mara, stated that the prisoner had been trying to escape from custody and when Monks refused to halt was fatally shot by a sentry. Evidence of identification was given by a fellow prisoner, but no detainees were asked what really happened. This was the first of many fatalities in the Curragh Camp.

An article titled 'Silent Bishops' in the anti-Treaty *Poblacht na hEireann* announced: 'Most Rev. Dr Foley, Bishop of Kildare and Leighlin has not denounced the murder of Vol. R. Monks when a prisoner at the Curragh ...'[8]

Patrick Mulrennan (30) died of gunshot wounds in the Curragh Military Hospital, on 3 November 1922. He was a member of the East Mayo Brigade and a native of Kiltymaine, Lisacul, Co. Roscommon. Mulrennan had been shot and injured after a disturbance among prisoners at Athlone Military Barracks on 6 October. The National Army claimed the men were trying to escape. Mulrennan was brought to the Curragh Military Hospital, where he died from gunshot wounds.[9]

In consequence, prisoners knew that their lives were at risk and even wrote black-humoured ditties about it. One went:

The only view from Tintown Two

Is the top of the Curragh Steeple

If we go near the wire, the sentry will fire

And 'tis all for the Will of the People.[10]

Future Taoiseach, Seán Lemass, was intelligence director when he was arrested on the quays near O'Connell Bridge in November 1922. He was sent to Hare Park Camp on 28 November, where his leadership qualities ensured his immediate election as a line captain – leader of one of the three or four lines of huts in a section of the camp. Lemass was not noted for sociability but was very much one for personal care and a sharp sense of self-improvement, his biographer John Horgan wrote. His toothbrush moustache earned him the popular sobriquet 'Charlie Chaplin', but he was also known as the 'Jewman', probably because of his dark Mediterranean looks and his love of economics. Despite his family owning a gentleman's outfitters, Lemass received no money from them while he was incarcerated. He had to learn the hard way to get money and as he was good at poker, the young

Lemass often relieved some of his fellow prisoners and military guards of their wagers.[11]

Another biographer, Brian Farrell, wrote that Lemass' imprisonment toughened the young man, and he became a typical IRA 'hard man' who 'was impatient of politicians, not unduly sensitive to the feelings of his companions, unwilling to complain about the harshness of his treatment and unshaken in his confidence'. (Not all good qualities for a man who served as Taoiseach and leader of Fianna Fáil from 1959 to 1966.) It was during his early imprisonment that the young Lemass turned from a gunman into a student. His political apprenticeship began when he developed his broader interest in public affairs and began to read any books he could lay his hands on dealing with economics.[12]

Robert C. Barton was also detained at Hare Park. He had been one of the Irish plenipotentiaries negotiating with the British government representatives in 1921 and had recommended the Treaty proposals to the Dáil. Personally, he was unconvinced it was the best settlement. However, Barton did what he felt was his duty, but then he switched allegiance and joined the anti-Treaty faction.

Barton had been appointed as minister for economic affairs when De Valera formed an 'Emergency Government' on 25 October 1922, as a rival to the Free State government and to give legitimacy to the anti-Treaty forces. The position carried no power as De Valera's government was not in charge of the country, but Barton received a call to attend a cabinet meeting shortly after its formation. Having surrendered in the Hamann Hotel in July 1922, Barton subsequently escaped from Portobello Barracks and was staying at the Oakley Road home of Áine Ceannt, widow of the 1916 executed leader Éamonn Ceannt. As Barton cycled away from his safe house, he was recognised by two National Army soldiers in a passing car. They stopped and arrested him and took him to Wellington Barracks, from where he was sent to Mountjoy Jail and subsequently Hare Park Camp.[13]

While he was detained, his cousin, Erskine Childers, was arrested at the Barton family home in Annamoe, Co Wicklow. Childers was found in possession of a pistol, which he claimed was given to him as a present by Michael Collins. Because he was found under arms, Childers faced the death penalty. He was a political scapegoat and, as the Republican head of propaganda, was blamed for anti-Treaty IRA activities and paid the ultimate price. The Emergency Act had been in operation for a month, yet no one had been executed for being in possession of unauthorised weapons or explosives. To pave the way for Childers' execution, four young Dublin volunteers, arrested with revolvers, were shot by a firing squad on the day of Childers' trial, 17 November 1922. That evening Kevin O'Higgins defended the action in a rambling exposition in the Dáil 'If they took, as their first case, a man who was outstandingly active and wicked in his activities, the unfortunate dupes throughout the country might say that he was killed because he was a leader, because he was an Englishman, or because he combined with others to commit rape.'[14]

Despite his trial, only one outcome was likely. Erskine Childers was executed by firing squad in Beggar's Bush Barracks on 25 November 1922. His execution was a political decision taken at the highest level. Robert Barton was disillusioned by the death of his cousin. He had always been close to Erskine Childers. Robert Barton's father, Charles, had been very much a surrogate father to Childers, and when he died, Erskine had become something of a father figure to Robert Barton. When Childers was married in 1904, Robert Barton was chosen as his best man, not Erskine's brother, Henry. The two cousins had been converted to the cause of Home Rule in 1908 and both had volunteered for British military service on the outbreak of war in Europe in 1914. Two of Robert Barton's brothers, Thomas

Eyre and Charles Erskine, were killed in France during the war. Robert was posted as an officer to Dublin during Easter Week 1916, serving at Richmond Barracks, where the rebel prisoners were held. Here he underwent experiences which led to him joining Sinn Féin in the summer of 1918 after his military service was complete. Erskine Childers also joined Sinn Féin, armed with a note of recommendation from Robert Barton.[15]

By November 1922, the estimated number of military prisoners was 8,338.[16] The *Leinster Leader* of 9 December 1922 reported that 350 prisoners were conveyed by special train during that week to the Curragh siding for internment at Hare Park Camp. It further stated that a 'man named O'Connor, from Kildare, is lying in a serious condition at Mercer's Hospital, Dublin, suffering from a bullet wound in the thigh. He arrived at the hospital from Kildare on Friday night'. There was no indication whether the military had shot the prisoner.

A letter from Col Comdt Dunphy, adjutant, Beresford Barracks, Curragh Camp, dated 10 January 1923, and in connection with a missing parcel, stated that they had distributed '1,486 parcels to prisoners during Christmas Season'. The parcel, which contained cigarettes and cake was addressed to Hare Park, but the prisoner, John Harmon, was in Hut 54, Newbridge. Seemingly, another prisoner named Harmon in Hare Park received the parcel.[17]

On 25 January 1923, Fianna Éireann scout Daniel Foley (17), died from illness at the Curragh Military Hospital. He was a prisoner at Hare Park Camp and had been admitted to the hospital on 23 December 1922, suffering from pleurisy. His cause of death was recorded as acute tuberculosis and syncope. Foley was active since 1919 and was imprisoned from September 1922 in Tralee and Limerick, and was then transported on board a merchant steamer, SS *Slievenamon*, to Dublin in late

November 1922. From there he was sent to Hare Park Camp. It was claimed that Foley was subjected to ill treatment while a prisoner in Tralee Jail and that the harsh conditions on the SS *Slievenamon* led to the illness which caused his death. Foley was removed from Limerick Jail on 24 November and was four days on board the *Slievenamon*. According to a pension application later made by his family 'neither food nor bedding was provided for 398 prisoners during the four days voyage'. Roger O'Connor (Tralee), the prisoners medical officer, claimed that he had recommended Foley's release on medical grounds to both the governor and medical officer of Hare Park, but that his recommendation was turned down.[18] Daniel's two older brothers, Timothy and John Foley, were interned at Tintown Camp. Timothy Foley was released on 18 December 1923.[19]

A period of guerilla warfare had begun in the autumn of 1922 after the National Army took all the major towns and cities in the conventional opening phase of the war. As the National Army broke up many of the large IRA units and gradually gained the upper hand in the fighting, the holding camps at the Curragh began to fill up. On 14 February 1923, another special train arrived at the Curragh Siding with 100 prisoners from Kilkenny Jail, bringing the total at the Curragh to 1,500 internees.[20] A week later, another special train with 200 prisoners arrived at Kildare railway station. They, too, were escorted to Hare Park Camp. Several hundred prisoners arrived by rail from the south and west that weekend, also, many of them from Limerick and Kerry. They too were conveyed to the Curragh.[21]

Since the number of detainees continued to grow, further facilities were required and work began on a series of new prison camps to be known as Tintown 1, 2 and 3. The huts were sheeted with corrugated iron (tin), hence the name 'Tintown'. This complex of huts dated from the British army period and had contained a veterinary hospital, horse baths, a segregation camp and lazarette stables.[22] Tintown No. 1 Camp opened in early 1923 and was designed to accommodate about 600 men. Tintown No. 2 and No. 3 were later located on the right and left of No. 1 Camp. Tintown 2 would hold 800; Tintown 3, had 1,600–2,000 men.[23] M. J. Burke, Chief Architect, Board of Works, designed the Tintown Internment Camp.

Construction on the camp began on 23 November 1922 and No. 1 Section was completed by 15 January 1923. No. 2 Section was completed by 24 January 1923. The construction was carried out in part by Dublin building contractors. Their work consisted of lining the inside of the huts with felt and timber sheeting, and later, fitting felt to the roofs. The sheeting of the huts left a space between the outside galvanised iron and the inside sheeting of about four inches. Continuation of the concrete floors was to render tunnelling an impossibility, although the floors were serrated rather than flat. The converted stables made very large huts – roughly 180 feet by 29 feet – each accommodating more than 100 prisoners. Control of electric light was completely in the hands of the camp authorities, with a power switch being placed outside the compound.

Comdt William 'Billy' Byrne was appointed on 28 January 1923 as military governor, of Tintown No.1 Camp.[24] Some internees remembered him 'as a very decent man'. Mick O'Hanlon said, 'When he threatened you, you knew he did because he had to do it'.[25] Byrne received little or no instructions on how to run the camp and only received index cards for each internee on 18 April 1923. (Most of the internees were from Mayo, Limerick, Kerry and Dublin.) Orderly officers were present at the morning count and monitored those prisoners, appointed by their own line officers, carrying out their fatigues. The orderly officers were to oversee the general running of the camp during the day and then were present at the evening count at 7 p.m. before prisoners were locked in for the night.[26]

According to Joe Keane (Stradbally, Co. Laois), 'there is a leader for each hut, then a leader for each 300 men and then the camp staff who deal with the entire management'. Keane, as a member of the camp staff, had no fatigues or menial chores to carry out and was involved in the administrative side of the camp organisation.[27] Prisoners were eventually allowed to organise themselves in a variety of activities, including education. The only legitimate way out of the camp was to sign a declaration not to take up arms against the government. A few did sign, but in doing so, they were barred from the IRA and dismissed in disgrace if they were already a member.

Each prisoner was supplied with a bed mattress, pillow, sheets and three blankets. Toilets were located thirty metres from each hut. Wash houses with cold water and bath-houses with hot water in a separate building were always open. There was a kitchen for every four huts and a dining hall with tables and benches adjoining each kitchen. Six wooden huts were used as an infirmary, staffed by three military doctors and nurses with daily visits. Two censored letters and a parcel were allowed per week.[28]

Life in Tintown, like any camp or prison, was monotonous and unpleasant. Sanitation was inadequate for the thousands incarcerated. Internees were cramped together with little or no privacy. The huts were leaky, draughty and some of the windows were broken. Joe Keane wrote in a letter to his sister Brigid, that it 'was very cold and the rain gets in easily. It's just the same as a hayshed'. In the Irish winter, freezing blasts of air coming across the flat plain of the Curragh penetrated the cracks in the walls, forcing the men to sleep in their clothing. Rations received by the internees were supplemented by parcels from home. Throughout his stay in Tintown Joe Keane requested all kinds of food and his own toiletries – a comb, toothpaste, soap and razors.[29]

Food was a common source of complaint. Rations were the same as those issued to the National troops, but the prisoners were eventually allowed to cook their own food. When asked in the Dáil by Wexford TD Richard Corish to state the amount of food allowed per day to prisoners, Richard Mulcahy replied, 'the following is the normal ration scale for prisoners in the internment camps:

Milk 0.5 pints
Bread 16 ozs
Meat 12 ozs
Tea 0.5 ozs
Sugar 2.5 ozs
Vegetables (fresh) 8 ozs
Potatoes 12 ozs
Oatmeal or rice 2 ozs
Fridays:
Fish 8 ozs
or eggs 2

Corish then asked if the rations varied; in reply, Mulcahy said he was unaware. Ceann Comhairle (Speaker of the Dáil) Michael Hayes said it could sometimes be larger or smaller but did not elaborate on how he knew.[30]

The supply of foodstuffs and milk to the internment camps was a recurring problem. Lt D. O'Kelly, quartermaster, Tintown No. 2 Camp, complained to the governor that 294 tins of condensed milk were requisitioned on 11 March 1923 and that the central stores at the camp were only able to supply eighty-four tins, leaving a balance of 210 tins due. The following morning, he asked for 147 tins of condensed milk but received none. In a letter of complaint, Lt O'Kelly stressed, 'I may add this state of affairs is continuous since opening of Camp, and it is impossible to guarantee supplies.'[31]

Michael 'Mick' O'Hanlon arrived in Tintown No. 1 in

the spring of 1923. The Tintown camps were enclosed by two high metal fences running parallel. Between them was a coil of concertina barbed wire. Three-storey guard towers were manned by armed guards with powerful searchlights. Mick wrote to his cousin Paddy O'Halnon at the family farm at Mullaghbawn, Co. Armagh.

Hut A
Tintown No. 1
Curragh
1st March 1923
Dear Paddy

Just a line to let you know that I have arrived at the above address and having a fairly good time here. We are allowed papers, parcels etc so we are as well off here as on the *Argenta* [a prison ship in Belfast Lough]. My brother Pete and Johnnie McCoy are in No. 2 camp. We can walk up and down twenty yards about (barbed wire and sentry in between) but dare not talk or signal to one another across without serious risk.

I hope the ploughing is going ahead. I am sorry I cannot give you a hand this Spring. I hope you don't get fed up with the extra work but the weather is not too bad. Did anything happen Gerry lately? I heard the other day that he was in bad health. You might remember me speak of Peadar O'Donnell, Tirconnail, he is in the same hut with me. [*sic*.]

With the best of wishes etc etc to everybody.

Paddy O'Hanlon had been wounded in a confrontation with National troops in August 1922 at Dungooley Cross on the Louth/Armagh border. He was shot several times and was lucky to survive. The soldiers left him lying beside an outhouse while they searched the area. When he was finally taken to Dundalk Infirmary, Paddy's loss of blood was so severe, his leg had to be amputated above the knee. With the aid of Bridie Agnew, a friendly nurse, Paddy O'Hanlon was smuggled out of the hospital and brought back to Armagh.[32]

Tomás Ó Maoláin (Thomas Mullins), who had spent several

months in the Curragh's Rath Internment Camp during the War of Independence, wrote '… daybreak, one wintry morning found me again face-to-face with my old friend – and enemy – the Curragh. Tintown 1 proved to be reconditioned Cavalry stables, the floors of cement and studied with concrete blocks. That was my first disappointment.' Ó Maoláin had escaped through a tunnel from the Rath Camp in September 1921 along with over fifty other prisoners. He maintained that if it could be done before, it could be done again, and he wasted no time in getting his bearings for the inevitable escape attempt.[33]

Tragedy was soon omnipresent behind the wire. Tubercurry Rural District Council (Sligo) voted a motion of condolences to one of their members, Thomas Pat Gallagher, on the death of his son, Patrick Gallagher (22), who had died from an accidental head injury in the Curragh Military Hospital on 4 March 1923. A group of prisoners had been play-acting outside Hut 43 in Newbridge Barracks, and men were being tossed in turn in a blanket. Gallagher had fallen out of the blanket, which split inwards, while being tossed in the air. He struck his head in the fall, received a brain compression and was brought to the Curragh Military Hospital. The young farm labourer from Cashel South, Tubercurry, had been active locally from 1920 with Tubercurry Company and had been arrested in August 1922 and interned in Newbridge.[34]

5

THE EXECUTIONER'S SONG

Early in the morning of 13 December 1922, the searchlight from the Curragh Camp picked up a group of men near Rathbride on the edge of the Curragh plain. Hours later, National troops from the Curragh arrived at a farmhouse at Mooresbridge, the home of John and Mary Moore. The soldiers searched the farmhouse where Annie Moore (daughter of John and Mary) and one or two men were arrested. They then went into the stables across from the front entrance of the farmhouse. A soldier banged his rifle butt on the floor and heard a hollow sound. After a quick search, the soldiers found an entrance to a 'dug-out' and threatened to throw grenades in unless the occupants surrendered.[1]

Ten men and one woman, Annie Moore, were arrested and the 'dug-out' yielded ten rifles, 200 rounds of ammunition, four bombs, two grenades, and food supplies. Two .45 revolvers with fifty rounds of ammunition were also found. Annie Moore had a Webley revolver, possibly slipped to her by one of the men. The soldiers assaulted several of the detainees – Annie Moore was allegedly struck by a rifle butt, as also was Tom Behan. Annie Moore claimed Tom Behan was killed by a blow of a rifle butt on the head at the scene, while the official version is that he was, 'shot while trying to escape', from the Military Detention Prison, known as the Glasshouse. The authorities claimed that Behan was shot dead while trying to escape through a window in a hut at Hare Park Camp, and issued the following official statement later on the same day:

> An irregular named T. Behan, Rathangan, County Kildare, arrested at Moore's Bridge, near the Curragh, on the occasion of

the discovery of a dug-out containing men, arms and ammunition, endeavoured to make good his escape this morning by trying to remove the sash from a window in the hut in which he was detained at the Curragh. He ignored the warning of the sentry to desist, and was fired upon and fatally wounded.[2]

Mick Sheehan (Newbridge) was a prisoner in the Glasshouse – so-called because of its glass roof – at the time and thought it highly unlikely that an experienced volunteer like Behan would try to escape through such a small window. Other sources, including an eyewitness, claimed Behan was killed when he was arrested at Rathbride and not in the Curragh, and that this was a fabrication to cover up his unlawful killing.[3]

Annie Moore was taken in a lorry to Mountjoy Jail, in Dublin, while the men were roped together and brought by lorry to the Curragh Camp. The men were members of the anti-Treaty unit which operated in the Kildare-Curragh area and was known by the Free State authorities as the 'Rathbride column'. It was led by Comdt Bryan Moore, Rathbride, and consisted of Tom Behan and Joseph Kelly, Rathangan; Pat Moore (brother of Bryan) and Patrick Nolan, Rathbride; brothers Stephen and Jimmy White, Joseph 'Jackie' Johnston, Patrick Mangan, Patrick 'Paddy' Bagnall and James O'Connor, all from Kildare town.[4] At least five of the men were actively employed or had casual employment on the local railway.[5]

The Rathbride column operated against the railway line, goods trains and the National Army in the vicinity of Kildare. In October, the group had sent a runaway engine down the main Kildare line. A railway bridge near Kildare was blown up and an engine and some wagons, from which the driver and fireman had been forcibly removed, were sent crashing into it. On 11 December 1922, two engines were taken from a shed at Kildare and sent down the line towards Cherryville. One engine ran out of steam and did no harm, while the other overturned and blocked the line for some time. A third engine was also removed at Kildare and driven into the turntable pit at the station; additionally, a wagon of coal was run into the pit. On another occasion, the column ambushed a party of troops at the Curragh siding, wounding two. It was also alleged that goods trains had been looted and shops robbed in the area, a claim denied by the supporters and families of the men.[6]

The Rathbride column's campaign against communications to and from the capital was quite successful. As the main priority for the Provisional Government was law and order, Kevin O'Higgins provided the clearest view on the situation from Government Buildings. He told his colleagues: 'We are dealing with anarchy under cover of a political banner.' His colleague Eoin MacNeill, whose son was killed in action fighting with the anti-Treaty forces in Sligo a month earlier, counselled a brutal solution: 'The Irregulars have acted very intelligently. Defeated on what we may call the military front, they have shifted their whole campaign to the sabotage front.' He advised giving priority to the execution of the culprits. 'This should be done now and on a sufficient scale to strike terror into the plunderers and destructionists.'[7]

On 3 October, the government had issued a proclamation, published the next day in the newspapers, offering an amnesty 'to all those in arms against the State, who deliver up the weapons in their possession, and cease to take part in armed opposition to the Government on or before' 15 October. Anyone found under arms after this date would be tried by Military Courts and could face execution. Furthermore, prisoners could also be freed if they agreed to take an oath 'that I will not use arms against the Parliament elected by the Irish people or Government for the time being responsible to that Parliament'. The response was limited.[8]

Gen. Mulcahy said the increasing bitterness of the conflict had resulted in soldiers taking the law into their own hands and that this new Act was a means to stop the killing of prisoners in this way.[9] On 15 October, the day the amnesty offer expired, special powers regulations were put into effect immediately. A month later, the first official executions took place. Four young Dublin volunteers arrested in the city were found guilty of carrying loaded revolvers without authorisation and were shot by a firing squad on 17 November. When Republicans retaliated against TDs who had voted for the Special Powers Bill, killing Seán Hales and wounding Padraic Ó Maille, the authorities executed four interned IRA leaders: Rory O'Connor, Liam Mellows, Dick Barrett and Joe McKelvey.[10]

The authorising of the use of execution as a weapon in the arsenal of the government was, for many, a step too far. As a form of reprisal, it was described by Thomas Johnson of the Labour Party as 'murder most foul, bloody and unnatural'.[11] Kevin O'Higgins explained that 'a certain number of men were garrotting this country and they had to deal with them with the only weapons at their hands. It would be criminal to allow the Government to be garrotted for want of using that weapon in a sufficiently strenuous manner.'[12] The execution policy was met by silence from the Catholic church, although Dr Edward Byrne, archbishop of Dublin, objected in private, saying it was 'unjustifiable from the moral point of view'.[13]

A decision was taken to execute seven men of the Rathbride column. It was to be the largest single execution of the Civil War. Sometime between 13 and 18 December, seven of the ten men arrested at Mooresbridge – Bryan Moore, Stephen White, Jackie Johnston, Patrick Mangan, Patrick 'Paddy' Nolan, Paddy Bagnall and James O'Connor – were charged before a Military Committee of being in possession, without proper authority, of ten rifles, 200 rounds of ammunition, four bomb detonators, and one exploder. They were found guilty and sentenced to death. The sentence was carried out at 8.30 on the morning of

19 December. It is not known which army unit supplied the firing squad, but it appears that they were brought in from another command. It is possible that it was the 'Dublin Guards' – a crack unit formed around members of Michael Collins' old assassination group 'the Squad.' Comdt Daniel McDonnell, a former intelligence officer for the Squad, was present at the execution and, at least in the case of Stephen White, was the informant to the registrar. Their bodies were buried in the yard adjacent to the Glasshouse.[14]

Before their execution, Fr Donnelly, chaplain to the troops on the Curragh, administered to the seven condemned men. They were shot by a firing squad, one by one. It is said they sang 'The Soldiers' Song' and shook hands with their executors before being shot. As the officer in command, Bryan Moore volunteered to be the last to be executed. Two of those arrested at Mooresbridge, Pat Moore and Jimmy White, were spared. The question remains why. It is possible that Jimmy White was on guard, slipped his revolver to Annie Moore, and so was not armed. But it was probably a step too far to execute two sets of brothers at the one time. The public outcry would have been too great.[15]

In their final hours the men were allowed to write letters to their relatives. Bryan Moore wrote one last letter to his mother and father on 18 December 1922, with the address of 'Hare Park Prison.'

> Dear Mother and Father, – I am about to be executed in the morning and I wish to bid you good-bye, and to ask you to pray for me and the rest of the boys.
>
> I had the priest this evening and will see him again tonight. I am resigned to die. God comfort you both.
>
> Tell Johnny to pray for me. – Your loving son, Bryan.[16]

Paddy Nolan had for some time a premonition of his fate and was striving to reconcile his friends and comrades on his imminent death. He was engaged to be married to Bryan Moore's sister, Annie Moore, and said: 'If I died for Ireland, wouldn't you be proud?' Paddy and Annie were to be married on Christmas Day 1922, but it was not to happen.[17] On 18 December, Paddy wrote to his 'Elder Brothers and Sisters' from 'Curragh Camp Prison'.

> My Dear Brothers and Sisters, – Now that I am about to part from this world, I ask you for one favour – be kind and good to Father and Mother, and never dishonour the Cause for which I die – a Free and Independent Ireland. I bear no ill-will to any person. Fond Sisters and Brothers, pray for me. Good-bye forever. Paddy.[18]

One prisoner, Paddy Bagnall, was a two-time escapee, having been released from Dundalk Jail in August when Frank Aiken's men had captured the town from the National Army, and having been recaptured and interned in Newbridge Barracks, he fled there through a tunnel in October. This time, there was no escape. Of his execution, Bagnall said, 'We are all here, seven of us – Johnston, Mangan, White, Moore, Nolan, Connor & I. We are all to go "west" together … I hope it lets old Ireland free. We are not afraid to die … We are dying happy anyway. So goodbye old Kildare …'[19]

The Curragh killings brought the toll of executions for December to nineteen. By the end of the Civil War, the Free State had authorised the execution of seventy-seven; this was fifty-three more than the British had executed during the War of Independence.[20] In a similar situation in Co. Kerry, a group of volunteers captured under arms were pardoned, having undertaken an oath not to attack Free State troops or cause damage to property. Because of their part in robberies of local businesses, it is known that the Rathbride column was not well regarded in the locality. The executions might have been the government's way of firmly stamping out insurrection and putting a halt to lawlessness in the area.

Jackie Johnston's mother wrote a scathing letter in the Republican newspaper *Éire. The Irish Nation*, in reply to a *Leinster Leader* report, which accused the men of local robberies:

> When he was taken prisoner (no arms been got on his person), he and his companions were cruelly beaten by First Staff Officer (vouched for by an eye-witness), tied up with electric wire and taken off to the Curragh to be executed six days afterwards.

> His parents received no notification of arrest or execution until long after the foul deed was carried out and the first and last letters permitted by him to write were not received until eight days afterwards.

> The dug-out was described as a huge warehouse containing several tons of food and loot – where in reality it was no more than able to contain the men who were captured, and who used it only as a refuge in any emergency. His mother can empathically state that her son never did any looting in the surrounding district and was in no way connected with any of the robberies of shops in Kildare as stated in the Press.[21]

Jackie Johnston was only eighteen years old; two of the other men executed – Bagnall and White – were nineteen. Sinn Féin referred to the executions as 'One of the most ruthless acts of the Free State Government in the whole course of their war on the Republic ...' The remains of the seven executed men were exhumed in October 1924; six were re-interred in Grey Abbey Cemetery, Kildare, while James O'Connor was re-buried at Bansha Cemetery, Co. Tipperary. Seán Lemass delivered the oration at Grey Abbey. At the conclusion of his oration, Lemass said that the mothers and relatives of these men would be prepared to give them up again in the same cause, and they were proud that their sons had given their lives bravely for the Republic.[22]

6

TINTOWN TUNNELS

Comdt Byrne was determined that there would be no repetition of the escape via a tunnel of about fifty men from the Rath Internment Camp, at the Curragh, in September 1921. More powerful searchlights were used and there were regular inspections for tunnels. Potential escapees were not discouraged, though.[1] Several tunnels were constructed. A tunnel started at Hut 18, where Mick Sheehy (Rhode, Co. Offaly), was the chief engineer. When that tunnel was discovered in March 1923, after clay was uncovered during a routine search, military policemen shot into the tunnel's exit. They then proceeded to demolish the interior of the hut, move the men out, and closed up the hut.

Another tunnel was started nearby in Hut 17, with Jim Foley, of the Dublin Brigade, in charge.[2] The most successful tunnel was begun by Peadar O'Donnell, the prominent Donegal Republican who had been captured in the Four Courts in June 1922. O'Donnell became involved in Irish Republicanism through his initial participation in socialism as an organiser for the ITGWU. When he was unsuccessful in establishing a branch of the Irish Citizen Army in Derry, he joined the IRA and led guerrilla activities in Donegal and Derry during the War of Independence. O'Donnell, a member of the Executive of the anti-Treaty IRA, was in the Four Courts when it was attacked by National troops in June 1922. He was arrested shortly after the fall of the Four Courts.[3]

O'Donnell was moved from Mountjoy Jail to Tintown No. 1 on 12 January 1923. He had been hoping he would be transferred to Newbridge Barracks, where his brother Joe was interned, but instead Peadar was sent to the Curragh. On the train journey to Kildare from Dublin, O'Donnell slipped through the crowd of prisoners organising groups to stick together by county for accommodation. About twenty-five men from Limerick and another twenty-five from Mayo banded together and were in O'Donnell's hut, No. 1. As a senior officer, O'Donnell was appointed as Officer Commanding (OC) of the 600 prisoners at Tintown No. 1 and 'set to work fixing things up'. Internees in camps had more control over their living conditions than those in jails. O'Donnell wrote: 'Our living huts were large and had concrete floors serrated like stable floors, and we had spring beds. We could cook and distribute our own food and organise the camp life generally.' Discipline, in the beginning, was strict, with according to O'Donnell, '... strange as it may sound during my time in Tintown, everybody was out, and most of them at [physical] jerks, at 8 o'clock every morning.[4]

The new internment camp was surrounded by heavy rows of barbed wire, with sentry posts on platforms at intervals. Powerful lights illuminated the boundaries of the camp at night, as military police patrolled around. Prisoners were locked in their huts, and during the night, the military police would unlock the doors and stage head counts, often flashing lamps on the faces of sleeping prisoners or pulling down the bedclothes to ensure that a bed was occupied. At 7 a.m. the doors were opened and the men went outside for exercises and washed with running water behind a street of huts. Orderlies carried in breakfast for men, or men prepared their own. Hut inspections were carried out around 10 a.m. and all huts were expected to be clean and tidy, with beds made and all men indoors. The internees stood at ease at the foot of their beds and, at the command of their hut leader, sprang to attention and numbered off, while National Army officers checked the count. Each hut supplied orderlies for drawing food, for the cookhouse, for fatigue work and for latrine duty. What most prisoners found the worst was the noise and bustle and the lack of privacy. Escape occupied the minds of most internees and there were to be many successful escapes.[5]

O'Donnell was approached by Mayomen Tomás Ó Maoláin and Paddy Cannon, who suggested they dig an escape tunnel. Ó Maoláin had successfully escaped from the Rath Camp in September 1921, and brought his tunnelling skills to this new escape bid.[6] Patrick 'Paddy' Cannon, from Cornacushlan, Islandeady, had been captured at Castlebar in August 1922 and, with six others, had quickly escaped from Athlone Barracks, but was recaptured.[7]

Ó Maoláin said, 'Our quick survey of conditions, during our settling-in period, convinced us that specific precautions had been taken to dealing with tunnel possibilities. Our cement-floored huts were flat on the ground so there would be no repetition of the Rath Camp repository for clay. Mathematical calculations became highly important, as we sought a dump for the 5,000 cubic feet of refuse that would accrue from a tunnel almost 200 yards long.

'Another obvious precaution was the unusual distance of the barbed wire from the huts. On the opposite side of the only entanglements under which a tunnel might be possible a new internment camp was already under construction. So, we were once again face-to-face with that inevitable race against mankind's eternal enemy – Old Father Time.'[8]

Ó Maoláin knew time was of the essence, as this meant that even if the tunnellers succeeded in escaping from Tintown 1 Camp, their exit would lead them into a similar camp under construction, which was surrounded by a further series of entanglements and obstacles, for which wire cutters would be needed. So, the word went out through Edward 'Dixie' Wallace, that a wire cutter was essential for the escape plan to work. His sister, Newbridge Cumann na mBan activist Nellie Wallace, smuggled in a double-action wire cutter through a friendly army guard.[9]

Peadar O'Donnell quickly identified one of the three huts assigned to the 'hospital wing' as the ideal location to begin digging a tunnel to freedom. The huts were then almost empty, so one, according to O'Donnell, could accommodate an escape tunnel. He approached the camp medic, Dr Francis P. Ferran, a Derry native active in Co. Mayo.[10] Dr Ferran was a TD for Sligo-East Mayo, and had been interned in the Rath Camp in 1921, where he was the camp doctor. Arrested again in 1922, he was now the camp doctor in Tintown No. 1. Once again, Dr Ferran focused his energies on the well-being of his fellow internees, which soon numbered above 600. His own health was neglected as a result, and he suffered from bronchitis and lingering chest pains.[11] O'Donnell approached Dr Ferran to use his hospital huts to assist with a tunnel escape. O'Donnell's plan involved some of the men pretending to be unwell to facilitate their transfer into the hospital hut, from where they would begin their tunnel. Dr Ferran listened attentively and then replied, 'That can't be. I won't have any part of the hospital used for that.' O'Donnell pressed his case but was to discover that the Derryman's principles would not be so easily compromised. Ferran even offered to resign as medical doctor if O'Donnell pressed ahead.

'It was no good,' O'Donnell wrote in his memoir *The Gates Flow Open*: 'Dr Ferran would not have any part of his hospital improperly used. He had accepted the huts from the enemy M.O. as a hospital, and as a hospital he would use them ... I had never met Dr Ferran before we came together in Tintown,' recalled O'Donnell, '... but there was no mistaking the mettle of the man.'[12]

O'Donnell declared he would be quite prepared to see

an escape tunnel started under the altar in the prison chapel. Since he was housed in Hut 1, the Tintown tunnel originated there, not from the hospital huts as initially planned. Tomás Ó Maoláin and Paddy Cannon proposed that they sink the shaft of the escape tunnel in their hut. As there were 116 occupants – mainly from Dublin, Mayo and Limerick – in the hut and no option to keep the escape secret, O'Donnell gathered all the men around him. They were all sworn to secrecy and vowed not to speak of the tunnel outside the hut.[13]

Comdt Owen O'Brien (32), Holycross, Bruff, Co. Limerick, was in command of the Limerick tunnelling contingent. O'Brien was captured by the National Army in September 1922 and detained in Limerick, Kilmainham and Mountjoy prisons before being transferred to Tintown. He was a member of the Irish Volunteers since 1917 and was vice-commandant of the East Limerick Brigade during the War of Independence. According to Michael 'Mick' O'Hanlon (Mullaghbawn, Armagh), O'Brien a 'fair-haired and very nice man' worked on the escape tunnel from Hut 1 but died before it was completed.[14]

O'Brien contracted a slight cold on 4 March, which developed into double pneumonia. He recovered but had a relapse on 13 March and died at 3 p.m., on Good Friday, 30 March. His relatives were left in ignorance of his illness until a telegram reached them the following day to say Owen had died. The prisoners rejected the coffin provided by the National Army authorities and had their own coffin made. *Éire* reported: 'The scene was touching, as the body of their dead comrade was taken on their shoulders from the hospital to the morgue and thence to the lorry which removed it to where it was given in charge of the relatives of the deceased.' The funeral took place from St John's cathedral, Limerick, on Easter Monday, to Mount St Lawrence Cemetery where Owen O'Brien was interred in the Republican Plot.[15]

The first job of the would-be escapees was to make an entrance before beginning the tunnel. Tomás Ó Maoláin said, 'Number one was, of course, the mouth of our shaft, which, necessarily, would be within our hut, with its concrete floor.' The floor was serrated in nine-inch squares, and eight of these were cut out in one piece and set on a piece of flattened corrugated iron, upturned at the sides to form a container which fitted exactly into place. This was an exceedingly labour-intensive task carried out by Jimmy Kilroy with a large nail and a piece of cloth-wrapped metal instead of a hammer. The improvised trapdoor, with a hidden wire handle which enabled it to be lifted up and down in position over the mouth of the shaft, was soon completed.[16]

The tunnel was started from the doorstep entrance to the hut, as according to Mick O'Hanlon, 'the Staters never searched the doorstep'.[17] The mouth of the tunnel began in front of a large stove, which stood in the centre of the hut and faced the main entrance. This position protected the trapdoor from footsteps and offered cover for the many squatters, who always sat around such a stove in cold weather. To prevent the trapdoor from being walked upon, a tin mug or stool was generally placed on it, and Ó Maoláin said, the arrival of 'visitors from other huts, from whom our activities were concealed, was a constant irritation'.[18]

Concealing the uneven edges of the trapdoor became an urgent problem, and the solution was to apply soap along the crevices and over the wire handle. The weekly soap ration of the hut was commandeered, and beards became the fashion. A five-foot shaft was dug and an estimated forty yards of tunnelling was to follow.[19] Mick O'Hanlon said, 'The Mayo fellows did most of the tunnelling'. Among those he mentioned were Jimmy Kilroy, Paddy Cannon (a teacher), Paddy Hegarty, Jimmy Donnelly, Big Paddy Cannon and his cousin Willie Malone (OC Westport Battalion), Tommy Reidy and Tomás Ó Maoláin, some of whom were professional miners and had worked on a tunnel while held in Athlone. 'Two men worked at a time below,' O'Hanlon said, 'one digging and the other hauling. They made bags out of sheets and the bags were brought back filled to the shaft and there they lay until night came.'[20]

Jimmy Kilroy solved the problem of earth dumping from the tunnel by stating that there was about 7–8 inches of space between the outer and inner walls of the hut, which was where the clay from the tunnel could be concealed. By chance, the tunnellers had procured the most efficient of all tunnelling tools, a bayonet which sped its way through the wall of clay, which was fairly dry because of sand in it. The wooden panels in the hut wall were removed and replaced one by one as occasion demanded for the receipt of the clay. The corrugations outside were short of the ground, and some had to be packed from the outside of the hut to keep the earth from slipping down. Groups of potential escapees ran around the camp to keep themselves fit for the escape.[21]

Work on the tunnel proceeded with lookouts kneeling on their beds to keep an eye on the approaches to the hut, a patrol being announced by a few short whistles. Those below stopped working, waiting for the signal to begin again. O'Donnell re-called a humorous story when, during a night of tunnelling, the alarm was raised by a sharp whistle. 'Everybody sprang to his task at one,' O'Donnell wrote, 'the shaft was sealed, the boards in the wall replaced, watchers flopped into bed and in a few moments everything was still. And again came the warning whistles: softer, less urgent. Red John Gallagher who had been in charge of the work was up on his elbow, Mick O'Hanlon beside me made a sharp movement of his hand and whispered an enquiry. And then again came the whistles. Red John got out on the floor to cross over and question the whistler …' to discover that Jerry Purcell whistled while deep in a slumber. Gallagher cursed in frustration and put his hands around Purcell's throat, waking the sleeper in a panicked roar.[22]

A few hand-picked footballers were placed outside the hut, on sentry duty, in case a ball hit the hut and dislodged the clay hidden behind the partitions. At night, at least two workers were underground – one at the face and the other to haul back the clay. Lookouts placed their beds under the windows of the hut, knelt on them and peered into the darkness for the approach of the nocturnal military police who made frequent counts at every unlikely hour. When the military policemen arrived for a sudden inspection or raid, the signal was given, and the tunnellers ran to the mouth of the tunnel and waited there while the count was taken. Dummy beds were made up in the corner of the hut where the electric bulb was intentionally broken in case men working on the tunnel could not get up in time. According to O'Hanlon, 'dummies' made up to represent a person, that were 'authentic works of sculpture' were placed in the absentees' beds in the gloomiest corner of the hut.[23]

When the military police went for a tea break at 3 a.m., the tunnellers would then pack their gear away for the night and get some sleep. Time had been lost constructing the trapdoor and shaft, and time was running out as a new compound, Tintown No. 3, was nearing completion. Subsequently, the tunnel became a twenty-four-hour job, in shifts of two hours underground at first, but shortened considerably as conditions worsened. Tommy Heavey (Westport) said, 'How long did we remain down at a time below? About an hour for it was hot and clammy'. The tunnel took about six weeks to dig after the construction of the trapdoor and shaft, and ran for forty-two yards.[24]

The tunnel was dug without supports, so was kept low and arched. When the air became too bad, a fan system was achieved for ventilation. Holes were made in the walls of the hut with a hot poker to allow air to circulate. Tunnelling was difficult and dangerous work, where the sandy soil of the Curragh was prone to shifting, resulting in quick tunnel collapses. Occasionally, there was a frightening cave-in, but the main thing was not to panic when this happened. Peadar O'Donnell was caught in one such cave-in, but his head was free, so he avoided the terror and waited until the man behind him freed his body from the clay.[25]

Acting on information supplied by a military chaplain, raids were conducted by engineers looking for the tunnel. The raids were on surrounding huts, but Hut 1 only received a brief visit. In the early hours of the morning of 18 March 1923, however, the doors of the hut were suddenly flung open and several guards marched in. The sentries had seen them coming and warned the tunnellers who were quickly in bed. Lights were switched on as the guards made their way to the centre of the hut and stopped at Peadar O'Donnell's bed. An officer said, 'You are Peadar O'Donnell, dress immediately and come with me.' As O'Donnell was leaving, he said resignedly to Tomás Ó Maoláin, 'I suppose I am for it.' He was right. O'Donnell was transferred to Mountjoy Jail and missed the impending escape.[26]

Mick O'Hanlon replaced Peadar O'Donnell as OC. As a precaution, the tunnellers suspended all activities for two days. They then returned to tunnelling and had more problems – direction, lighting and fresh air. Jimmy Kilroy solved all three simultaneously. Candles provided light, but Kilroy suggested that the tunnel could be lit by electric light. His fellow inmates shook their heads in despair. Electric bulbs were few in those days and electricians were even scarcer. Then, one day, Kilroy appeared with a cache of electric wire, bulbs, fuses, and other electrical implements. To the surprise of his comrades, he began hooking up the wire to the tunnel.[27] Kilroy laid the wire inside the wall and under the roof, where Tom Scanlon (Sligo Town) made an electric connection. They then ran the wire with attached bulbs along the ceiling of the tunnel. When the bulbs, viewed from the shaft, ran straight, the tunnellers knew the tunnel was also straight. Tomás Ó Maoláin said, '… it is easy to picture our pride and joy as that heavenly beam lit up the innermost recesses of our underground lair'. When the light switch was turned off, the men in the tunnel knew a raid was in progress and stopped work and began again when the light came back on.[28]

7

ZERO HOUR

Meanwhile, the new internment camp beside Tintown No. 1 was almost ready, and the lighting over the new barbed wire barriers indicated that prisoners and additional guards would soon occupy the camp. Spurred on by this, the tunnellers forced a bayonet, which they had acquired for digging, to the surface, revealing that they had gone about thirty-five yards to a spot beside the last wire entanglement. Another day's work would take them clear of the wire, but close to the new glaring lights. They had no option but to go the following night. Zero hour was set for 10 p.m., Saturday, 21 April. Mick O'Hanlon had given a workman £1 for a wire cutter. Civilian workers were escorted into the camp by military police, and this workman 'lost' a wire-cutter while on duty.[1]

The bayonet was once again forced to the surface and this time it came up beyond the wire. Jim Boyle (Foxford, Co. Mayo) had a copy of P. W. Joyce's *The Geography of the Counties of Ireland*, in which roads and rail lines were located for the escapee's countrywide route to freedom. Landmarks had been picked out to make for when escapees got out of the camp.[2] (The Curragh was described as 'a gently undulating plain, covered with a fine velvety elastic sward, perpetually green'.) Once escapees had left the camp, Ballymore Eustace village on the Liffey served as the gateway to the Wicklow Mountains; Celbridge, in the north-east of the county – the route to the west – had safe houses at Cardwell's and O'Connor's; the railway line at nearby Kildare Town was the route to the south.[3]

At 7 p.m. on the night, the prisoners received their final count, and the orderly officer reported there were 479 internees in No. 1 Camp and thirty-seven prisoners in the hospital huts. Those in the huts who were leaving through the tunnel said their goodbyes to those remaining due to illness, wounds, or duty.[4]

The night of the escape was quite stormy and misty, with occasional heavy showers. A sentry was positioned just beyond the wire, and as each sentry met one another at intervals during the night, they called out 'No. 1 Post and all's well.' The escapees were instructed to move in groups of six at a time, with a man in charge of each group, and a ten-minute interval between each group. The man who oversaw each group stood by until his party left, then he followed. (Some other prisoners recorded that they went out in groups of ten, or eleven.)[5]

First into the tunnel were Tomás Ó Maoláin and Tommy Reidy, armed with their newly acquired wire cutters. Tommy Reidy was known as the 'Prince of Tunnellers' after his experience tunnelling in Athlone Barracks. When the tunnel was discovered before he could escape, Reidy was moved to Mountjoy Jail and then to Tintown.[6] Ó Maoláin crawled behind Reidy, his face and hands blackened, and his boots tied around his neck. Reidy pulled back the last layer of earth from the exit shaft and slowly stuck his head up, only to withdraw it immediately and whisper: 'It's as bright as day and there's a sentry not five yards from us!'

The exit hole – fourteen to eighteen inches wide – was about three yards inside the wire of the new camp, at a point where there was complete darkness at night. Reidy and Ó Maoláin waited patiently until the sentry moved away on his rounds, presumably to keep warm. Reidy exited the tunnel, followed quickly by Ó Maoláin. He said, 'So ever on the alert, we forged ahead to the entanglements on the far side of the new Camp … By the time we had cut our way through the entanglements, there was a bloodstained trail in our wake, but that was a minor detail just then.' With the wire cutters, they cut their way through the barbed wire into the new compound and tied a handkerchief to the opening so those following would find the hole in the wire.[7]

Tommy Heavey oversaw the fourth group of six designated escapees: 'Instructions were issued as the sentry passed up and down, and you waited until you heard his steps retreating, then you dashed to the washhouse of Tintown 2 camp which was about twelve to fifteen yards away, and there you waited for your six men. Then you made for the far lower corner of the wire which we had been warned that there was surgical adhesive plaster which was to mark the spot where Tom Mullins had cut his way through. Then when we got through we crawled under the wire and we waited for our six, and off we started to make our way.

'We travelled in what we thought was the best way. We ran for quite a while … we went along blindly for there was nothing to guide us … At first we saw the old Water Tower (which is visible high up on the plain of the Curragh in the Curragh Camp), but then we lost it. I thought that would be a guide, but we could not see it.' The group slept in a thicket on a landed estate and, having been discovered by a worker the next morning, headed for the Wicklow mountains in the Kilcullen direction. Hungry and desperate, they went to an isolated cottage where they received food and were directed towards Blessington, in Co. Wicklow. At a house near Lacken village, a local schoolteacher volunteered to bring the group to meet Plunkett O'Boyle's Column.[8]

Billy O'Sullivan maintained he was the twenty-third man out of the tunnel. Arrested on 2 July 1922, he was held in Mountjoy Jail until his transfer to Tintown with Peadar O'Donnell. 'There were only 3 huts in our camp, and 100 in each hut, and only one hut knew of the tunnel … I was in charge of No. 3 section for 11 men were to escape at a time, 10 men and a leader. We had a big ball of twine to the mouth of the tunnel, and the last man out would pull the twine to tell the men at the head of the tunnel that they could now go ahead as the tunnel was clear … I told my group we're not going far, for if we do get out we don't know where to go. I went less than a mile where we lay in the furze. There was a main road outside and we didn't know it was a main road till we saw the lorries on it.' O'Sullivan's group hid in the furze for the night, avoiding troop searches. That night, they moved out towards Ballymore Eustace and approached a house where they asked for assistance. A woman there said, 'you're some of the escapees', and gave them a cake of bread. Pointing north-east, she said, 'You can see the Wicklow Mountains from here'. The group headed towards Wicklow, but it would be twenty-nine days before Billy O'Sullivan made it back to his home area in Kerry.[9]

Each group of escapees went their separate ways towards their respective home areas. Tunnellers John Bird (Dublin) and Willie Malone (Westport) were not recaptured. Malone returned to his home area in Mayo and was on the run until 1924. John Bird, a member of the 3rd Dublin Battalion, died of tuberculosis in 1927, aged thirty. His poor health was blamed on his captivity and tunnelling practices.[10]

Another batch of escapees headed to the north Kildare home of Cardwell's of Celbridge.[11] Mick O'Hanlon claimed he was the last man out of the tunnel. He lost one of his boots and, tying the remaining boot around his neck, O'Hanlon walked over twenty-two miles (36km) to the home of Art O'Connor, Elm Hall, Celbridge.[12] Jim Colbert and Liam O'Callaghan were with him. Jim Boyle caught up with them as they crossed the Curragh plain. O'Hanlon said, 'We could see the lights of the Curragh [camp] and we waded across the Liffey catching each other's hands. Then we lay in the furze and slept. We found the Kildare people were good whenever we called in for food. We came to a cottage and the sons of the house were in the Free State army. But they gave us milk and bread and told us where our supporters lived and the people who weren't so good.'[13]

Some escapees never even got out of the new camp compound. A military police patrol came across six escapees in the Riding School. Several more military police arrived, and they rounded up four more prisoners who were hiding behind some cement blocks in the new camp. None of the prisoners had their boots on.[14] Subsequently, troops rushed into Tintown 1 Compound and, on opening No. 1 Hut, discovered that the entrance to the tunnel was fully exposed. A count was taken which revealed seventy-one men missing from the previous rollcall of 114.[15] Two men, Patrick Brennan and John McCoy, were also found to be missing from the hospital. McCoy had been certified by Dr Comer as having scabies and was placed under Dr Ferran for treatment, but it was a ploy to get him to the hospital so he could escape.[16]

Tomás Ó Maoláin, Paddy Cannon, Paddy Hegarty, M. Heneghan, Gus Hughes, Jim Browne, Tom Scanlon and Paddy Kelly made their way towards Kilcullen. Ó Maoláin said, 'Now that we were technically free, it was a case of each group for itself … Once again our luck held, even in one extremely tight corner. Soon, the whinny of horses was music in our ears, as we hastened past a famous Racing Stable. But, it was only when we crossed a main road, and headed for the open country, that we really began to breathe freely.' In Kilcullen, they hid in the roof of a two-storey vacant house, owned by a brother of Patrick Brennan, the hut commandant. According to Cannon, Patrick Brennan's brother arrived the next day and brought them to a house where the escapees had a wash-up.[17] The group proceeded towards north Kildare, where, by chance, they met Joseph Doyle herding sheep. Doyle farmed at Sillagh House, Killashee, outside Naas, and had been interned in Hare Park Camp and the Rath Camp, the Curragh, during the War of Independence.[18] He brought them to a hayshed where they hid until night. Cannon said, 'At dark we went to his house and we wrote our names in an autograph album which he had from Hare Park in the British times.' Doyle brought the group to the home area of Jim Dunne, of Greenhills, Kill.[19]

Jim Dunne commanded an anti-Treaty column operating in the Kill area of Co. Kildare. Dunne had previously escaped from Dundalk Jail with help from John McCoy. He took control of Ó Maoláin's group of escapees and led them to Cardwell's, in Celbridge. In his witness statement, Dunne said:

> Prisoners escaped through a tunnel from the Curragh ... about 15 of these men, from the west of Ireland and north of Ireland, were brought to me and were guarded by the column. One batch of 10 men from the west of Ireland I brought to Cardwell's of Celbridge, and while having tea at 6 a.m. we were surrounded by a column of Free State troops from Naas. Myself and Tom Kealy of Celbridge were the only ones who were armed. We managed to keep the Free State troops engaged for an hour while the unarmed escaped prisoners, after getting their directions for home, retreated. When we retired after an hour's fighting, we took one of the escaped prisoners with us, as his feet were swollen and he was hardly able to walk. The troops did not attempt to follow us but went after the unarmed prisoners, whom they captured after a ten mile chase. The next escaped prisoners to reach us were: Seán McCoy, afterwards on the Military Pensions Board, Liam O'Callaghan, and Jim Colbert, afterwards T.D. for Limerick. I succeeded in getting these men through our area, and O'Callaghan and Colbert reached Limerick in safety, dressed as greasers on a canal boat. Seán McCoy was captured afterwards in another brigade area.[20]

Escapee Liam O'Callaghan was the brother of Donal O'Callaghan, lord mayor of Cork (1920–24). Jim Colbert was the brother of the executed 1916 leader Con Colbert and was quartermaster of the West Limerick Brigade. Despite being elected for Limerick City in the August 1923 general election on an anti-Treaty ticket, Colbert did not take up his seat and remained on the run until 1924, fearing re-arrest.[21]

Leonard Cardwell and most of his family members were anti-Treaty activists. His first wife was Mary Anne Aiken, half-sister of Frank Aiken. After her death, Leonard remarried and moved to Celbridge to farm at Beatty Park.[22] His daughter Anne (18) was accidentally shot dead on 7 December 1922 by Patrick Brady's service rifle when he visited her home, while he was armed and in the uniform of the National Army. Patrick Brady was arrested and held at the Curragh Camp until mid-1924.[23] A patrol of nine National Army troops was fired on when they approached Cardwell's. Leonard and his young son, Leo (13), were subsequently arrested; a quantity of arms and ammunition was also found. It appeared that whilst he was in custody, Leo received a slight bayonet wound in the neck and was admitted to the military hospital in Naas Barracks. A member of the military was arrested and court-martialled for the incident.[24]

Cardwell claimed that he was on guard duty for several prisoners who had escaped from Tintown and who were staying at his father's house when he was arrested by National Army troops and taken to Naas Barracks. While in custody, Cardwell claimed that he was ill-treated and taken out of his bed at midnight and brought to Jigginstown Bridge on the Naas to Newbridge road by Capt. Patterson and Military Police Officer Byrne. He said he was placed against the wall of the bridge and fired on twice by Capt. Patterson with a revolver. Both bullets missed, but Patterson then 'caught me by the throat with his left hand and fired straight through my neck'. Capt. C. Ellison treated him for his wound.[25]

Six escapees, including Tomás Ó Maoláin and Paddy Cannon, were recaptured in follow-up searches near Cardwell's, but nine more managed to get away safely.[26] Cannon said they were having breakfast between 7–8 a.m., while a 'a little boy' was outside on sentry duty. 'I got up from the table to wash my hands which were dirty from the rafters,' he said. 'The young lad shouted the military are coming in, and he pointed to the way they were coming. We went out, and we ran across an open field with two lads who were on the run in Kildare. The military opened fire, but they didn't hit any of us.' The local volunteers were armed with a rifle and a revolver and returned fire. The recaptured escapees were brought to Naas Military Barracks, where they were held for a week before being re-interned at the Curragh and Gormanstown Camp.[27]

Some escapees were quickly recaptured in the Ballymore Eustace and Harristown areas of Kildare, while one prisoner was arrested in Naas on 23 April.[28] After a night's rest, Mick O'Hanlon's group headed towards Blackchurch, near Kill, and after another night sleeping in some furze bushes, approached a shepherd's house. Here they were fed bacon and eggs and then guided to an outlying house of the O'Connor family, at Elm Hall, Celbridge. John McCoy and Jim Rush met them there. Sympathetic guides arrived and brought the group of six to Dunboyne, Co. Meath, where they stayed at the farm of Molly Nugent, near Fairyhouse Racecourse, for two weeks. On 5 May, the farm was raided by a detachment of National troops from Navan and literature and field dressings were found. The escapees took to the road heading north, but two, John McCoy and Tom Scanlon, were spotted by sentries. McCoy resisted arrest and attempted to seize the rifle from one of the soldiers; the other soldier opened fire, wounding McCoy in the upper thigh. The two were taken to Trim Barracks, where McCoy received treatment at the infirmary. The other four men escaped.[29]

John McCoy had been incarcerated, having led an attack on Dundalk Jail on 27 July 1922. He said, 'After a few days as a prisoner in Dundalk, I was removed to Dublin and eventually sent on to Maryborough Prison in Leix. I was removed from Maryborough Prison to Tintown Camp, the Curragh, Co. Kildare. In April 1923, I escaped from Tintown Camp by means of a tunnel.' McCoy claimed he was the twelfth man to escape from the tunnel and, along with Jim Rush, stayed the night in the hay loft of Kildare footballer Paddy 'Boiler' White's father before hiding out at MacDonnell's, a milk contractor to the camp. From there, he went to 'an old lad's place near Maynooth whose son was in the Free State army', who also put him up for the night. McCoy said he went on to Hazelhatch, in Celbridge – although Mick O'Hanlon said it was Elm Hall – where he met O'Hanlon and Tomás Ó Maoláin. McCoy said, 'I was recaptured about two weeks afterwards ... Scanlon and I were in front... we ran into two soldiers, a soldier rushed with a bayonet ... another fellow shot me high up in [the] thigh and I fell down ...' He was sentenced to two years' imprisonment and, after a spell in the infirmary, was brought back to the Curragh Camp, to Tintown No 3.[30] O'Hanlon continued his journey and walked home to Mullaghbawn. He was not recaptured.[31]

The medical officer, Dr F. P. Ferran, opted to stay with his patients back at the camp hospital. Tomás Ó Maoláin said, 'As I shook his hand, his Northern voice sounded sad as he said, "I'll be watching from the window and saying a wee prayer for you".' He should have gone, for Dr Ferran fell dangerously ill in the summer and died of pneumonia on 10 June 1923.[32]

Among the escapees re-captured was Ed 'Dixie' Wallace of Newbridge. Having been returned to the Curragh Camp, Wallace spent fourteen days in handcuffs in the Military Detention Barracks. The camp authorities claimed that as the prisoners were dangerous, they were handcuffed only during the night. Dixie Wallace's sister, Nellie, smuggled in wire cutters, but she was unaware of the escape as Nellie and her sister Lily were arrested at their Newbridge home on 6 April 1923 and imprisoned in Kilmainham Jail.[33]

A total of seventy men escaped that night and while try-ing to determine the names of the men who escaped, the camp authorities met with considerable opposition from the prisoners. That this opposition was because of orders issued by the prisoners' leaders was proved by a document found on one of the prisoners, containing instructions to hinder any attempt at discipline by the camp regime. During hut inspections, prisoners were supposed to stand beside their beds. They refused to leave their beds, with the result that the military police would walk on top of them as they lay in bed. The non-co-operation campaign lasted about two weeks.[34]

As a disciplinary measure, the prisoners' diet scale was reduced as follows: Butter was reduced by 1 oz, sugar by one-half oz, and milk from one tin for ten men to one tin for fifteen men. The camp commandant said the full ration would be restored in a few days.[35]

Subsequently, two days after the escape tunnels were discovered in two more blocks, while in the following month another 'drain exit' had to be filled in. (Later the same month, a tunnel about seven feet deep, along with various implements for digging, was discovered underneath a fireplace in G Block in Newbridge Barracks.) To effectively prevent another tunnel escape, the camp authorities issued orders for steps to be taken, including the prisoners at the Curragh camps digging trenches around each camp. The prisoners' leaders were removed from the camps before the prisoners began this work, and some of those leaders were transferred to the Military Detention Barracks. Known as the Glasshouse because of its glass roof, the Military Detention Barracks was used as a punishment block and had a notorious reputation for ill-treatment by the Military Police guards.[36]

Johnny Grealy (Coongawnah, Co. Mayo) was sent to Tintown No. 2 from Mountjoy Jail in 1923. He was there when a tunnel was discovered and said military policemen ill-treated those who refused to dig the trench. Around thirty prisoners were delegated to dig this trench. An armed guard, under the command of Comdt Lynham, deputy governor, and Comdt McCormack, accompanied them. Grealy mentioned that 'McCormack, a Commandant, a tough fellow from Kilcock with a sallow face, was there at the digging of the trench also … McCormack rounded us up in the compound, and there he was swinging his Parabellum in his hand. "You'll get me for this I suppose when you get out of here." When they were searching for a tunnel they put us out in the compound. Then they scattered everything around in our huts. They smashed our little boiling tin cans and they threw the tea around and splashed water around as well. They fired over our heads when we were out in the open, with machine guns, and we were herded there until the night time when they allowed us back into our huts. Afterwards the PAs would come into our huts and put our tin cans which had tea in them flying around the place with sticks.'

Another prisoner Greg Ashe was also on the trench dig. He said, 'They hurled us out until 10 in the evening on the first night and a bad night it was … when I came back to my hut everything was gone as regards kettles, razors etc. They looted the hut.' Not all the guards were hostile, some were sympathetic to the internees. Greg Ashe recalled that 'P.A.s' and 'Hunt, an officer from Mayo would bring in a good share' of tobacco. Fr Buckley also brought him in a pound of tobacco on a visit.

Seán Lemass was involved with another internee, Alfred McGloughlin (Mac Lochlainn), in drafting an affidavit on prison conditions after the discovery of the tunnel and the mistreatment of some prisoners. Nine prominent prisoners were subsequently dragged from their huts by camp guards. They were: Alderman Charles Murphy, Seán Lemass, Alfred McGloughlin, Alfred Power and Mick Price, Dublin; Jack Cantillon, Barrack Street, Cork; Joe Considine, Ennis, Co. Clare; Desmond Murphy, London; Tomás Malone (Seán

Forde), Limerick. A statement alleging ill-treatment, vouched for by several prisoners in Hare Park Camp, was issued to the newspapers: 'It is not long since "A.E." and James Douglas and other "humanitarians" were calling loudly on us to cease warfare, though we were merely defending a position which we were bound in honour to defend. Now these "humanitarians" are silent when things are being done behind prison walls which are a disgrace not only to Ireland, but to humanity.'

The statement claimed that the camp authorities hung the nine prisoners by the wrists from the rafters in the Military Detention Barracks, for two-and-a-half hours. They were then cut down and chained to the wall for three days and nights. When they were released from this position for their meals, they had to run between two files of military police, where they were punched and kicked. During this time, they were denied use of the lavatory. As a result of their torture, Desmond Murphy and Joe Considine had to be removed to a hospital in Dublin.

Alfred McGloughlin was subjected to this same treatment. On 21 October 1922, McGloughlin was arrested at his home in Dublin by National troops and brought to Wellington Barracks. McGloughlin had joined the Irish Volunteers in November 1913 and was involved in the Howth gunrunning. He was Sinn Féin's director of elections in south Dublin for the 1918 and 1921 elections and stood as a candidate during the local elections of 1920; he was also a Republican justice during the War of Independence period. McGloughlin was a nephew of Pádraig and Willie Pearse and grew up in the Pearse household. In November, McGloughlin was transferred from Wellington Barracks to Hare Park Camp, where his guards ill-treated him. On 6 November 1923, a letter from McGloughlin (9 Newgrove Avenue, Sandymount, Dublin) refuting Gen. Mulcahy's denial of ill-treatment of prisoners at the Curragh was published in the *Irish Independent*:

Gen. Mulcahy's statement ('Irish Independent', Nov. 1, 1923) re treatment of prisoners in the Curragh military prison last April is so outrageously inaccurate that it is difficult to imagine that it is not a deliberate and intentional distortion of the facts. I am one of the Hare Park prisoners referred to. In spite of what Gen. Mulcahy says, I slept on bare boards in the Curragh military prison for five nights – April 24 to 28. I did not get 3 blankets; I got one and a piece about 1 yard square. I only got bed-hoards and one trestle on the last night I slept there. I was handcuffed night and day (day behind, night in front) from Tuesday, April 24, until Saturday morning, April 29. My handcuffs were not off for meals; they were off one wrist for alleged dinner, except Thursday, April 26, when they were both off at dinner, but on that day I was hanging handcuffed by the wrists to a kit-rack about 6ft. 6ins. from the floor for 4½ hours. I did not get soldier's rations. I got dry bread and tea (and broken bits of meat on 2 days) ...

I was in solitary confinement the whole time and would not be let sit down, eyes on the floor, as if I tried to rest a guard presented his gun and ordered me to 'get up and exercise yourself'. I was threatened with a gun and told several times I was to be shot. I have made an affidavit, as to the facts of my treatment in the Curragh military prison, and am taking steps to convince Gen. Mulcahy that flagrant departures from the truth do not pay. As to the General's statements re the happenings in Mountjoy, as there are many other witnesses to their inaccuracies and distortions, I will not refer to them more than to say that they, too, bristle with 'outrageous falsehoods'.

As I have publicly stated the true conditions of prison treatment and Gen. Mulcahy's statement charges me with 'outrageous falsehoods', I must ask you to give as much publicity to this denial as you did to his report. As to the inquiry he alleges was held into the happenings in the Curragh, I never heard of it until I read of it in your report.

I was arrested unarmed in my bed on October 21, 1922, taken to Wellington Barracks, and have been confined in various prisons and camps since that time, and have suffered various periods of punishment and ill-treatment until my unconditional release from 'C' wing, Mountjoy, on Oct. 13. 1923, and during all that time I have never been charged with anything, nor told why I was detained or punished.

Alfred McGloughlin later obtained a position as a draughtsman with the Office of Public Works (OPW). He remained active as a political journalist and was a regular contributor to the

Republican newspaper *An Phoblacht*. His health never recovered from his time in prison and he died from heart disease, aged forty-four, on 5 August 1932 at his sister's residence, Emmet's Fort Hermitage, Rathfarnham.

Seán Lemass later told Ernie O'Malley in a series of interviews O'Malley conducted with Republican veterans, it was 'an offence punishable by death for attempting to escape. We thought we were going to be shot. Handcuffed around wrist. I could get my toes on the ground but Desmond Murphy couldn't. We were left there for four or five hours then the guard kicked up about it. A bastard named [John] Leonard from Athy. Then they threw water over us. Price and Enright were beaten up. He was in the first cell and got a hammering. Joe Considine there also but Enright did not come over with us. We were there a while. Things eased off. One day humped into a lorry and brought to the Joy and we saw the "Cease Fire" order'.

Éamon Enright, from Tralee, Co. Kerry, was OC Tintown No. 2. When he refused to give the names of the hut OCs, he received the same treatment as the other nine prisoners and was then handcuffed to a rack outside his cell, and was threatened to be shot with a revolver pushed into his chest. Enright was beaten by two officers and had two buckets of water thrown over him. He was returned to his cell, his clothes saturated with water. Leonard was present during the beating and according to a letter from Charlie Murphy, he was 'Governor or Deputy-Governor of the Glass House'.

According to Denis Quille (Listowel), 'Éamon Enright was our O/C. He was very sincere … They took him to the Glass House, hung him up by the wrists and beat him. I think his arm was broken.' Enright was later moved to Mountjoy Jail.

Following the movement of the prisoners' leaders, the camp authorities ordered the prisoners put in batches of eighty to dig a trench around the camp. However, the prisoners refused and were then put back into their huts, which were fired on by the military. Several prisoners were wounded and others had narrow escapes. The prisoners were then subjected to beatings with rifle-butts and batons and fearing that someone would be killed, the prisoners' OC, Tom Hales, ordered them to dig the trench. Medical treatment for injuries was refused. It was alleged Capt. Guiney shot a prisoner named McCann, of Dublin, 'through the shoulder and lung, for refusing to dig a trench'. McCann was removed to a Dublin hospital for an operation. Prisoners alleged their medical orderly, Seán Healy (Cork), was knocked unconscious with a blow of a shovel; J. Stack (Kerry) had his glasses broken from a revolver butt; and Tom Heavy (Galway) was beaten unconscious.

Tension continued in the camp with raids on the different huts and the occupants being moved from one hut to another. Personal belongings, meagre at the best of times, were often destroyed by the military police whose actions did not endear them to the prisoners. Joseph Campbell wrote about the raids and shootings as 'Zizz-z-z-z over our heads – heavy calibrated bullet ... A good deal of firing all night ... picks & shovels all morning ...' He was bedridden with influenza in the Hospital Hut when Campbell recorded a diary entry for 3 June: 'Camp returning to normal after the dreadful happenings since 24 April. No guns, no intimidation.'

8

AN ESTEEMED VISITATION

Despair, disillusionment and economic necessity drove many prisoners to sign the form of undertaking not to engage in hostilities against the Free State government. Christmas came early for some Republican prisoners when 328 'military' captives, including four women, were released on 23 December 1922, having signed the form of undertaking.[1] At times, local newspapers divulged the names of prisoners who had signed to gain release. It was a major issue for die-hard Republicans, as the following letter suggests.

> To the Editor, 'The Nationalist and Leinster Times.' Patrick St., Mountmellick, 7th September, 1923. Sir – A rumour is current that I signed the Form of Undertaking prior to my release by the military from Tintown No. 3 Camp on the 22nd ult. I wish to contradict this, and to state that my release was unconditional. –Yours truly, Jos. Moore.[2]

Charlie O'Neill, who was interned with his friend, Joe Carey, in Newbridge Barracks, received a letter from Joe's father, Joseph. The interesting part of the letter was that some of the text had been marked out by the censor's pen. The possible reason it was censored was that Joseph asked Charlie to ensure that his son did not agree to sign the undertaking that he would refrain from any involvement with the anti-Treaty IRA and not take part in attacks on the government if released. As far as can be ascertained, the censored text said, 'I hope you will keep an eye on Joe and see that he does not do anything that can be chalked up to him. I mean about signing any papers as I have been told that he has already done so but do not believe it ...'[3]

The governor of Hare Park Camp sent a letter to the Prisoners' Department, Office of the Adjutant General, at Parkgate, Dublin, stating that 'it is futile to ask prisoners to sign Forms of Undertaking at this stage unless they approached us on this matter themselves'. He was referring to the case of ten men recommended for release but then baulked at signing the Form. The governor continued, 'The idea has apparently been instilled into them by their "Officers" that they must sign nothing and only accept unconditional release … In practically every one of these particular cases, the prisoners would sign the Form only for fear or other influence of the others.'[4]

Local commanders took it upon themselves to be lenient in parts of the countryside. A column of seventeen Republicans led by Michael Pierce, who surrendered to National forces at Ballyheigue, near Tralee, and signed the form of undertaking, were allowed to return to their homes immediately.[5]

There was growing dissatisfaction, however, about overcrowding, poor food, sanitation, ill-treatment and indiscriminate use of firearms by prison guards at jails and camps throughout the country. Concern was voiced not only by Republican supporters, but also by several pro-Treaty senators, among them W. B. Yeats, Lord Granard and Sir Bryan Mahon. Both Mahon and Lord Granard had suffered at the hands of the anti-Treaty IRA in February 1923: Mahon's house at Mullaboden, Co. Kildare, had been burned down, while Lord Granard's Leitrim mansion had been partially destroyed in an attack.[6]

William Butler Yeats had been appointed a senator in the Free State the month previously, a fact which infuriated his lifelong friend, Maud Gonne MacBride, who condemned him for accepting the legitimacy of a state 'which voted Flogging Acts against young Republican soldiers still seeking to free Ireland from the contamination of the British Empire'. As a senator, Yeats regarded himself as a representative of order amid the nation's chaotic, slow progress towards stability. Still, he had to speak out for injustice, including appealing to W. T. Cosgrave when Maud Gonne MacBride was jailed. Maud was among several prominent Republican women arrested on 10 April 1923. In Kilmainham Gaol, she joined a hunger strike initiated by Nell Ryan, Richard Mulcahy's sister-in-law. Yeats urged President Cosgrave to release Maud, saying that she was no longer a young woman and would not be able to stand up to fasting. Cosgrave retorted that it was not possible 'to consider these women as ordinary females' and that 'women, doctors and clergy ought to keep out of politics, as their business is with the sick'.[7]

In early December 1922, Dr Kathleen Lynn and Kathleen O'Brennan, of the Irish Women's Republican Federation, visited the International Committee of the Red Cross (ICRC) offices in Geneva, Switzerland, to appeal for intervention on behalf of Republican prisoners. The International Committee of the Red Cross was founded in Geneva to protect international and internal victims of conflict. It aimed to assist war-wounded combatants, prisoners, refugees, civilians and other non-combatants. During the First World War, the ICRC set up an International Prisoner of War Agency to work with prisoners-of-war (POW), which included inspections and visits to POW camps. It was in this capacity that the ICRC was invited to visit Irish prisons and internment camps.[3]

Armed with lists of detainees and details of ill-treatment and torture, the two Irish women argued that the Free State government was acting in contravention of the 1921 Geneva Convention on the treatment of prisoners-of-war. They urged the ICRC to investigate Ireland's prison conditions and issue an 'expose' as a 'moral force'.[9] The ICRC has a duty to intervene when an appeal is made to it, and as a result of the numerous representations on the treatment of prisoners in Ireland, the ICRC subsequently appointed M. M. Schlemmer and Rodolphe A. Haccius to go to

Dublin and to obtain authority from the Free State government to institute an inquiry of a purely non-political and technical nature into the position of its prisoners.

According to the ICRC, the belligerents should recognise the principles of humanity as much during wars as following them. Because the nature of the ICRC and the experience gained by it offered a guarantee of impartiality of its inquiries, the government reluctantly decided to grant the authority requested and to accord to the delegates every facility for visiting the prisons and internment camps and for making a report on the treatment of those detained in them. A mutual understanding was arrived at as to the nature of the facts to be investigated and the character of the intervention of the ICRC.[10]

The Red Cross delegation arrived in Dublin on 16 April to an 'agreeable, if slightly frosty' reception. The delegates of the ICRC were received by Desmond Fitzgerald, Minister of External Affairs; Mr Walshe, Secretary, and Gen. Morris, Director of Army Medical Services. They were informed by Desmond Fitzgerald that the situation in Ireland was not a civil war but a police operation. Nevertheless, Fitzgerald agreed to a 'technical' investigation of prisons and internment camps on the condition that the ICRC delegate, Rodolphe A. Haccius, could not speak to any prisoners. As International Commissioner, Haccius had visited political detainees in Hungary in 1919 and drew from this experience for his Irish visit. Between 18 and 25 April, he visited the internment camps at Newbridge, Tintown and Gormanstown, as well as Mountjoy Jail.

Mr Schlemmer subsequently returned to Geneva to report on the result of the negotiations and on the welcome accorded to his delegation by the government. The first visit by Mr Haccius was to Newbridge Barracks where he reported there were 1,969 men interned in several buildings and huts where, 'some of the doors and windows have been intentionally damaged by the prisoners'. Haccius gave a favourable description of accommodation and conditions, stating that, 'There are lavatories with water installation (partly destroyed), hot water baths, and douches always in working order. Soap is supplied.' He went on to say that there were thirty men in the infirmary and that they were cared for by two army doctors and several army nurses who offered daily medical visits and that there were 'No epidemics'. Haccius commented on the neatness of the rooms, to which the governor replied that 'it depended entirely on the prisoners themselves'.[11]

On 20 April, Haccius visited the Tintown Internment Camps, where the 7,369 held there, according to the government, were being treated as prisoners of war 'devoid of all hostile spirit'. In general, his reports were favourable and he concluded that 'the government refuses the status of "prisoners-of-war" to prisoners, but in reality treats them as such'. However, there was an important proviso in his reports which was his comment about Tintown that, 'I have not had any complaints to register concerning the food, medical care, or treatment, not having been authorised to question the prisoners.' The ICRC reported that the kitchens at the camp in Tintown, for example, were 'well run' and that the dining hall had both benches and tables. Food provisions were said to be of good quality and that the 'quantity of food supplied is amply sufficient'. Haccius commenting on the wholesale availability of washing facilities said that he 'was surprised to see that in spite of these facilities many prisoners neglected their own personal cleanliness'. He concluded in saying, 'My visit to the camp made a favourable impression on me. The conditions correspond to the normal treatment of prisoners of war, in conformity with the principles which inspired the Convention of Geneva.'[12]

The ICRC report released to the government in June was the subject of debate in the Dáil on 3 July when Gen. Mulcahy felt it necessary to place before the House a report of its visit:

> M. R. Haccius was delegated to visit the prison camps from the point of view of their organisation and accommodation, and of the sanitary conditions of the internees. The total number of prisoners and internees is about 11,500 men and 250 women. Our delegate visited the principal camps, comprising a total of 7,369 prisoners.
>
> The treatment of these prisoners is devoid of all hostile spirit, and the general principles adopted by the 10th International Conference of the Red Cross are observed. The Government refuses the status of 'prisoners-of-war' to the prisoners, but in reality treats them as such. The delegate particularly draws the attention of the Committee to the fact that nowhere did he find a wounded or sick prisoner left without medical treatment. On the contrary, he found everywhere a carefully organised medical service. The serious accusations made on this subject appear to him unfounded.

Although conditions in the women's prisons had formed part of the appeals to the ICRC, Haccius did not visit Kilmainham Gaol, where 300 women were held and a hunger strike was on-going. However, his report said that he has no reason to believe that the treatment there is different to that adopted at Mountjoy. Thirteen of those prisoners had been on hunger strike since the day of their arrest to obtain their release or immediate trial, and not as a protest against the prison regime. This fact, is moreover verified by their written statements. The delegate did not consider it his duty to insist on getting into touch with these prisoners, fearing that his intervention, misinterpreted, would only encourage them to persist in their attitude, and give rise to a new case of strike. During his sojourn three of these prisoners were released'.

Instead, Haccius was brought to the vacant site at North Dublin Union (NDU), which was to be the new home for female political prisoners. He described the NDU as spacious with plentiful facilities:[13]

> The buildings of the old North Dublin Union are in the course of alteration for the reception, of those detained in Kilmainham. These buildings, with the surrounding garden, will fulfil all

desirable hygienic conditions. The instructions given by the International Committee of the Red Cross to the delegate exclude certain representations and sworn inquiries bearing on individual complaints.

It is a fact that searches have taken place in various private hospitals, but the working of these hospitals has not been interfered with. There are grounds for the complaints of overcrowding in Mountjoy Prison.[14]

There are no epidemics. A certain number of men who arrived lately are affected with scurvy, and have been isolated from the rest while being treated … The wounded, who are submitted to surgical treatment, are nursed outside the camp in a pavilion isolated from the barracks hospital. The rooms are fitted with every comfort, and contain from 4 to 5 beds. The patients seem to be very grateful to the doctors for their devoted care and attention … I have not had any complaints to register concerning the food, medical care, or treatment, nor having been authorised to question the prisoners. The men are not obliged to do any compulsory work, and are at liberty to walk about the enclosure of the camp. I was present at a football match.

Haccius concluded by saying, 'My visit of inspection to the [Tintown] camp made a favourable impression on me. The conditions correspond with the normal treatment of prisoners-of-war, in conformity with the principles which inspired the Convention of Geneva.'

Overall, Haccius concluded that the 'serious accusations' made by Republicans were unfounded.

Continuing, Mulcahy quoted from a report with reference to the Internment Camp at Tintown as follows: 'Sick – seventy-two men in the infirmary, twenty-five men in the surgical hospital. There are six wooden barracks used as an infirmary; these buildings are in good condition and well heated. The Military staff is composed of three medical doctors (Head Dr Comdt Maguire) and army nurses. A medical visit daily, which anyone wishing to see the doctor could attend.'

Mulcahy also read extracts from letters written by women and other prisoners, testifying to the comfort of the conditions under which they were detained. Denis Lane, interned in Newbridge, wrote to a friend: '… this place is splendid. Just imagine to have acres of ground to roam about, kick football, or play any game you want to. The concerts in the evening are very good.' Patrick Cummins wrote: '… I may tell you we are very snug here. We can be out on the playfield from 7.30 in the morning until 8 in the evening.' Patrick O'Mahoney wrote to Mrs P. O'Mahoney, Dunmanway, Cork: '… The soldiers down here are very kind to us.'[15] Mulcahy thought it necessary that the information he had given should be disclosed, so that the public and the House should not be misled regarding the prison conditions.[16]

When the report appeared in the *Revue Internationale de Croix-Roux* in July 1923 it was lauded by the *Freeman's Journal* as 'sane, balanced and moderate in tone'.[17] A delighted Free State executive council published the report in the press, even going to the length of stating that 'prisoners actually receive full prisoner-of-war treatment'.

Critics of the government were considerably less enthusiastic about the report and were highly critical that prisoners were not interviewed and that some of the prisons where the most serious complaints had been made were not investigated. The ICRC report was undoubtedly a blow to the anti-Treaty side and a victory for the government. In the Dáil, George Gavan Duffy questioned the veracity of the ICRC report and asked whether the local councils could perform another, more impartial inquiry.

Prisoners, however, claimed that many of the men had scabies and lice and that impetigo was rampant. An epidemic of influenza hit Tintown from April to May, during which 200 prisoners were stricken, but luckily no deaths occurred. Tintown No. 2 Camp had no shower facilities and internees there had to go to Tintown No. 1 to bathe.[18]

A delegation of concerned senators, including W. B. Yeats, was more circumspect, however. Oversight and improvements were needed, Yeats maintained in May 1923, but he also accepted that 'many statements by critics could not be relied upon as to their accuracy'.[19] This was probably true, but critics of the government would not be silenced.

In a letter to the editor of the *Irish Independent*, published on 11 July 1923, Mr L. H. Kerney, Republican delegate in Paris, stated, 'In view of the use made by Mr Mulcahy in the debate on Tuesday last of a report on the treatment of prisoners in Ireland from the International Committee of the Red Cross it is important that the public should be informed of certain facts concerning that delegation. We ask you, therefore, in justice to the prisoners, to publish the following statement.'

> On April 7th, 1923, the International Committee of the Red Cross wrote informing me that the memorial presented to them by the Government of the Irish Republic had had their attention; that they were studying with interest the problem submitted to them; that they were contemplating certain steps which required further consideration; and that they would not fail to communicate to me with the least possible delay the decisions which would be taken. On 7th May I wrote to the Red Cross Committee reminding them of their promise. On May 11th this latter communication was answered, and I received a copy of the communique, which, I was informed, was being sent to the Press that very day concerning the visits paid to internment camps in Ireland by one of their delegations at the end of the month of April. The decision to send a delegation, to Ireland was not communicated to me.

Maud Gonne MacBride added her voice to the statement, adding that 'Finding that even after the terrible evidence of ill-treatment of prisoners, of the shocking over-crowding and unsanitary conditions in many of the jails disclosed before the Commission of Inquiry instituted by the Dublin Municipal Council, nothing was being done to remedy these evils.' Charlotte Despard also stated that she had written to the ICRC asking them to obtain proper 'prisoner-of-war' conditions for the thousands of Republican prisoners in Free State custody.

Mrs Despard had received several letters from Geneva

and The Hague, and finally a message sent through Kathleen O'Brennan stating that the ICRC was sending delegates to investigate the conditions of prisons in Ireland. These delegates would communicate with her immediately upon their arrival in Ireland to gather all the information she could provide. Mrs Despard did not learn of the presence of the two Red Cross delegates in Ireland until after they had left, and they had not contacted her.

She subsequently wrote to Geneva saying that she had not had an opportunity to see the delegates and give them the information she possessed. Mrs Despard requested that their report be sent to her and further stated that the complaints she had voiced were chiefly about prisons and barracks where thousands of prisoners were detained and that she had not made a complaint about the 'show' internment camps. This letter, she claimed, was ignored by the ICRC.

In a letter to the editor of the *Irish Independent*, published on 11 July 1923, Dr Lynn stated:

> I was one of the delegates sent by the Irish Women's Republican Federation to Geneva to draw the attention of the International Red Cross to prison conditions in Ireland. The International Red Cross Committee, before whom we made our statement on December 8, 1922, promised an enquiry and said that their representatives would get in touch with Mrs Despard, on their arrival in Ireland On 19th April, 1923, I heard by chance that two representatives of the International Red Cross were in Dublin; I called on them at once, accompanied by Mrs Ceannt and Miss Ffrench-Mullen, and learned that Mr Schlemmer was in London (it would be interesting to learn how many days he spent, in Ireland) from Mr Haccius, whom we saw, and who appeared rather taken aback at being discovered by us.

> He took down more recent details of conditions in Maryborough and Kilmainham. I stressed the fact that there were about 300 women in Kilmainham and that this prison, was in Dublin. At the end of our interview, Mr Haccius asked me, and those who accompanied me, to keep secret for a few days the presence of the Red Cross delegation in Dublin, saying it might interfere with their admission to the prisons. We consented, little thinking it

would be our first and last interview with the Red Cross delegates and that they would see no other Republicans or representatives of the prisoners while in Ireland, Mr Haccius stated that he did not wish to attract attention by receiving prisoners or their relatives at the hotel, but he would take any written statements and forward them to Geneva. In his report, he states that the International Red Cross did not allow him to receive any sworn statements; how does he reconcile these two assertions?

One can understand his not wanting to attract attention before he entered the prisons, but surely, afterwards, he should have seen and interviewed as many prisoners as possible. Impartiality surely demands that both sides get a fair hearing.

Dr Lynn claimed that contact with the ICRC and the Free State government was close and thorough as shown by Mulcahy's announcement that, 'A mutual understanding was arrived at as to the nature of the facts to be investigated and as to the character of the intervention' of the ICRC 'so as to determine the exact lines in which the activity of the delegates should be directed ... A study of the report will show the spirit in which the "investigation" was carried out.' Dr Lynn went on, 'Commissioner Haccius had not visited Kilmainham, but did visit the North Dublin Union, then in the preparation process for the arrival of 300 female prisoners. Haccius said the NDU would "fulfil all desirable hygienic conditions". Lynn asked if three baths, according to Red Cross standard, would be suitable for 300 prisoners. She said uncleaned wards, unemptied refuse bins, rat-infested dormitories, an unequipped hospital and intolerable over-crowding in the NDU were hardly desirable conditions.'

Lynn also pointed out that the Red Cross had been requested, specifically, to inspect, the jails where complaints had been made, but delegates 'visited, it appears, only certain internment camps – selected for them by the Free State government. No complaints had been made by Republicans against Gormanstown or Newbridge Camp. Were not these visited by the delegates in preference to prisons against which accusations had been made? The Red Cross had been urgently requested to deal with the practice of executing prisoners and bodily ill-treating them as punishment, and for purposes of interrogation. Both these matters are completely ignored in the delegates' report.'[20]

In consequence, Commissioner Haccius asked his superiors for the opportunity to return to Ireland to re-investigate the complaints, but the ICRC refused, not willing to become further involved in Irish affairs.[21]

Meanwhile, the lax conditions in the jails and internment camps took a horrifying toll on prisoners. Tintown camp doctor Frank Ferran's health deteriorated in the summer of 1923. Joseph Campbell wrote in his diary: 'Cool, windy morning. Bad unseasonable weather still continues. After Mass Dr Comer came over to me & said, "The F.S. M.O. has a bad a/c [account] of Dr Fearon [Ferran]. Dying at 7 o'clock last evening. Mother & wife sent for. It will be providential if he pulls through." I said that if he died it would stop the idiotic mockery about "amenities in prisons". The hardship of his previous terms in jail telling on him now. The constitution of a horse would break down under it. The fact that the Local Govt. Ministry under sealed order deprived him of the M/O ship of Swinford district told on a sensitive man, no doubt. Little provision for wife & children as he was a man that gave no thought to money & attended the poor free in big areas of Connacht. L. G. Ministry's action mean & contemptible – no thought for previous services to Nation, or for wife & small children of a man who remained faithful to his oath as a Republican.'[22]

On 10 June, Dr Frank Ferran, TD, passed away in the hospital hut of Tintown No 1, at the age of forty-six. The cause of his death was recorded as septic pneumonia. Ferran's funeral took place two days later. Large crowds attended the requiem mass in the Whitefriar Street Carmelite church, Dublin. A party of uniformed Cumann na mBan formed a guard of honour and marched on each side of the hearse to Glasnevin Cemetery, where he was laid to rest in the Republican Plot. Frank Ferran's wife, Eleanor Mary, their young daughters, his mother and his three sisters were joined by sympathisers from Dublin, Mayo and his native Derry. Among the notable figures in attendance were Mrs Pearse (mother of the 1916 martyrs P. H. and Willie), Peadar Toner Mac Fionnlaoich (president of Conradh na Gaeilge) and Irish language writer Alice Furlong.[23]

The events surrounding the death of Dr Ferran were raised in Dáil Éireann on 10 July 1923, a month after his untimely passing. Patrick McCartan, Tyrone-born TD for Laois-Offaly, asked General Mulcahy, Minister for Defence, if he was aware that Mrs Ferran had not been informed of her husband's rapidly deteriorating condition and that '… a physician desired by Dr Ferren's family was not permitted to see him'.

Gen. Mulcahy told the House that 'absolutely nothing had been left undone to save Dr Ferran's life', that he had been attended by a senior physician named Dr Carroll. He claimed that a message had been sent to Mrs Ferran via her husband's brother-in-law, Dr James O'Kelly.

The following day, a lengthy and scathing letter to the editor of the *Irish Times*, penned by Ferran's brother-in-law, Dr James O'Kelly, went to print. The sole purpose of the correspondence was to outline, in painstaking detail, the many inaccuracies in Mulcahy's statement in Dáil Éireann.

Dr O'Kelly insisted that no contact whatsoever had been made with Mrs Ferran, and that it was only a result of repeated pleas for information from her that news of Dr Ferran's ill-health was finally conveyed to his family, on 6 June. Sustained requests for permission to visit Dr Ferran, or send a doctor of their choosing, were left unanswered. Dr O'Kelly even delivered a letter by hand to the relevant authorities in a desperate attempt to hasten a reply.

Finally, at 8 p.m. on Friday, 9 June, Gen. Mulcahy conceded, and the family were given permission to attend the deathbed of Frank Ferran. It was an agonising case of 'too little, too late'. Ferran had already slipped into a coma at 3 p.m. and never regained consciousness.

In his letter, Dr O'Kelly called on the Minister for Defence to amend his comments and offer a full explanation to the Dáil. Gen. Mulcahy did not take such action.[24]

On 28 June 1923, Owen Boyle (20), who had been interned at Newbridge Barracks for several months, died in the Curragh Military Hospital of tuberculosis and cardiac failure. Boyle was a native of Lackenagh, Burtonport, Co. Donegal, and had served with the 1st Northern Division, IRA, during the War of Independence and Civil War. He was captured by National Army forces in September 1922.[25] Capt. Denis Ryan (Bouleen, Tipperary) died at the Military Hospital, Curragh Camp on 19 July 1923. He had been seriously wounded on his capture at Bohercrowe, Co. Tipperary, the previous January, in an encounter with National troops in which Comdt Martin 'Sparky' Breen had been killed. Ryan's prognosis was not good and in May he had been brought to the Curragh from St Vincent's Hospital, Tipperary, where he died of infection and heart failure. According to his death record, Denis Ryan was twenty-one.[26]

Four days later Matthew Ginnity (31), Rathkenny, Co. Meath, died of pneumonia at the Curragh Military Hospital. He had been in custody since his capture at Curraghtown House, Co. Meath, in July 1922 and was held at Tintown No. 2 Camp. During the War of Independence, Ginnity was a section leader with Birkenhead Company and operated in Liverpool, acquiring and smuggling weapons to Ireland. The IRA in Liverpool also carried out arson attacks on timber yards and warehouses in Merseyside in revenge for Black and Tan activities in Ireland.[27] Ginnity was taken prisoner in November 1920 and appeared in court with his head swathed in bandages; he was released under the general amnesty in December 1921. He returned to Ireland and joined the Meath anti-Treaty Active Service Unit on the outbreak of the Civil War.[28]

Two more prisoners died at the Military Hospital within a week. Peter Maher (19), Gooldscross, Co. Tipperary, died of pulmonary tuberculosis on 25 July, and Daniel Downey (22), Dundalk, who died on 31 July from septic pneumonia. Peter Maher was active from 1919 and had been jailed during the War of Independence. He was arrested by National Army forces in February 1923 and was held at the Fever Hospital in Cashel and then at Templemore, Co. Tipperary before being transferred to the Curragh. His mother, Mary Maher, in a pension application, claimed that Peter was mistreated by his captors during his imprisonment. His brother, Patrick Maher, also served with the IRA.[29]

Daniel Downey was active during the War of Independence with the Dundalk Battalion. According to material on file in the Military Archives, Daniel Downey received a beating while a prisoner in March 1923, resulting in lower jaw injuries, which resulted in his admission to the Curragh Military Hospital on 7 May 1923. Downey developed and died from septic pneumonia following an operation for his condition. There had been some suggestions that he was on a hunger strike protest at some stage during his imprisonment.[30]

9

TINTOWN TIMES

Jack Comer was among 200 prisoners who arrived in Tintown No. 2 Camp from Maryborough Jail, on 22 February 1923. Born in Williamstown, Co. Galway, Comer had studied medicine in University College Galway. He was a medical officer of the 3rd Southern Division when he was arrested on 2 February 1923.[1] He recalled how 'the old lad with the shit bucket' offered to take out a man a day in his refuse cart, but there were few takers. This 'old man' smuggled out dispatches hidden in brown OXO bottles in the excrement. He shovelled out the excrement at the dump, where he would pick out the hidden dispatches and post them to the covering addresses. According to Comer, not one of the dispatches was ever discovered.[2]

The day started for prisoners at 7.00 a.m. with a roll call. Internees would stand at the foot of their bed while the military police took a count. The prisoners were then dismissed by their own officers. For the rest of the day until lock-up, the internees were under the unofficial authority of their officers. A senior officer was in command of each compound, and answering to him were the hut commanders, each responsible for a hut. These elected officers acted as go-betweens in negotiations with the camp military authorities.

Books, newspapers and magazines were allowed through the post, although political newspapers were not distributed. Canteens operated in the camps, which were controlled by the prisoners, from which they could purchase cigarettes, tobacco, food, writing material and stamps. Forty-four letters were posted out by prisoners from Tintown No. 2 in November 1923, while a further thirty were posted in December, including one addressed to the 'Chairman Release the Prisoners Committee, Dublin'. Postage was 2d, which was a lot of money for those without financial means.[3]

There was a certain hostility in the camp towards visiting priests; some prisoners refused the sacraments and even stole a wooden confessional that had been brought in to provide priests and their confessors with more privacy. The prisoners believed the confessional box was designed so that men would be persuaded to sign the undertaking form secretly. No trace of the confessional box was ever found, and it was not replaced. Jack Feehan said, 'the Tintown priest was bad, very bad. It was he who came into the camp in full uniform, and all the men refused to go to Mass to him, so we had no Mass on that Sunday. Another day, he made remarks from the altar, and they stood up the men, and they all left the church hut.'[4] Jack Comer said that Fr Hughes was very nice, but he 'refused to give confession in Tintown'. Fr Dunne, a Dominican, 'gave a very tough sermon so we had to keep the lads quiet. He addressed us as if we were convicts in Sing Sing'.[5]

The Belfast playwright and poet, Joseph Campbell, was arrested in Bray, Co. Wicklow, on 7 July 1922. He was a veteran Republican, having joined the Irish Volunteers at their inception in 1913 and served as a justice in the Sinn Féin courts and as a councillor in Co. Wicklow. Campbell was held in Mountjoy Jail until 20 February 1923 when he was transferred to Tintown No. 2 Camp, where he did clerical work for Seán Ó Tuama (Cork), the camp's OC.[6]

Campbell kept a hidden diary and his first entry in Tintown was on 7 March 1923 which recorded the bleakness of the Curragh: 'Bitter, raw March day ... Bitter wind sweeping – with rain squalls – across open Curragh plain. Tin huts and muddy roads of camp very desolate …' Two days later, Campbell recorded in his diary that he was informed by his hut leader '… Garraghan that the internees were not to interfere with sheeting boards on the hut roof as the "horses stalled in Hut before British Occupation of the Curragh had suffered from ANTHRAX!!! – and the prisoners were liable to get the disease".'[7]

Campbell recorded that on 20 March, after tea, there was 'great excitement over shooting of one of the sentries in Hare Park compound, by his comrade in a block house'. Eighteen-year-old Pte Michael James Doherty (Co. Donegal) died after being accidentally shot in the head by a fellow soldier. Campbell remarked that these accidents would continue to happen as the National Army troops were severely lacking in training with weapons. Before joining the National Army, he had served with Derry City Battalion, Fianna Éireann, and was employed as an apprentice shipwright.[8]

Seamus Maguire was released from Hare Park Camp on 10 April using another man's name, and despite the winding down of hostilities, immediately went back to the guerrilla campaign. With three other volunteers, Maquire formed a small unit which engaged in several skirmishes with National forces. Maguire had been arrested on 29 June 1922 but escaped from Athlone with eight other Republicans on 24 August 1922 and resumed command of the anti-Treaty 5th Brigade (Mullingar). He was re-arrested on 8 November 1922 and held in Kilmainham Gaol and subsequently transferred to Hare Park Camp. Maguire remained active throughout 1923–4, organising the area and was on the run until he married Shelia Fitzsimons on 12 November 1924.[9]

There had been peace approaches early in the year when Liam Deasy, OC 1st Southern Division, was captured in arms at Tincurry, in January 1923, and imprisoned in Clonmel. Deasy was sentenced to death, but successfully requested a stay of execution and following negotiations, signed a document agreeing to aid in an immediate unconditional surrender of men and arms, convinced that further bloodshed was futile. He further appealed to Liam Lynch and the Republican Executive to end the war. Although his appeal was unsuccessful, and he was heavily criticised by some of his former comrades for what they considered a betrayal of his beliefs in the face of imminent execution, it had a demoralising effect on the IRA. In his book *Brother against Brother*, Liam Deasy wrote, 'In the intervening years I can honestly say that I have never regretted the decision. I made it without fear or favour and in the best interests of the country as I saw it.'[10]

On 10 April, Liam Lynch, the IRA chief-of-staff, was mortally wounded in a skirmish with National troops in the Knockmealdown Mountains, in Co. Tipperary. Word filtered into Tintown the next day, which Joseph Campbell recorded in his diary as a 'BLACK DAY. Liam Lynch's death'. It was the topic of conversation all that day and further demoralised and depressed the internees. Campbell wrote, 'in the wash-house (where I washed handkerchiefs), I could feel the sorrow in the men's hearts as they rubbed their shirts, etc. on the boards – they emitted an aura of low-spiritedness.' Campbell began to sing an old 1798 ballad 'Kelly the Boy from Killane' which helped lift the spirits of those present. As Campbell left, he was cheered by the remark from one of the men, who said, 'well they can't plug us all.'[11]

On the outside, bodies of various councils and corporations paid tribute to the fallen IRA leader. A message of sympathy was also sent from imprisoned members of the East Limerick Brigade in the Curragh Camp, who asked his mother, Mary, to let them 'share your grief, for if you have lost a loving member of your family, we have lost a loving and beloved Chief'.[12]

One of those picked up in follow-up sweeps after the

death of Liam Lynch was C. S. 'Todd' Andrews, a member of GHQ staff and adjutant to Lynch. Andrews had attended the IRA Executive meetings in relation to ending the war. He was captured, having spent the night in a safe house near Ballinamult, Co. Waterford. Andrews was brought to Cork Jail, and from there, he was transferred by railway car to Newbridge. He arrived with a group of about fifty other prisoners who were marched under armed guard from the railway station to the military barracks. Andrews noted that the guards were a 'brusque, bullying lot' as they were processed into the barracks.[13]

Andrews was assigned a number and a billet in one of the barrack blocks, but on meeting captured friends, he was told not to worry about his billet allocation, and he was whisked off to share the quarters of his old comrades. Hut No. 60 housed about thirty Dubliners, mainly men from the Four Courts garrison, all anxious for news of their friends and outside events. Word had passed around that Andrews had been adjutant to Liam Lynch, and he was often asked about the general's last days and at times had to correct the impression that he was with Lynch when he died:

> By the time I had been fed and settled in I knew that relations between the prisoners and the Camp authorities were very bad. A few weeks earlier following the discovery of a tunnel some of the prisoners had been beaten by the guard and others, caught more or less in the act of escape, had been taken to the 'glasshouse' in the Curragh where they were very roughly treated before being returned to Newbridge. Parcels and letters were stopped though they had been resumed just before I arrived. The prisoners had been given a bad time by parties of Staters who raided their huts or dormitories, upsetting the furniture and scattering their belongings … The prisoners' O/C Tom McMahon, with the entire prisoners' Camp Council, had been removed to Mountjoy Jail. The prisoners had not got around to choosing a new O/C and the consequent lack of discipline tended to aggravate the general discontent which was never far from the surface in any internment camp at that time.

Andrews maintained that morale was low in Newbridge and that many prisoners neglected their appearance and did not bother to shave or bathe. The usual prisoner preoccupations of making crafts, macramé bags, rings, bone crosses and harps were also absent. He said a considerable number of prisoners were not Republicans and should not have been interned in the first place. An effort to counter this began after Andrews arrived. Jim Moloney (Tipperary), who had been communications director before his capture, was appointed Camp OC. He appointed Andrews as camp adjutant and Luke Masterson (Dublin) as camp quartermaster. The new camp officers, with the help of the more responsible men in the different billets, re-established discipline, implementing the necessary fatigues, such as washing out billets weekly and clearing litter from the compounds.

As camp adjutant, Todd Andrews became the repository for his fellow prisoners' complaints: personal problems, theft of belongings, a change of billet and rations not being doled out fairly. He also received men who wanted permission to 'sign the form' which would enable them to be released. Andrews explained that the signatory would be recognising the legitimacy of the Free State government, an act which was forbidden by the IRA. However, many prisoners insisted on telling their tales of woe, and some had legitimate reasons; families on the outside were in dire financial circumstances with the main breadwinner locked away.

Andrews was relieved when lock-up time arrived, and he could relax away from the mental strain of listening to 'so much human misery'. He relished the chat around the bedsides in the evenings with his friends in Hut 60 and enjoyed their 'agreeable company'. Andrews said that the food was the same as that given to the guards and that the meat, vegetables and butter were of a high quality. The prisoners had beds instead of bed boards and plenty of blankets and sheets. Gaelic football, soccer and even rugby were played regularly, while concerts and theatrical shows also provided entertainment. Boxing tournaments were organised from time to time.[14]

Outside the jails and camps, efforts were continuing to end the war. On 20 April, the Executive of the IRA met and decided to call on De Valera, as head of the Republican Government and of the Army Council, to make peace with the Free State authorities. Of the twelve deputies named as the Republican Government Council of State, only five were at liberty, of which three were in America or Australia. The following were in custody: Austin Stack, Robert Barton, Count Plunkett, Seán T. O'Kelly, Seán O'Mahony, Kathleen O'Callaghan and Mary MacSwiney. The only two at liberty were P. J. Ruttledge (Mayo North) and Michael P. Colivet (Limerick).[15]

Ten days later, Frank Aiken, who had replaced Liam Lynch as IRA chief-of-staff, ordered a suspension of all operations. Negotiations began between both sides, but nothing came of them. In the end, Aiken ordered on 24 May that 'arms that we fought the enemies of our country are to be dumped. The foreign and domestic enemies of the Republic have for the moment prevailed'. Accompanying the order was the following proclamation from Éamon de Valera:

Soldiers of the Republic, Legion of the Reartguard:

The Republic can no longer be defended successfully by your arms. Further sacrifice of life would now be vain and continuance of the struggle in arms unwise in the national interest and prejudicial to the future of our cause. Military victory must be allowed to rest for the moment with those who have destroyed the Republic. Other means must be sought to safeguard the nation's right.[16]

De Valera's statement gave the impression that the ceasefire was merely tactical and that the war could be resumed if conditions proved favourable. In reality, the Civil War was over, but it would be some time before peace prevailed. The next stage of the Civil War would be fought in the jails and internment camps.

On 5 May 1923, Michael McGrath (33), from Powerstown, Clonmel, Co. Tipperary, died in the Curragh Military Hospital of a gunshot wound to the lung, which he received when captured near Slievenamon on 27 April. McGrath was brought to Clonmel and then transferred to the Curragh Military Hospital for an operation, but he died from shock and haemorrhage. McGrath's relatives arrived at the Curragh to collect his remains but refused an inquest into his death. The County Kildare coroner agreed that it was not necessary once the medical doctor had given his death certificate. The remains were brought back to Powerstown by the family, and his funeral was held on 7 May. An inquest into Michael McGrath's death took place that afternoon in Clonmel but was adjourned when one of the jurors stated: 'We are here to inquire into the murder of McGrath.' A row ensued, saying that an inquest could only be held where the person died, and since McGrath died in Kildare, an inquest should have been held there. A relative then said that the McGrath family had not made any statement regarding not having an inquest at the Curragh. A military legal adviser said that Clonmel had no jurisdiction to hold an inquest on a body brought from another county. After another adjournment two days later, the inquest was abandoned, and the coroner's jury discharged.[17]

Despite the continuing arrival of prisoners to Newbridge and the Curragh – forty prisoners arrived in Newbridge in the first week of June, along with another forty who went to the Curragh – a large number of workmen who had been employed for around five months on the internment camps were let go.[18] The internment camps were a regrettable source of employment for civilian labour and the presence of the prisoners and military also helped the local economy. With the reduction in prisoner numbers, the military authorities were also left with surplus equipment like stoves, latrine buckets, and washing basins, which also had to find further use. Many items were sold off locally.[19]

With the war won, the government felt confident enough to call a general election for August to replace the Third Dáil with the new state's first regularly constituted parliament. On the day Daniel Downey died, 31 July, Kevin O'Higgins announced that 'the lists of prisoners were analysed very carefully with a view to releasing as many as possible and that before the elections they would try to release every man it was considered safe to release'. He further stated, 'it was not fair to suggest, as had been suggested that they were out to lock-up anti-government votes'.[20]

In the immediate aftermath of the Civil War, the government became concerned that the use of internment might be illegal, particularly as the Free State constitution neither explicitly permitted nor prohibited it. The High Court ruled on 31 July 1923 that a state of war no longer existed, and consequently, the internment of Republicans was now illegal. The following day, 1 August, the Public Safety (Emergency Powers) Act received the Royal Assent, but a ruling by the Court of Appeal held that its mode of enactment was defective. A serious constitutional crisis was created when the Court of Appeal granted writs of *habeas corpus* in the case of two anti-Treaty prisoners who had been in military custody for several months, on the ground that a state of war no longer existed. President Cosgrave said that the demand for action was urgent as the thousands of prisoners who were recently at war against the government would have to be released. As it happened, the Public Safety Bill, which gave the government power to continue the detention of Republican prisoners, was due to complete its final stage in the Seánad on 1 August when the Court of Appeal announced its decision.

The bill, however, was not yet law, and so the Public Safety (Emergency Powers) (No. 2) Act was introduced in the Dáil late on the night of 2 August. At a further sitting the following day, the Public Safety (Emergency Powers) (No. 2) Act, 1923, was rushed through and passed its various stages later that day without discussion. When the Dáil reassembled that evening after a short recess, there was a strong muster of government members, but the Labour benches were completely, and suspiciously, empty.[21] The passing of the Emergency Powers Act enabled the government to continue detention in peacetime of unconvicted Civil War prisoners in military custody, restoring its right to suspend *habeas corpus* and to set up new procedures to begin releasing those it considered the least dangerous prisoners.[22] Without a formal peace, every person who was held in military custody could be further detained, 'if the authorities are of opinion that his detention is a matter of military necessity … the public safety could be endangered by such person being set at liberty.'[23]

It was not all plain sailing for the government. At a special meeting of Kildare Co. Council, the following resolution was passed unanimously: 'That we, the Kildare Co. Council, call upon the Government for the immediate release of the internees in order that they will be able to exercise the franchise at the forthcoming elections.' Labour Senator Michael Smyth (Kildare) said they wanted to have the elections complete, and not have people saying when it was over that it was not a free election. It could not be a free election, he said, with 15,000 men and women locked up.[24]

The chairman of Mountmellick District Council proposed the following motion: 'That we call on the Government to immediately release all political prisoners, their detention, in our opinion, being a great obstacle in the way of establishing a lasting peace and moreover is unwarranted, as in every country where anything in the nature of good government exists the liberty of the subject is respected …'[25]

Calls from local authorities fell on deaf ears, and in the

camps and jails, men continued to die needlessly. On 2 August, Joseph Whitty (18), William Street, Wexford Town, died at the Curragh Military Hospital. Whitty had been active with the anti-Treaty forces since August 1922. His two brothers, both IRA volunteers, were the targets of a National forces round-up in October 1922, but in their absence, Joseph was taken instead and was initially held in Wexford Jail before being transferred to Newbridge Barracks.[26] He contracted tuberculosis and was moved to the Curragh Military Hospital. Although there had been suggestions that he was on a hunger strike protest at some stage in his imprisonment, his death certificate recorded that he died of pulmonary tuberculosis and heart failure at the Military Hospital. Whitty's mother visited him in the Curragh, but he was so ill he didn't recognise her. On 22 July, a public meeting in support of Whitty and his fellow prisoners was held in New Ross, addressed by Cumann na mBan activist and playwright Dorothy Macardle, who had been released from imprisonment the previous May for health reasons.[27] The Free State government refused all appeals for his release, and on 2 August 1923, Joseph Whitty died of pulmonary tuberculosis at the Military Hospital. His remains were interred in Ballymore Cemetery, Killinick, Co. Wexford, where three volleys of shots were fired over his grave. There was only one mention of his death in the newspapers.[28]

The following day, Frank O'Keefe (35) died in the Curragh Military Hospital from pneumonia, having contracted tuber-culosis. Frank was the son of Patrick O'Keefe, proprietor of the Ormond Hotel, Clonmel, and had served an apprenticeship with a local motor works before joining the British army, where he was commissioned as an aviator during the First World War. After the war, he returned to his native Clonmel, where he joined the IRA. National forces captured him in the winter of 1922. Frank O'Keefe was described as a 'kindly genial young man' and 'a great favourite in Clonmel'.[29]

Former president of Sinn Féin, Éamon de Valera, came out of hiding to contest the general election, which was set for 27 August. Jack O'Sheehan, a prisoner in Hare Park Camp, wrote an election campaign song, 'The Song of the Legion of the Rearguard. The Rallying-song of the Republic', dedicated to De Valera. A note at the end of the published sheet music reveals it was first performed by the Hare Park Camp Choir on 5 August 1923, and performed in public for the first time at the Four Martyrs' Anniversary Concert at Dublin's Theatre Royal on 9 December 1923.[30] De Valera was arrested while addressing a public meeting in Ennis, Co. Clare, on 16 August and while interned at Kilmainham Gaol became one of the many Republican prisoners running for election.[31]

Jailed candidates, naturally, found it hard to canvas for votes. The following letter from Dulcibella Barton, the sister of anti-Treaty candidate Robert Barton, appeared in the *Irish Independent* on 14 August: 'My brother, Robert C. Barton, the Republican T.D. for Wicklow and Kildare, who is interned at Hare Park Camp, the Curragh, is a candidate for Co. Wicklow at the forthcoming election. He is anxious that his silence may not be misunderstood by his old friends and neighbours. He cannot publish an election address, since he cannot communicate same to me or anyone else outside, as appears from the following extract from a letter to me, dated July 26, from Commandant Seán Ó Caomhanaigh, the Military Governor of the Camp, namely "I am instructed that literature or correspondence of a political character cannot be allowed to pass between prisoners and their friends, outside".'[32]

Not only did candidates have to deal with censorship, but, in moments reminiscent of the War of Independence years, Republican posters were torn down, election meetings broken up, and canvassers and candidates harassed and beaten up. The culprits this time were the National Army and garda síochána.

Despite the government crackdown, the surprising election result boosted Republican morale. Sinn Féin polled better than expected, winning 27.4 per cent of the vote with forty-four TDs returned.[33] The number of seats had been increased from 128 in June 1922 to 153, yet the new Cumann na nGaedheal party of the outgoing government managed only to increase its representation from fifty-eight to sixty-three seats, while the Republican representation increased from thirty-six to forty-four. Eighteen of these seats were won by prisoners, including Ernie O'Malley, elected in North Co. Dublin.[34] For Sinn Féin, the forty-four seats 'heralded the first step back, proving that all the people had not turned from 1916 or swallowed the whole Treaty line'.[35]

A general election, however, did little to end the despair of prisoners. On 4 September, Patrick Joseph O'Hanlon (16) died in the Curragh Military Hospital of a gunshot wound inflicted by Pte Joseph Barry in what was termed the 'execution of his duty' at Kilkenny Jail. The sentry had shot the teenager in the leg for no apparent reason, while O'Hanlon was reading a letter from his mother written before her death. In July, Patrick's mother, Mary, became ill and died within a few days. Despite being only sixteen years old and being detained less than thirty miles away at Kilkenny Jail, O'Hanlon apparently was not given temporary release to attend his mother's funeral. At the inquest held on 16 September, the coroner for South Kildare, Dr F. Kenna, wrote on Patrick O'Hanlon's death certificate: 'We consider the order issued a disgrace with regard to prisoners. We consider the other prisoners in the cell should have been provided as witnesses.'[36] Patrick O'Hanlon had joined Na Fianna Éireann in 1920 and was arrested in March 1923 after a cache of arms and secret documents were found in his hometown of Carrick-on-Suir, Co. Tipperary.[37] His death was one of many deemed reckless, inflicted by military guards with little weapons training or discipline.

10

Hunger for Release

Despite the ceasefire and arms dump order in May, the thousands of Republican prisoners held in jails and internment camps across the country faced their indefinite detention with a sense of basic unity. They were, in effect, almost hostages to prevent the resumption of Republican hostilities. Their ongoing imprisonment created a significant challenge for the government. If released hastily, Republicans might resume the war as they had only 'dumped arms', not admitted defeat. Many anticipated a return to action when the time was right. If held indefinitely, however, the prisoners would attract increasing public sympathy and there was already evidence of rising tension within the prisons and camps.[1] Although there were several applications for *habeas corpus* after the ceasefire and disarmament order, each was refused. Lord Justice O'Connor discharged an application on behalf of detainee Nora Connolly O'Brien on 15 June 1923, concluding that there was still a state of war: 'The Irish Republican Army did not state that a state of war had ceased to exist.' He added that the affidavit filed on behalf of O'Brien was insufficient and that the only evidence produced that the war had ended was an *Irish Times* article on 29 May 1923.[2]

Despite the collapse of morale due to executions and on-going imprisonment, what happened in the prisons was considered highly significant for the Republican cause. The next round of the Civil War was to be fought in the jails and camps throughout the country. With the war over, prisoners felt they should be released; the government thought otherwise.

On 1 July 1923, the number of Republican prisoners in the Free State was officially estimated as 11,316.[3] Of those held, 3,101 male prisoners were from Dublin; 2,275 were from Cork, 997 from Tipperary and 784 from Limerick – all areas that had been amongst the most active during the War of Independence. Counties that showed a high upsurge in activity during the Civil War, as indicated by the number of prisoners, included Kerry (936), Mayo (860), Louth (537), Sligo (475) and Wexford (407). The county with the lowest representation of prisoners was Fermanagh, with eight. The majority of those deported from Britain, male and female, who were then imprisoned in Ireland, came from Glasgow, Liverpool, London and Manchester.[4] The government began releasing prisoners as early as June 1923, and the numbers gradually fell.

New procedures were also set up to begin releasing those the government considered the least dangerous prisoners in dribs and drabs. The government had decided to class internees into four groups: those no longer regarded as a threat to the state; those who might be released on signing an undertaken to desist from armed resistance to the state; those who might be released when the country had returned to normality; those who might be held indefinitely, against whom a serious charge was, or would be, preferred. A committee of army officers and members of the Protective Corps reviewed the cases of internees, which saw around thirty-five of the least dangerous prisoners released every day. Within three months they investigated 1,100 cases and recommended continued detention in twenty per cent of them.[5]

Initially, pressure was exerted by demanding that prisoners sign the declaration renouncing armed resistance to the state. Prison discipline was tightened, privileges were revoked, and ordinary prisoners were introduced to wings where political prisoners were held. Most prisoners still refused to sign the declaration. While large-scale releases began in August, these were not happening quickly enough to defuse the rising anger among men in the prisons and internment camps at the fact that they were still detained after the courts had agreed with a captured document from the new anti-Treaty chief-of-staff, Frank Aiken, stating that the war was over.[6]

President Cosgrave was initially in favour of general amnesty, but he soon came to the conclusion that such a gesture would completely oppose what seemed to be the 'intense feeling there is against release of these prisoners' amongst government supporters'. He felt it was challenging to see how an immediate amnesty would win Republicans over to non-violent ways. Furthermore, the government's policy was calculated to demoralise the Republican movement further while reducing public sympathy. In this, it succeeded.[7]

As part of this new government strategy, the camp authorities in Tintown No. 2 demanded that the prisoners' OC of each hut should salute National Army officers. The prisoners refused, so the authorities decided to run the camp themselves. They cleared out the prisoners' staff from the cookhouse and ordered other internees to take their place. They, of course, refused and were marched off to the Military Detention Barracks, where there were allegations made that the men were beaten. Consequently, the prisoners refused to parade or co-operate with the camp authorities. Internees were locked in their huts for five days, not even being allowed out to the latrines. According to a report from the camp officer: 'At the end of this period, as the terrorism was of no avail, the attempt to break up the prisoners' organisation was abandoned.'

An officer's report, dated 29 August, also mentioned that three prisoners had gone insane and had been taken from the camp: Michael O'Hara, Ballinasloe, Co. Galway; George Fitzsimons, Dundalk, Co. Louth; and Henry Carraher, Cullyhanna, Co.

Armagh. The report said, 'we attribute this to the conditions which prevail here.'[8] Mental breakdown began with a demoralising melancholia, a feeling of being hopelessly trapped. In its most destructive form, it devolved into a captivity psychosis that left a victim unable to concentrate. Afflicted men became apathetic and inattentive and would spend entire days in their beds staring vacantly at the walls. The inherent uncertainty of confinement aggravated the condition. Unlike prisoners in a civilian jail, internees had no release date. The main thing was to keep busy, attend classes and have friends who supported you. Most internees bore up under the pressure and a few actually profited from the experience.

At the recent general election, Republicans had won forty-four seats to the government's sixty-three, giving them a renewed hope that the people were still supportive of their efforts. The Republican Movement believed that the people who had voted for them would back a hunger strike, use it as a rallying point and force the government to yield to public pressure. This pressure began over the autumn in the form of multiple petitions and resolutions from local government bodies calling for the release of internees. Daily, several county councils, urban councils or rural district councils passed resolutions calling for the immediate and frequently unconditional release of all political prisoners. The reasons given were: no justification for holding internees now that hostilities were over; the cost to the government of maintaining so many prisoners; the financial hardship faced by families whose main source of income was imprisoned; and the likelihood of increased bitterness and possible retribution the longer prisoners were held.[9] By mid-November, four county councils – Meath, Mayo, Clare and Offaly – at least fourteen urban district councils, sixteen rural district councils, ten trade union branches and farmers unions, and many other public bodies and groups passed resolutions demanding the immediate and unconditional release of all political prisoners.[10]

There were also ten *habeas corpus* applications before Justice William Huston Dodd, including one affidavit by Denis O'Moore, father of Patrick, Éamonn and Anthony O'Moore, against the commandant of Newbridge Barracks. Patrick (24), Éamonn (21) and Anthony O'Moore (20) had been captured at the surrender of the Four Courts in June 1922 and had been detained since then without charge or trial. Mr Lynn, acting on behalf of Éamonn O'Moore, submitted that his client was being held illegally and that his detention was a violation of the Constitution. In reply, Richard Mulcahy said that he felt that if Éamonn O'Moore were released, he would be a danger to public safety. The attorney-general, Hugh Kennedy, agreed. Justice Dodd said he was bound by the law to keep people in jail who were deemed a danger by the government; the order of release was refused. In the matter of Patrick and Anthony O'Moore, Justice Dodd, in refusing their release, said, 'like case, like result …'[11]

On 21 September, Richard Mulcahy announced that all women Republican prisoners would be released, but there were no assurances for the men that they would have a release date. Two days later, on 23 September 1923, West Cork Commandant Dan Hurley, Hut 15, Tintown No. 2 Camp, wrote to his mother that: 'The weather is getting cold here already and I'd want a new cardigan in a few weeks' time. I have clothes, shirts, flannels, caps and boots enough so it is for the winter which in all probability we will spend here.' Dan's brother was interned at Hare Park Camp, and also spent the winter of 1923–4 in captivity.[12]

Dublin City Council passed a motion on 24 September calling for the release of all Republican prisoners and condemned Mulcahy's refusal to allow visits, 'a right accorded to them during the Black and Tan regime'.[13] Patrick Hogan, Labour TD for Clare, told the Dáil that he was in possession of a memorial signed by 30,000 Clare residents calling for the release of political prisoners. Kevin O'Higgins responded to Clonmel No. 2 Rural

District Council's resolution calling for the release of prisoners with a letter stating that their release would constitute a danger to the country.[14]

According to Tom Garvin, 'in Newbridge Barracks prisoners were being taught courses in constitutional law, local government, and Irish history, under the aegis of Dan O'Donovan, a well-known Dáil civil servant who went anti-Treaty, by September 1923. He and other lecturers suggested that the military victory of the Free State could be reversed by peaceful means. Non-violent penetration of the local government apparatus would, in the long run, deliver the new state into the hands of its enemies. Local organisational centres were already being set up all over the twenty-six counties. This mixture of the military and the political, a central characteristic of Fianna Fáil, was a prime result of the Civil War. If there had been no conflict, Irish party politics would have been very different, almost certainly even more localist than it actually became.'[15]

September also saw a riot in Mountjoy Jail against the military authorities' attempt to treat Republicans as ordinary criminals and to adhere to regular prison regulations. Furniture was smashed and cells were damaged. During the disturbance, the water hoses were turned on the protesting prisoners on the bottom landing.[16] The riot and new regulations resulted in increased prisoner discontentment and the belief that release was not likely.

Some Republicans became more convinced that extreme measures were necessary – there were 9,697 prisoners still in custody on 1 October 1923.[17] Buoyed by their unexpectedly good showing in the August general election and continuing public sympathy, the IRA made a major mistake. On 13 October 1923, Michael Kilroy (Newport, Co. Mayo), OC IRA Western Command and recently elected TD for South Mayo, called for a hunger strike in Mountjoy Jail by 300 IRA prisoners protesting their continued incarceration and for unconditional release. Ten of the Mountjoy Jail hunger strikers, including Kilroy and Ernie O'Malley, were TDs. O'Malley reasoned 'a cease fire order had been issued in May, and it was now October. The Free State had little excuse for still keeping large numbers of men in prison'. The hunger strike quickly spread sporadically and without co-ordination or instruction to over ten prisons and camps, but as O'Malley later realised, 'it would have been better to have selected a number of really determined men, who might have been more fitted for such an ordeal than the heterogeneous complement of the four wings'.[18]

Veteran guerrilla leader Michael Kilroy (38), described as 'puritanical and ascetic', was the right man to lead a hunger strike.[19] A statement released by Kilroy made the position of the prisoners clear:

> Each of us, to himself and his comrades, solemnly pledges to refrain from food until he is unconditionally released. In taking this grave decision we, as citizens of Ireland, know that lovers of human liberty the world over will understand and respect our decision. Our lives and the suffering we shall endure we offer to God for the furtherance of the cause of truth and justice in every land and for the speeding of the day of Ireland's freedom.[20]

Because of government censorship, accurate information from the jails was slow in coming forth. The *Irish Times*, of 17 October, reported that it was the 'biggest hunger strike in history' and that 380 men were refusing food.[21] The protest soon spread to other jails and internment camps, and within two weeks, 7,003 prisoners had embarked on a hunger strike. The figures given by the Republican news sheet *Sinn Féin* were:

Mountjoy Jail:	462
Cork Jail:	70
Kilkenny Jail:	350
Dundalk Jail:	200
Gormanstown Camp:	711

Newbridge Barracks:	1,700
Tintown:	123
Curragh Camp:	3,390
Hare Park Camp:	100
North Dublin Union:	50 women[22]

The Free State authorities, knowing well the power of hunger strikes in Irish history, kept publicity for the protest to a minimum, preventing sympathetic media coverage. They also maintained a hard line against the prisoners' demands, insisting that early release would be denied to those taking part. The Executive Council drew no comparison between the hunger strikers of the War of Independence against an occupying British government and those who challenged the legitimate, democratically mandated government of the Free State. Their views and their intransigence were supported by the Catholic Church.

Despite the commencement of the strike, the main daily papers were largely and predictably indifferent to the prisoners' plight. Still, the Republican new sheets such as *Éire* and *Sinn Féin* ran regular commentary on the progress of the fast and the prisoners' determination. Nightly vigils were held at prisons throughout the capital. The Sinn Féin Ard Fheis opened at the Mansion House on 16 October and a unanimous motion of support was passed by the party. Mary MacSwiney, rather ambitiously, asked that all Republicans across Ireland refrain from alcohol as a means of impacting financially on the Free State Exchequer, but her suggestion was not put to a vote.[23] However, another suggestion to recite the Rosary publicly for seven days in all the towns and villages in the Free State, was taken up, with reports during the following weekend indicating that demonstrations of the kind were held in many districts.[24]

At 6.10 p.m. on Friday morning 19 October, a letter was

handed to a sentry at the gate of Hare Park Internment Camp:

To the Military Governor,

SIR,

The Republican prisoners in this camp will go on Hunger Strike at 8 p.m., Saturday evening for unconditional release, in sympathy with our comrades and political leaders in Mountjoy jail, upon whom your authorities are endeavouring to fix the status of criminals.

Every man in making this decision is clear within himself that the part he took in the recent war was prompted by the highest motive of patriotism, and by the faith which convinced him that to maintain the sovereignty of Ireland was his first duty as a soldier and an Irishman.

We realise that could your authorities succeed in Mountjoy Jail, an endeavour would be made to fix the same status upon us, and our present action has, therefore, been forced upon us in order to defend our position and honour that of our comrades.

The efforts made since our internment in this camp to degrade us from the status of prisoners of war, coupled with our prolonged detention, and this latest attack upon our comrades, notwithstanding the fact that the military campaign ended several months ago, proves to us that it is not an admission of military defeat that is required from us, but a renunciation of the principle for which we have fought and for which we shall be always willing to sacrifice ourselves.

It is now six months since the cessation of hostilities was ordered by our leaders. That order has been faithfully obeyed and is accepted by all who now make the decision to sacrifice their lives rather than accept for themselves or their comrades the status of criminals.

Signed, TOM HALES, Prisoners O/C.[25]

Tom Hales was the brother of TD Seán Hales, whose assassination on 7 December 1922, led directly to the retaliatory executions of Rory O'Connor, Liam Mellows, Dick Barrett and Joe McKelvey.

Not all prisoners were happy with the outcome of the hunger strike. Greg Ashe, from Kinard, Lispole, Co. Kerry, said, 'they went on hunger strike by the vote of huts. They were told that it would be over in a couple of days. In Hare Park, Paddy Paul Fitzgerald forced the bloody strike on the camp. And in 8 days, he walked out the gate, signed a paper, and went home. He was one of the Council inside. Paud O'Donoghue was, I think, in charge of us in Hare Park, and Con Moloney was his Adjutant.'[26] In his military pension application, Fitzgerald, an experienced activist since 1920, stated he was captured on 2 August 1922 and was released from internment in November 1923.[27]

In Newbridge Barracks, Todd Andrews wrote that Aiken's appeal for support for the Mountjoy hunger strikers was 'interpreted in the internment camps as an invitation to support the Mountjoy prisoners by joining the hunger strike and in Newbridge over two thousand decided to do so.'[28]

On the morning of 20 October, 1,858 prisoners in Tintown No. 1 refused food, while the entire 1,346 men on the rolls in Tintown No. 2 joined the hunger strike.[29] The camp committee in Tintown No. 2 had decided on joining the strike, and when put to the prisoners, they backed the action with a majority vote. Jack Feehan (Rossow, Co. Mayo), in Tintown 2, recalled that: 'Orders came in, as far as I remember, and we were to go on [hunger strike] in sympathy with the lads in the 'Joy. I think that it was left to a vote of the officers. Petie McDonnell was O/C of Tintown 2 then. We communicated with the next camp by a stone which was hurled well over the wires with a message in it, and we had to be very careful that the sentries didn't see us when it was thrown.'[30]

The determination of those who chose to go on hunger strike was to be sorely tested in the grim days that followed. The hardest part of the hunger strike was the first week, when the effects of a diet of warm water, salt and pepper began to take their toll on the men's will. Many prisoners survived on a diet of cigarettes and chewing gum, which helped dull the eternal craving for food.[31]

'There was an enforced fast,' Jack Comer said, 'for the Cook Houses were closed by Christie Byrne, and there was no cooking so you had to go on hunger strike.'[32]

Among the hunger strikers was sixteen-year-old Jack O'Brien, whose condition on 3 November was described as 'delicate'. O'Brien, a schoolboy from Minard, Dingle, Co. Kerry, had been arrested in February 1923. 'This child is hardly a danger to the Public', *Éire* harked. 'He has also been served with a Detention Certificate, which enables his jailors to keep him.'[33] The *Freeman's Journal* reported on 31 October that 'sixteen boys, not 16 years of age were in a bad condition' due to fasting.

The Re-organising Committee of Sinn Féin announced 'on reliable authority' that 1,301 prisoners at Tintown Camp had joined the hunger strike.[34] On 19 October, Martin McGrath, Ballina, Co. Mayo, a prisoner in Tintown No. 2 Camp, wrote: 'My dear Mother – This is going with young Brogan. It probably will be the last for some time, as we decided entering on hunger strike tonight for unconditional release, whatever the consequences entail. Our enemies have tried to fool us too long and break our moral spirit, so we will either smash them by this strike or die. The Staters would release me on Sunday last if I signed their infamous document. I wrote them today pointing out that if the signing of the document was to be a condition precedent to my release, whenever it does come, [release] must [be] unconditional absolutely. This is written on eve of hunger strike. Good-bye now, dear Mother. Say some prayers for our success. I just got this chance of sending you this. – Your fond son, Martin.'[35]

In the early hours of 20 October, 130 hunger strikers arrived from Mountjoy Jail in open lorries to Tintown No. 2. Twelve were removed to the camp hospital and had to be put to bed by their comrades who were already twenty-four hours on hunger strike. The rest were accommodated in Hut 18, a disused chapel with a concrete floor. Each man received a thin mattress and two blankets. The hut was unbelievably cold, and the men shivered under their meagre covers throughout the night. A doctor appeared the next morning, and according to reports, went away uninterested, while a military doctor refused to treat a sick hunger striker.[36]

According to *Éire*, fifty-two of the hunger strikers were brought to Tintown No. 3 Camp at 7 p.m. on 19 October. The prisoners who had been on hunger strike for seven days were brought from Mountjoy Jail to Broadstone Railway Station, at Constitution Hill:

> They were driven to Broadstone, poorly clad, in open lorries, and when at Broadstone they were kept for about an hour in the open before they were removed to the train. When they got to the Curragh they were kept in the train, famished with the cold, for over three hours. They were then put into lorries and kept another hour in the open-air before being driven to Tintown No. 3 Camp. The whole party were in a pitiable plight from cold and exposure. At the camp they were then kept in the open-air for another hour before they were shifted into a hut, into which most of the men had to be carried at 4 a.m.
>
> The doctors also in this camp will not treat any man 'who refuses food'. Hot water was cut off from the strikers for three days.
>
> The men are so weak they are confined to bed practically all day. The sanitary conditions are deplorable, and the men are now too weak to clean huts and remove refuse. Several are housed in stables and suffer intensely from cold. There are no stoves or heating apparatus of any kind. Purgatives supplied are totally insufficient.[37]

In Tintown Stephen Keys had major doubts about a fast to the death. He said, '… I thought to myself that I would not go on hunger strike I was married at the time and I said, "I am not going on hunger strike and have to go out of this place as a cripple". Dr Jim Ryan was Medical Officer of the Camp, and any men with any repute that did not want to go on hunger strike would have to go before him. There was a lot of people there who were not in the I.R.A. at all, mixed amongst us. There was quite a good queue of us outside, awaiting medical examination. I went into him.'

Keys claimed that he had a recent stomach operation and so could not go on hunger strike, but after an examination by Dr Ryan, which found no evidence of this, the doctor said sternly, 'you're a quartermaster … Give a good example to the men.' Keys had no choice but to go on a hunger strike, but after fifteen days, he had had enough. He went to the cookhouse, said he was coming off the hunger strike and was given a little Bovril – a thick and salty meat extract paste diluted with water – to begin the slow process of going back on food.[38]

Despite the high morale and determination of the leaders, as the days wore on, the number of men driven by hunger to break their fast began to mount. When a hunger striker broke, he was transferred by the authorities to another camp, and his companions were gleefully told by the military guards that he had been released. Prisoners who came off the protest were released upon signing a form promising to abstain from activities against the state. With the prospect of release for those willing to end their fast, many men could not see the point of starvation after their original enthusiasm faded.[39]

In Newbridge Barracks, Todd Andrews wrote: 'Within days men found they couldn't endure the lack of food and abandoned the hunger strike in increasing numbers until one day, after about a week had passed, a mass hysteria swept the camp. The cookhouse with its very abundant stock of food was raided by the prisoners transformed into an uncontrollable mob. It was a most unedifying and humiliating sight.

'Some men persevered but day by day more dropped out.

After fourteen days Jack Plunkett and I decided that the whole effort was futile and was creating division and personal animosities in the camp. We decided to come off the strike. Fourteen days without food ... left me with no disabilities, real or imaginary, beyond the discomfort of hunger which became less after a few days. We lived on tobacco and cigarettes and "hunger strike soup". I didn't have to stay in bed. I walked round the compound as usual.' Because he was camp adjutant, Andrews was approached by other hunger strikers asking him to give them permission to end their fast. He explained that hunger striking was voluntary and that there was no disgrace in ending their fast, but many felt they had let their comrades down by giving up. Those who gave up, grudgingly, resented those who continued to fast.[40]

Initially, the government had been releasing prisoners in a steady stream, but with the commencement of the hunger strike all those on the protest were denied release, even if they had been earlier recommended.[41] On 21 October, the government finally made a pronouncement on the subject of the hunger strike: that the government would not yield to this attempt to secure the 'unconditional release' of prisoners and there would be no concessions. Speaking in Dublin W. T. Cosgrave said that the prisoners had caused death, destruction and misery. They were in jail because neither life nor property was safe while they were at large – and they would remain in prison until life was as safe in the Free State as it was in any other country in the world. The hunger strike was a fraud, he claimed. Brown bread and pastilles were found in some prisoners' pockets! He maintained that if a prisoner died, it would be his own fault, and not the government's.[42]

Regardless of appeals from many quarters, including Dr Daniel Mannix, the Catholic archbishop of Melbourne, Archbishop Edward J. Byrne, of Dublin and Cardinal Michael

Logue, archbishop of Armagh and primate of all Ireland, the government was unanimous in its aim to remain immovable in the face of the strike.[43] Nevertheless, the large number of prisoners on hunger strike alarmed the government, which was afraid that if a massive number of deaths occurred, public opinion would swing away from them to the Republican Movement and could jeopardise the little stability the state had gained.

On 25 October, IRA chief-of-staff Frank Aiken sent a message of support and encouragement to the thousands of internees throughout the country. In referring to a campaign of alleged disinformation that had been waged against the hunger strikers by the news media, Aiken implored the men to remain steadfast:

> Listen to the lies but do not heed them ... Smile at the threats of the enemy to put you on the lists of the country's historic dead. Smile at their sneers that you will be forgotten by the people who are proud, beyond all else, of being citizens of the Nation for which Tone, Pearse and MacSwiney died. Smile at the threats that God, Whose Son died to save mankind, will punish you for following his example.

Aiken had chosen his timing – it was the third anniversary of Terence MacSwiney's death on hunger strike – and his words invoked the men's Catholic faith of self-sacrifice for others.[44]

While some hunger strikers' determination had waned, *Sinn Féin* reported that there were ultimately 7,843 prisoners on hunger strike, including fifty women at the North Dublin Union. The news sheet said there were 3,300 on strike at Tintown Nos 1, 2 and 3; a further 1,000 fasting at Hare Park; and 1,700 on strike at Newbridge Barracks.[45] (The decision to go on hunger strike was not universally welcomed by the prisoners and while over 7,800 joined the fast, around 3,000 did not participate.) To counteract Republican propaganda, the Free State Publicity Bureau daily announced the toll of prisoners giving up their hunger strike, making sure the day-to-day newspapers received the up-to-date figures.[46] Todd Andrews said, 'some of the men simply refused to give in. They carried on for over forty days reacting to the prolonged fast in very different ways. Some suffered from hallucinations, some were just wasted from hunger, some were apparently unaffected physically or mentally.'[47]

From the beginning of the protest, the large number of prisoners on hunger strike was a problem for the IRA leadership. Some officers sought to limit the number joining the protest, but the request was turned down in case it caused bitterness among the prisoners if one was picked over the other. Some prisoners participated in the hunger strike without fully considering its implications. Within days, men found they could not endure the lack of food and abandoned the hunger strike in increasing numbers, further dividing the prisoners and adding to their de moralisation.[48]

Michael Hopkinson wrote: 'The strike became an ill-defined and poorly planned sympathy one, which imposed enormous strains on individuals and their consciences. There was little clarity about its purpose, or about when it could be called off, by whom, and on what grounds.'[49]

A meeting of the camp committee was held on the eleventh day of the hunger strike in Tintown. For the sake of morale, it was decided that those who felt they could not carry on the hunger strike should end it immediately, while those who felt they could carry on would take the burden. On the final count it was found that sixty-seven men elected to remain on strike, while the remainder ended their fast. Two of the men were Denis Sheerin and Thomas Loftus, Bonniconlon, Co. Mayo, while the rest were men from Cork and Kerry. Following the decision, the sixty-seven hunger strikers were transferred from their usual billets and lodged in Hut 16.[50]

Embarking on a hunger strike meant long-term health con-sequences. The effects of abstaining from food were lifelong and heralded premature death in many cases. IRA leader Austin Stack died prematurely in 1929, partly as a result of the deprivations he suffered in prison.[51] Peadar O'Donnell noted, 'I think the main pain of hunger strike must be the apprehension of death ... the greatest sensation of a hunger strike is the exhilaration the mind achieves'.[52]

Boredom was one of the most common complaints of internment, but the hunger strike protest gave many prisoners new meaning. The budding writer Francis Stuart was captured after a running fight in Dublin on 9 August 1922. He received a copy of Fyodor Dostoevsky's *The Brothers Karamazov* hidden in a food parcel. For Stuart, prison was a perfect setting to read and later discuss Dostoevsky's philosophical novel that examines free will, morality and the existence of God. Having spent six months in Maryborough Jail, Stuart was transferred to Tintown, where he found more literature that had been smuggled into the camp. Stuart came under the influence of writer Joseph Campbell, to whom he read some of his poems. Because he was so skinny and looked sickly and tubercular, Stuart was declared unfit for work and, along with other idle prisoners, read and discussed the writings of Pearse, Connolly, John Mitchell and Thomas Davis.[53]

'In the mornings across the wire we could see the race-horses out at gallops,' he later wrote. 'And far away, climbing a small hill, I saw a woman in a red dress, and I watched her in astonishment, not having seen anyone but men for a long time ... I became very bored in the internment camp. To me it was much worse than the prison. There was no privacy. I was never a moment alone for the nine months I was kept there. As I had not been sentenced there was no way of knowing when I would be free. And it seemed useless to go on dreaming about a future that seemed as far away as ever.

'... I became ill and went to hospital. There I lay in bed all day for weeks reading. What I read I don't remember. For days I lay not reading, not doing anything, just thinking. The only thing that interested me in the camp was the boxing tournaments in which I used to take part. I even used to get up and leave the hospital to box in them. The military doctor was very friendly and kept me in hospital long after I was well.'[54]

When he joined the mass hunger strike, Stuart was no longer bored but was happy now as he had embarked on what he called a 'game'... 'staking our lives against public opinion. That I believe was the object of the hunger strike – to stir public opinion in favour of our release. It was,' he said, 'about the slowest game I have ever played'. Stuart could no longer read as it made him dizzy, but he gave himself away to his thoughts on food, of course, and other things, too. Where was the mysterious, romantic life that had lured me? Where had I got myself? Into bed in a filthy stable in a prison camp without food for a week.'

Suart drank hot water with pepper and salt, which he said tasted like soup, but after a few days the taste disgusted him and he could no longer drink the concoction. His friend Joseph Campbell visited him for the first few days, but then stopped visiting. 'He began to conserve his energy for the final act,' Stuart wrote, 'as he put it in a note which he sent to me by a Free State soldier.'

'I lay under the grey verminous blankets, unwashed and un-shaven, for after the first few days few of us had the energy to walk to the wash house which was some distance from our hut. I suffered, too, from cold, which when there is no replenishment of warmth in the body appears to grow intense. We kept the windows shut. The air grew stale, but not warm. My tongue became coated and felt horrible and unclean in my mouth ... When it rained a trickle of water came in under the converted stables and lay blackly between the cobbles. Down the centre of the hut the urinal buckets stood at intervals and when we became too weak to carry the full buckets out Free State soldiers kicked them over.'[55]

On 20 October, Joseph Campbell wrote: 'Did not sleep well during the night. Heart's action accelerating – blood pounding.' A group of 130 hunger strikers from Mountjoy Jail had been transferred the night before to Tintown and were housed in Hut 18 where Campbell visited them. 'Went in – picking steps between men stretched on mattresses, wrapt [*sic*] in blankets on the floor. Middle of hut cluttered too – sides full – blankets overflowing everywhere. Like a casualty-clearing station after a battle. Men with white, waxen, death-like faces (some lying, some sitting up against wall) & yellowed eyes. Iodine-stained bandages. Neckcloths round heads with headache. Lips, cracked, dry, blood-caked. Mugs of water. Tintown prisoners setting up beds … Opinion rife that F.S. may let 300 men die. They're bankrupt in policy; bankrupt in humanity; bankrupt in civilisation.'[56]

The government, bankrupt morally in Republican eyes, stuck to its hardline attitude. It fell to the Minister for Finance, the passionate *Gaeilgeoir* Ernest Blythe, to outline to the fasting prisoners in Newbridge Barracks the consequences if they did not end their fast: 'We are not going to force-feed you, but if you die we won't waste coffins on you and will put you in orange boxes and you will be buried in unconsecrated ground. So have sense and come off it.'[57]

As part of the government's continued show of determination, the release of all prisoners on hunger strike was suspended on 26 October. However, prisoners who came off the strike were released once they signed the form promising to abstain from activities against the state.[58] While the strike continued, morale had deteriorated. A meeting of the camp council in Tintown was planned for 28 October to decide whether to continue the strike, but according to Joseph Campbell there was a 'great stampede of food-takers during the night. It began after lock-up … It continues this morning. The men don't care if they are seen now, so many are going.' Campbell voted to continue the hunger strike, one of 253 who did so; many others did not even bother to vote. Rumours circulated that the strike was over. Campbell said he would wait until the official announcement, but when he saw many of his comrades heading towards the military police hut, he went, too. Milk and eggs were ladled into tin mugs followed by tea and soup.[59]

Francis Stuart wrote, '… on the eleventh day, the general hunger strike was called off. It had apparently failed. At the same time from then on prisoners began to be released. And now that freedom was close I seemed to have lost all interest in it. I was even frightened at the idea of it. I felt tired, dispirited, suffering from nostalgia.'[60]

National Army Headquarters issued a statement on 30 October saying that 376 men in Tintown No. 1 and forty-three men in Tintown No. 2, had abandoned the strike. A further thirty-five in Newbridge had also discontinued their protest. The statement continued, 'in all, approximately 3,200 prisoners have gone off hunger strike in the past five days.'[61] The *Irish Times'* Newbridge correspondent reported that twelve prisoners from Newbridge Barracks were released along with thirteen from Tintown, and when they arrived at Newbridge Railway Station, two of them collapsed.[62]

The collapse of the hunger strike was inevitable. At Tintown No. 1 Camp one of the prisoners, on behalf of the other hunger strikers, gave the governor the following written note: 'This is to inform you that the hunger strike is terminated.'[63] When the strike collapsed, an officer in Tintown No. 3 declared: 'Of course, the main mistake was to allow so many men to go on in the beginning. Joe Harrington and myself pleaded at the Camp Council for a limit to be put on the number of men (I suggested

700) but this was turned down on the plea that it would cause a lot of bitterness because some good men were afraid to be overlooked, and also every day we lost we were letting down the boys in the Joy'.[64]

By the evening of 3 November, only 1,531 remained on hunger strike, with the Hare Park Camp protest collapsing that day. The next evening saw the number on hunger strike down to 671.[65] Joseph Campbell wrote in his diary for 4 November: 'I'm convinced that a hunger strike is not worthwhile. The cost is too great; the conditions too bad, the value set on human life or on mere humanitarianism too trifling in Ireland today.'[66] One major problem was that large numbers of hunger strikers could not stay the course after the original enthusiasm faded. The prospect of release for those willing to come off the strike also removed the purpose of the protest.[67]

Newbridge Barracks contained some men still on hunger strike and outside the grey stone walls support for them persisted. On 4 November, a resolution was passed in favour of the release of all political prisoners in Irish and English jails at a meeting of the Co. Kildare Labour Party and Workers Council in Newbridge. A planned public meeting in the town in support of the release of political prisoners, which the government proclaimed with the civic guard preventing people from entering the town unless on legitimate business, drew further resolutions and protests.

A steady stream of hunger strikers continued to abandon their fast until only 328 remained on the protest by the second week of November.[68] Johnny O'Connor (Farmer's Bridge, Tralee) said, 'after 14 days strike, a crowd, one night, broke out to the quartermaster's stores [in Newbridge] where parcels were piled up since the strike began. They ate raw meat and fistfuls of butter. Then we shrank in numbers until we had 2 huts.'[69]

A statement issued by the Ministry of Defence on 8 November said that: 'fifty-five prisoners ceased hunger strike during the last 24 hours, leaving 430 still on hunger strike. It is learned that amongst those who were on hunger strike and are now taking food are – Messrs R. C. Barton, T.D.; Seán T. O'Kelly, T.D.; P. Barrett, Thos. Hales, P. J. McDonnell (Connemara), S. Gaynor (N. Tipperary), M. Kelly (brother of Mr S. T. O'Kelly), and C. Traynor.'[70]

On 17 November, *Sinn Féin* reported that there were still thirty-three men on hunger strike in Tintown No. 2:

All are determined to remain to the end. The conditions here are intolerably inhuman.

The men on strike are all now herded in Hut 15 – a disused Depot for diseased horses. It is cold, cheerless, and miserable. The wooden lining that once existed is now practically torn away, revealing raw gaping patches of corrugated iron, covered in moisture in damp, and hoary with ice in frosty weather. The floor is rough cement, on which the least footfall sounds intolerably loud to weak and ailing men. One can then picture what it is like when the military, seem bent on an interminable count of us, stamp in six and eight times at the time, many times during the day and every hour during the night. Even our own orderlies, who attend during the night, cannot forbear from breaking the rest of light sleepers amongst us as the rough stoves have to be kept going and stirred up so as to keep up the hot water supply. The good lads are very attentive and doing all they can for us.

Our greatest enemy here is the medical profession who have prostituted their time-honoured calling and become mere tools of F.S. G.H. [Free State General Headquarters]. These doctors seldom visit the men; when they do they spend all their time trying to undermine their morale by stating 'They are all off in Mountjoy, Newbridge, etc.' Dr Nolan, of Dalkey, who started this policy, became alarmed at the steadfastness of some of the very worst cases, and ultimately threw up his brief and got transferred somewhere else. His successor, Dr Walsh, Ballina, went into every man's case and sent in an urgent report to his superiors, with the result that Dr Doyle was sent down from the Curragh Hospital. Doyle is a very truculent person who has done nothing to alleviate the sufferings of the men. He tells us if we do not give in we will be let die. Dr Boland, Adj. Curragh Hospital, also visits here. This man is sneeringly apathetic and will not even examine the men. There is another doctor named O'Brien who serves his F.S. masters in similar thorough fashion.

Fr Ryan, the Chaplain, refused us the Sacraments. I sent a letter to the Command Chaplain, Curragh, reporting the matter and asking if this procedure had his cognisance and sanction. If not, to make arrangements to meet the case at once. Result: Fr Hughes and another priest visited us next day and gave Confession. Holy communion is denied all hunger strikers on theological grounds.[71]

This letter was signed by Joseph 'Joe' Considine (Ennis) and while it paints a grim view of conditions and the medical profession, it is a real enough account of what faced the hunger strikers. Republicans would long blame the deaths of prisoners on the apathetic conditions and general neglect by camp medical staff. Considine came close to death after a forty-one-day hunger strike. He was released in December 1923.[72]

Inevitably, the hunger strike took its toll on the health of the protesting men.[73] Denis Barry, a veteran of the War of Independence in Cork, was arrested on 6 October 1922 in Courtown Harbour, Co. Wexford, by National troops and brought to Newbridge Camp, where he was detained without charge or trial. Denis was first detained in L Block, in old army huts which had no beds or heating. He was later moved to K Block, where conditions were a little better. Barry joined the mass hunger strike on 17 October 1923 to support his protesting comrades. On 6 November he wrote his final letter to his brother Bartholomew or 'Batt' ... 'I hope there is nobody worrying over-much, as for the present, thank God, I am as strong as can be expected, not having eaten for 21 days, but otherwise can sit up in bed, and get out while it is being dressed. The general state of my health, now at any rate, is really very good. I need nothing for the moment as friends I have by the hundred who attend me so my advice to ye is to do everything with a light heart, trust God for His hand is greater than those who hold me here.'[74]

However, the health of Denis Barry went into serious decline from 12 November and two days later, Fr P. Doyle, chaplain of Newbridge Barracks, gave him the last rites. On Saturday, 17 November, a telegram reached the Barry home in south-east Cork, which read: 'Your brother is now seriously ill in Newbridge Internment Camp, Co. Kildare. Every facility will be given to his family to visit him on making a personal application to the Governor.' Batt Barry left immediately to travel the 140 miles to Newbridge. On his arrival at the barracks, Batt met the military governor, Seán Hayes, who escorted him to a hut where he said he saw his brother and three other men lying on stretcher beds on a dirty floor. Denis Barry was conscious but could not speak, and when he tried, he went into convulsions. A doctor arrived and Batt had to leave.[75]

Batt Barry returned the next day and, having seen Denis again, asked Governor Hayes to move his brother to the hospital, but he was told that nothing could be done if he continued to refuse food. Batt then sent a telegram to the Minister of Defence, Richard Mulcahy, stating that Denis should be sent to a nursing home, but the reply was: 'No internee can force release by hunger strike.' He then signed a document in the presence of Gov. Hayes stating that his brother could receive food and treatment to save his life. According to Capt. D. L. Kelly, medical officer in charge of Newbridge Barracks, Denis Barry was given cardiac stimulants and some nutrient enemas. Capt. Kelly said he did everything possible short of forced feeding – which was forbidden by the authorities – to prolong Barry's life.[76]

Denis Barry was brought by ambulance to the Curragh Military Hospital the next day, Monday, 19 November, between 3 p.m. and 4 p.m., but he died at 2.45 a.m. the following morning. Batt arrived at Newbridge Barracks that morning to see Denis and was informed he had died in the Curragh Military Hospital. An inquest was held by Kildare coroner, Dr F. Kenna, who attributed death to heart failure due to inanition caused by his refusal to take food. Dr Kenna requested that the body be handed over to his relatives. When Batt and his brother-in-law, Walter Dain, arrived at the Curragh Camp the authorities refused to hand over the remains. The family consulted a legal team in Dublin and instructed them to act on their behalf, but when Batt again arrived to claim his brother's remains, he was informed that the military authorities had already buried Denis Barry at a site near the 'Glasshouse' Military prison. The Barry family members went to the grave and recited the rosary.[77]

During a debate in the Dáil, Gen. Mulcahy said that the bodies of any prisoners who died on hunger strike would not be handed over to their relatives at present, but later they might decide to hand over the body of Denis Barry. He said the government much regretted having to take this decision. However, on 26 November, following a High Court action, the remains of Denis Barry were exhumed from the site near the Glasshouse and handed over to his family. The remains were transferred from the coffin supplied by the military to a coffin provided by his relatives and removed to a mortuary in Naas, and then brought to Newbridge Town Hall, where the body lay in state overnight, flanked by a Republican guard of honour. Solemn requiem high mass was celebrated the next morning, and at 1.00 p.m., the remains were brought to Newbridge Railway Station and entrained for the 1.42 p.m. train to Cork.

The remains of Denis Barry arrived at Glanmire Terminus on the afternoon of 27 November, where they were met by a large crowd of sympathisers and the Tomás MacCurtain Pipers' Band. The body was to be taken to St Finbar's Catholic church, but more controversy awaited. Under the orders of the bishop of Cork, Dr Daniel Cohalan, the remains were not permitted to enter any church in the diocese, and all his priests were ordered to stay away from the funeral. Cohalan, a great supporter of a previous hunger striker, Terence MacSwiney, also forbade any of his priests to officiate at any religious ceremonies for the deceased. He wrote to the bishop of Kildare and Leighlin, Dr Patrick Foley, in whose diocese Denis Barry had died, asking whether Denis had received the last sacraments, as he did not trust a Republican statement that he had. Fr P. Doyle, prison chaplain for Newbridge Camp, confirmed in writing that he had administered the last rites of the church before Denis Barry's death, but Cohalan still refused to allow his body entry into his parish church.[78]

Having been denied the benefit of a Christian burial, Barry's remains were taken by a procession, headed by the Tomás MacCurtain Pipers' Band, to the headquarters of Sinn Féin, at 56 Grand Parade, in Cork City. In a letter to the *Cork Examiner*, Dr Cohalan wrote:

> I am not allowing religious exercises, which constitute Christian burial, to take place at the burial of Denis Barry. I regret very much to feel obliged to adopt this course.

> I knew deceased. I knew him to be interested in and to have a great knowledge of the social and moral question of dangers that beset girls in Cork and all through Munster. 1 knew him to be a very good man.

> But if it were my brother who had taken the course that Denis Barry chose to take, I should treat his burial in the same way. I am but enforcing the laws of the Church.

Demonstrating that he still believed Republican actions necessitated whatever punishments were available to the bishops, Cohalan concluded: 'I shall interpret the law of the Church strictly and refuse Christian burial. I feel bound to do it, especially on account of the challenge to the Church.'[79]

The funeral the next morning to the Republican Plot, in St Finbarr's Cemetery, was one of the largest seen in Cork for some time. Cinemas, dance halls, places of amusement and many businesses closed their shutters as a sign of respect. The *Cork Examiner* reported that 'it took in excess of six hours for the funeral to arrive at St Finbarr's Cemetery'. At the graveside, a decade of the rosary was led by Annie MacSwiney, sister of hunger striker Terence MacSwiney. Further prayers were recited by David Kent, TD, brother of Thomas Kent, executed in 1916. Before the burial, David Kent also sprinkled the grave with holy water. Mary MacSwiney, another sister of the hunger striker, Terence, gave a short oration.[80]

Denis Barry was forty when he died and had been on hunger strike for thirty-four days. His obituary, referring to Cosgrave's assertion that the hunger strikers were 'calling the bluff' of the Irish people, said:

> Commandant Denis Barry, 1st Southern Division, died on hunger strike in the Curragh Hospital today. It was with mixed feelings of sorrow and pride we heard the fatal tidings that Denis Barry had 'called the bluff' of Mr Cosgrave and his Ministers by giving all that he had – his life – to maintain the living Republic, which has forsaken so many. Thus has our sacred cause been further sanctified by a hero's blood, and Dinny Barry has gone to his eternal rest, where there are no bars or chains to bind his unselfish spirit.[81]

However, public outcry was almost non-existent, and there was no increase in anti-government sentiment afterwards. Coupled with Cohalan's stance, this reaffirmed to the government ministers that their hardline attitude to the hunger strike was the right course of action.

Meanwhile, the hunger strike had claimed another victim. Andrew O'Sullivan (38), died in St Bricin's Military Hospital on 23 November, having fasted for forty days. He was transferred from Mountjoy Jail while gravely ill and subsequently died of acute pneumonia. O'Sullivan, from Denbawn, Co. Cavan, had been working for the Department of Agriculture in Mallow, Cork, when he was arrested on 5 July 1923. By the time of his burial, on 27 November, the hunger strike had ended. It was reported that there had been unsuccessful attempts to 'feed' O'Sullivan after he slipped into a coma and this was sufficient in the eyes of Fr Patrick Casey to determine that his fast had ended, therefore, allowing O'Sullivan a Christian burial. Technically, in the eyes of the Church, O'Sullivan did not die on hunger strike, so his burial could go ahead in consecrated ground. His funeral cortege was reported to have been one mile long and was headed by sixty uniformed members of Cumann na mBan.[82]

With the deaths of Barry and O'Sullivan failing to elicit any positive response or concessions from the government, the IRA command ordered the strikes to cease. The hunger strike had been opposed by the leadership outside and even some of the men inside Mountjoy – Andy Cooney and Art O'Connor, TD, were against it. Andy Cooney, OC Republican prisoners on Mountjoy's C Wing, recognising its futility, had made his views known to Michael Kilroy as early as 13 November and again asked him to call the strike off.

Primate of all Ireland Cardinal Michael Logue had deemed the hunger strike foolish and 'of very doubtful morality' but urged the government to release all non-convicted internees. Politically active from an early age, but by no means a Republican, Logue resolutely opposed Republican violence in both the War of Independence and the Civil War. Although disappointed by partition, Logue firmly favoured the Anglo–Irish Treaty of December 1921 and was the architect of the Bishop's Pastoral of October 1922. He openly supported Cumann na nGaedheal during the 1923 general election.[83] In a letter read aloud at masses in his archdiocese of Armagh on 18 November 1923, Logue appealed to the hunger strikers to abandon the 'dangerous and unlawful expedient' of protest. His private contacts and visit to the hunger strike leadership in Kilmainham Gaol also helped ease the decision to call off the fast.[84] After much consultation with his comrades, Kilroy finally asked the governor of Mountjoy, Capt. Colm Ó Murchadha, to come to his cell, where he announced the hunger strike was to end.[85]

The military governor of Kilmainham Gaol subsequently received the following letter on 22 November:

> Dear Sir, I shall be greatly obliged if you endeavour without delay to obtain permission from your authorities for me to send two delegates to those prisons and camps where there are hunger strikers with a view to calling off the strike. In case this be granted, I am desirous that the delegates should travel tonight and with the least possible delay, and that they be provided with a closed motor car. I desire also that the interviews between my delegates and the prisoners' representatives should be private. The delegates will give their word of honour not to attempt to escape if a guard be not placed with them inside the motor – (Signed) Michael Mac Giollaruaidh [Kilroy], OC Prisoners.

The mode of transport chosen by Michael Kilroy were provided. During that night and the following morning, Tom Derrig and David Robinson, prisoners in Kilmainham Gaol, visited the men on hunger strike in Mountjoy Jail and the internment camps at the Curragh and Newbridge. Liam Hearty, who was interned in Mountjoy, travelled to see the men in Dundalk Jail. The women on hunger strike in the North Dublin Union also received a delegate. As a result of these visits, all prisoners who were on hunger strike decided to end their fast.[86]

The Newbridge correspondent of the *Irish Independent* wrote: 'I was informed this morning that two Republican officers called at Newbridge Internment Camp and the Internment Camp at the Curragh last night, and as a consequence of their visit, the hunger strike was called off.

'I was also informed that releases on an extensive scale were to begin immediately, and it is stated all the camp will be cleared before Christmas.'[37]

In Tintown's Hut 16, the men on hunger strike had fallen, through ill-health and breakdown, to twenty-one. At 3 a.m. on 23 November, Tom Derrig entered Hut 16 to end the thirty-seven-day ordeal of the remaining hunger strikers. Derrig was on the fortieth day of his hunger strike. Among those who remained were Denis Sheerin and Thomas Loftus. Sheerin said, 'No real I.R.A. man broke the strike between the 1st and 10th day while there was spirit left, and most of those who broke off were not members of the I.R.A.'[88]

From Mountjoy Jail, Michael Kilroy issued the following press statement:

> As the Officer Commanding Mountjoy prisoners on 13th October last, it was I who inaugurated the present hunger strike, and I wish to state:-

> The hunger strike was started in Mountjoy as a last resort against the inhuman conditions existing there, and was participated in by the free choice of each individual who went on it.

> It was neither order nor recommended by the leaderships of the Republican Party, or by G.H.Q., I.R.A.

> It has been carried on as was it started – by the free will of each individual engaged thereon.

> I record these facts in order to correct misstatements by members of the Free State Government appearing from day to day in the daily press.

> In response to the appeal by his Eminence Cardinal Logue, reinforced by the later appeal of Prof. O'Rahilly, I have decided to call off the hunger strike, as from Friday, the 23rd November, 1923.

> I ask every striker in every camp and jail to accept this decision, and inform them that on learning this has been done the strike will be called off in this jail also.

> For the sake of Ireland, and for the future, we must make this sacrifice, as we consider future deaths to Irishmen at the hands of brother Irishmen will only perpetuate unending bitterness in our loved country.

A note, signed by Kilroy, also accompanied the announcement:

> Tom Derrig, having been deputed by Michael Kilroy, TD, called on the men in Mountjoy and the several Curragh camps and Newbridge. It having been decided to go off hunger strike in these camps, the hunger strike is now terminated here.[89]

On hearing the news of the ending of the hunger strike, Josephine Plunkett placed an advert in the *Irish Independent* asking for donations of 'chicken and beef tea and the jelly of calves' feet to be brought to the prisons'.[90] Prisoners also reported that they were getting plenty of milk, tea and Bovril. The mass hunger strike had lasted forty-one days and included participants at ten locations. Two hunger strikers had died, Denis Barry and Andy O'Sullivan.

The next day Joseph Campbell recorded in his dairy that he was informed before the morning head count by the 'greasy cook' that the hunger strike was 'declared off in all jails & camps … About 10 a.m. the 22 men off strike were carried by prisoners & P.A.'s to Hospital 16. 3 cases removed to Curragh Hospital.' He mentioned that Tom Derrig and David Robinson had arrived in the camp that morning at 2 a.m. transported by government vehicle from Mountjoy Jail to meet with the hunger strikers.[91]

At the end, there were still 221 men on hunger strike.[92] Ernie O'Malley wrote that the strike ended with no promises of release: 'We had been defeated again, and although some wanted to continue the strike, yet they all agreed to fall in with the majority.'[93] Undaunted Peadar O'Donnell darkly quipped that the physical and psychological strain was worth it for his post-hunger strike feast: 'You have missed one of life's great moments if you haven't tasted a brandy egg-flip after a forty-one-day fast.'[94]

While the strike itself failed to win releases, it did begin a slow start to a programme of release of prisoners, the government being worried about the political impact of more deaths. Five hundred prisoners were released during the week ending 10 November. The Free State Publicity Bureau, eager to prove that the government did not want to keep Republicans in custody, published information showing that on 1 July 1923, there were 11,316 Republicans imprisoned and that by 17 November, this number had been reduced to 6,834. By 23 November, the last day of the hunger strike, the total number of prisoners was down to 6,124, with 2,303 having been released during the period of the protest.[95] The requirement to sign the form was quietly abandoned. While there was an increase in the number of prisoners released, the government decided that a mass release policy would have made it appear that the protest had been a success, thereby justifying and vindicating the Republicans' hunger strike policy.

With the ending of the hunger strike and no concessions gained, the discipline, which had held the prisoners together, began to erode further. Todd Andrews wrote that the will to escape had gone, interest in the Irish language had disappeared, and nobody spoke or tried to learn Gaelic.[96] In the jails and camps, the strikes' collapse had a demoralising effect on prisoners; many viewed the futility of resuming armed resistance once released. For the government, the hunger strike had involved enormous dangers. Many deaths could have produced a considerable sympathetic reaction in the tradition of Republican martyrdom, but the government gambled and remained firm. In the following months, the question of a general amnesty was often debated but always rejected in favour of what was known as the 'dribble' policy, in which prisoners were let out slowly. In some instances, officers were released, and the rank and file were kept. High-value prisoners like Ernie O'Malley and Tom Derrig were retained. It was all designed to disillusion the internees. Cardinal Logue's appeal for a general release of all prisoners by Christmas was largely ignored.[97] At the end of the year, there were 1,852 prisoners still in custody.[98]

The mass hunger strike had taken a huge toll on the prisoners over the forty-one days with nothing gained. There was little support for the strikers as the people were suffering from war-weariness by this stage. The independence struggle was now ten years old, and the population had had enough of violence and political discord. Any momentum Republicans had received from the general election was lost in the hunger strike. For government officials, the collapse of the hunger strike only served to bolster their resolve. They saw the strikes' outcome as a victory and a strong perception of their newly appointed power. With the end of the hunger strike, the release of prisoners was hurried up. However, the releases were only completed in the summer of 1924, and after that time, only those convicted of criminal acts remained.[99]

Many hunger strikers suffered ill-health due to their fast, and the lack of food had its after-effects, health-wise, too. *Sinn Féin* reported on 15 December that one of the hunger strikers, P. McElliot (Kerry), had lost his eyesight, while three others had gone insane.[100] Joseph 'Joe' Lacey, Wexford, continued to decline after the end of the hunger strike and died in the Curragh Military Hospital on 24 December 1923.[101] On Christmas morning at mass, the prisoners received the sad news that their comrade Joe Lacey had died on Christmas Eve in the Military Hospital.

'Lacey's death is a direct result of the hunger strike and the improper treatment given afterwards,' *Éire. The Irish Nation* said. He stuck the strike until called off and, in a couple of weeks, was brought into the hospital here, officially stated to be suffering from pneumonia. He was kept here for ten days and then removed to the Curragh Hospital. It was too late. The strike and the lack of proper treatment had so enfeebled what seemed to be a strong and vigorous man that he passed away on Christmas Eve ...'[102]

Fianna Éireann adjutant, James Pyne (19), returned home in ill-health to Cork from Newbridge Barracks where he had undergone a hunger strike. He died a year later of heart failure, on 11 November 1924, at his Old Youghal Road home, in Cobh, and was buried in the Republican Plot in St Finbarr's Cemetery.[103]

His death, like many others plagued by ill-health because of hunger-striking, passed almost unnoticed except in their home areas.

Richard Hume (25), Ballyduff, Camolin, Co. Wexford, died of heart failure due to pernicious anaemia on 9 November 1923, having been brought from Tintown No. 3 to the Curragh Military Hospital.[104] At the inquest held at Camolin, his brother, James Hume, a soldier in the National Army, had asked for the inquiry, as he alleged that his brother had been neglected while in the military hospital. James Hume, stationed at Kenmare, Co. Kerry, said that his brother had been interned for fifteen months, and on receipt of a wire from the commandant of the Curragh Camp, he visited Richard in the military hospital, where he found his brother in bed and very ill. James Hume said he spent five days there, and he did not see the doctor, although he had asked for him. While he was there, Richard changed for the worse, and before James left, he told him he had been neglected and would not recover. An internee named Philip Neill was the only patient in the ward with him.

Another internee, Dr James Ryan, called the immediate attention of the military doctor to the grave condition of Richard Hume, and that he should be released and sent to a hospital, which was not done.[105] The inquest was adjourned until both Dr Ryan and Philip Neill could attend. A later inquiry found that Hume had died of natural causes, but because it was not a majority verdict, this was dismissed.[106] His death was registered as 'heart failure' by a Cpl A. Williams, Army Medical Corps, who was present when Richard Hume died in the Military Hospital.[107]

On 28 November, at the monthly meeting of the Kildare Board of Health, a resolution of the *comhairle ceanntair* of Sinn Féin for County Kildare was read out. It called on the Board of Health to inspect the sanitary conditions at Newbridge and Tintown 1, 2 and 3 internment camps 'which is in your jurisdiction' following reports of neglect, including the death of Richard Hume. This resolution had also been read at the quarterly meeting of Kildare Co. Council on 26 November. The matter was referred to the District Council as the Sanitary Authority.[108]

11

MURDER MOST FOUL

Although the prison population was decreasing, problems persisted at the Curragh internment camps when, in December 1923, a military policeman suspected of passing information to Republican prisoners was brutally murdered. The body of Pte Joseph Bergin (23), from Camross, County Laois, was found in the canal at Milltown Bridge on 15 December. The medical evidence showed that he had suffered considerable violence and had been shot six times in the head. Bergin was an IRA intelligence officer and had been attached to GHQ during the War of Independence. He was identified carrying messages in and out of Tintown No. 3 on behalf of prisoners and conveying messages to Dublin. Bergin was watched and followed by Intelligence Department officers and was seen to enter the house of Michael Carolan, IRA Director of Intelligence.[1]

An intelligence officer, Capt. James Murray, made a verbal report to Col Michael J. Costello at Portobello Barracks that Joseph Bergin was in Dublin to meet a contact, Michael Carolan. Col Costello was the director of the Army Intelligence Department, and he directed Murray to go to Kildare Town, intercept Bergin at the railway station on his way back from Dublin, seize the documents he obtained from Carolan, and question him. Murray was to inform Bergin that Col Costello was aware of his activities on behalf of the Republican prisoners, but if he became a double agent, it would be in Bergin's best interests. Otherwise, he would be court-martialled for treachery, which carried the death penalty. A black Ford Touring car was

Group of republican prisoners, Hare Park Camp, 1924. Among the group is Jim Hurley (Cork); Liam Deasy (Cork) appears to be seated second row, far left. Photo: Cork Public Museum.

Bill 'Squires' Gannon (Kildare) and Michéal O'Hehir. Gannon escaped through a tunnel from Newbridge Barracks in 1922 and was the first man to lift the Sam McGuire Cup in 1928. Photo: Cill Dara Historical Society.

Joseph Bergin, a National Army soldier, assisted several republicans escape from Tintown Camp. He was killed by a group of National Army Intelligence men.
Photo: Kildare County Archives & Local Studies.

Mick O'Hanlon (Mullagh-bawn, Co. Armagh) was OC of the prisoners group who escaped from Tintown Camp in April 1923.
Photo: Michael Smyth/ Ruairí O'Hanlon.

*Rathbride Column volunteers, shot in the Curragh Camp,
December 1922.* Clockwise from top left: *Tom Behan,
Stephen White, Joseph 'Jackie' Johnston, Patrick Mangan,
Patrick Nolan, James O'Connor.*
Photo: Kildare County Archives & Local Studies.

Newbridge Barracks on the right. At the top left is the wooden sawmill building where the tunnel escapees exited in October 1922 and crossed the Liffey river.
Photo: Kildare County Archives & Local Studies.

Drawing by A. MacLoclainn of his Hut, Hare Park Camp, 1923.
Photo: Kildare County Archives & Local Studies.

Tintown Camps, No. 2 (on right) and No. 3 (left), the Curragh, c. 1924.
Photo: Don McAlistar.

Tom Harris, a 1916 veteran, was OC Kildare prisoners. He led thirty-four Kildare escapees through a tunnel from Newbridge in October 1922.
Photo: Kildare County Archives & Local Studies.

John McCoy (Mullagh-bawn, Co. Armagh) escaped from Tintown No. 1 Camp through a tunnel on 21 April 1923.
Photo: Art McCoy.

Souvenir of reunion of Civil War internees held in Jury's Hotel, Dublin, on 4 November 1950.
Photo: Kildare County Archives & Local Studies.

NEWBRIDGE BARRACKS, CO KILDARE.

*Newbridge Barracks, the former Methodist Garrison church on the right,
where Denis Barry lay in state after he died on hunger strike. On the left centre
are the prisoners' detention blocks.*
Photo: Kildare County Archives & Local Studies.

*Jimmy Whyte (Naas, Co.
Kildare) was rescued from
Dundalk Jail in August 1922,
recaptured and interned in
Newbridge, where he escaped
in October 1922.*
Photo: Kildare County
Archives & Local Studies.

Drawing of Newbridge Barracks prisoners S Block, July 1923.
Photo: Hugh McGinn.

Laurence Slevin, seated, a volunteer with Offaly No. 2 Brigade, took part in the mass hunger strike in Newbridge Barracks in October 1922.
Photo: Slevin family.

placed at Murray's disposal, and he drove off from Portobello Barracks at about 5.00 p.m. on the evening of 13 December, accompanied by two other intelligence officers, possibly Capt. William McAuliffe and Lt Joseph Mack. Murray never revealed who his accomplices were and Costello would later state that he did not know who these two officers were, not a very good sign for the Director of Intelligence.[2]

On his return from Dublin, Bergin called into the Railway Hotel, on Station Road, in Kildare Town, where James Kelly, the railway station ticket-checker, recalled seeing him. The ticket collector knew Murray and later stated he feared him because of an earlier altercation with the officer. There was one man with Murray, but he could not identify him. Around 8.30 p.m., Bergin called at the home of Peg Daly, at nearby Claregate Street, where he stayed about twenty-five minutes. Peg Daly was the officer commanding of Kildare Cumann na mBan, and most of the family were active Republicans. Bergin had left his bicycle at Daly's that morning on his way to Dublin and returned to collect it. He told Peg he was due on duty at 10 p.m. in Tintown No. 3. There was no light on the bicycle, which he had borrowed from a comrade, and Peg said, 'I will get a lamp for you'. Bergin replied, 'Ah, no. They will not mind me', and then left, taking the bicycle with him. He said he had to be on duty at 10.00 p.m., and would call back to see her the following night. Peg guessed that Joseph Bergin was dead when his blood-stained cap was thrown into her hallway the following day to point out to Republicans that their contact was eliminated.[3]

Patrick Nolan, the mess sergeant, later gave evidence that he saw Bergin in the officers' mess at Beresford Barracks late that evening, between 9.15 and 9.30 p.m.[4] It seems that Bergin was intercepted shortly afterwards on his way to Tintown No. 3 on the western side of the Curragh Camp by several men in a car. The motor car was seen driving with a bicycle on its roof near Milltown and seemed to be lost. Capt. Murray, driving the car, was looking for an unoccupied two-storey house in Guidenstown, near Milltown, used by Republicans as a safe house during the War of Independence. Because of this, there is little doubt that he had local knowledge of the house or information from someone local. James Payne, of Rathangan Demesne, later told the civic guard that a car had driven into the yard and a man alighted and asked for water for the car and directions to Thomastown Cross. Having filled the car with water from a bucket, the car drove away.[5]

When the car reached the abandoned house, Bergin was taken inside and was tied to a coat rack, which was nailed to the wall. He was interrogated, and at least two shots were fired at him to frighten or intimidate him into giving information. Bergin was released from the coat rack and brought to the kitchen, where he was beaten mercilessly before he was finally shot six times in the face and head, at close range. Three of these shots were probably fired while he was lying on the ground. His body was propped up, sitting in the car, and driven to Milltown Bridge, a short distance away, and thrown into the Grand Canal.

There was some effort to clean up the scene of the murder, but it seemed haphazard, possibly because the killers never expected the scene of the crime to be located. Very little effort was made to hide the body, making it clear the killers wanted Bergin's remains to be found. The next morning, several children going to school in Milltown village noticed blood on the parapet of the bridge and brought it to the attention of a man going to work. He looked over the bridge and saw Bergin's body in the water. The civic guards in Newbridge were called, and a murder investigation began.[6] The Civic Guard made an early breakthrough in the murder case by identifying that Bergin had been brought by car to Milltown Bridge. Casts were taken of tire tracks and sent to the Dublin Metropolitan Police (DMP).

When Driver James Cleary of the Transport Corps based at Portobello Barracks picked up a black Ford Touring at Crown Alley Telephone Exchange in the city centre, he found the back seat covered in blood. He reported this to his sergeant. It was not long before the DMP heard about this and linked it to the Civic Guard investigation in Kildare.[7]

Joseph Bergin along with two of his older brothers, Patrick and William, served with Camross Company, 6th Laois Battalion, during the War of Independence. He joined the National Army on 17 September in Portlaoise, then known as Maryborough, and was assigned as a military policeman with the rank of private, guarding Republican prisoners at Maryborough Jail.[8] It was not long before Bergin's Republican sympathies resurfaced; he smuggled in £200, which had been supplied by three priests and two lay people, to bribe prison staff at the jail to assist in the escape of Tomás Malone, the OC East Limerick Brigade. It was alleged that the prison governor, Jack Twomey, was involved in the escape attempt but baulked at the last minute.[9] Internee Jack Comer had been approached by Bergin, who told him he was 'one of our crowd' and that he could get a message to Malone, but Comer was unsure of Bergin and refused to co-operate. He later learned that Bergin was 'all right'. Bergin was subsequently moved to Tintown No. 3 Internment Camp, perhaps because he was under suspicion in Maryborough, and assisted Malone and Comdt Casey (Cork) escape from Tintown No. 3 on 12 July 1923.[10]

Comdt Tomás Malone, alias Seán Forde, had been captured in Nenagh in late June 1922. He was held in Maryborough Jail with 700 other anti-Treaty Republicans and because of his standing in the War of Independence, was elected OC of the prisoners.[11] On 29 August 1922, the prisoners rioted in Maryborough after an escape tunnel was discovered. They set fire to their mattresses and bedclothes. Five prisoners were subsequently wounded by

National troops who fired indiscriminately at the men inside the jail.[12] Several months later, many inmates were moved to the Curragh Camp. Among them was Tomás Malone. The day before they were moved [11 July 1923], Malone wrote a letter to his wife, Peig. Governor Jack Twomey, who censored all incoming and outgoing mail, knew Peig Malone and wrote a note on the letter, 'Dear Peig, Tom is fine, but he won't escape this time.'

According to Tomás Malone's son, Tom Malone, 'next day [12 July], when they were moved to the Curragh, Tomás Malone, when working in the kitchen, concealed himself in a rubbish skip and was covered in potato peelings, cabbage leaves and kitchen waste by Paddy Collins of Portroe and taken to the dump. He was home before the letter. The first Peig knew about his escape was when she awoke in the middle of the night and, in the dim light, saw the outline of a large figure at the end of the bed lifting their baby daughter Marie, who had been born while he was in prison, out of her cradle.'[13]

Stephen Keys was arrested in Dublin near the end of the Civil War and, after imprisonment in Mountjoy Jail, was moved to the Curragh, where he was quartermaster of Hut 12, in Tintown. He said of the escape:

> There was a P.A. in the Curragh by the name of Bergin. He was shot afterwards. I knew he was one that could be approached on matters of escape. If you approach him through the big shots. I heard of that. One evening I was told to be up at the cook-house early in the morning and don't bring any orderlies with you. I was told that by our Camp Adjutant; Malone, I think, was his name. I went up the next morning to the cook house or dining room, early. As I went up, the Camp Adjutant came up and said, 'Come on quick'. I went to the side of the cook house. There was a horse-drawn vehicle standing there, with rubbish. Commandant Malone, the Camp Adjutant, and our Camp Commandant got into the car and they lay down on the bottom of it. Myself, Bergin, the P.A., and two other people covered up the Camp Commandant and the Adjutant with cabbage leaves and all the refuse from the cook house. When they were covered up, they were driven right out and escaped.[14]

Keys said Bergin was known to the prisoners as 'Motorbike' and was someone who could be trusted. Joseph Bergin was involved in at least one other escape, that of Joseph Wilson (Loughlinisland, Co. Down), on 16 September 1923. Keys said:

> The next escape from the Curragh was made by Joe Wilson, a former Commandant of the Free State Army. I used knock around with him a lot because he was able to get a great lot of cigarettes from the soldiers. He said to me one day, 'I am going to escape'. We were sitting on the grass. He mapped out the whole Curragh on the grass. I said, 'Let me have your cigarettes before you go'. One evening while I was talking to him, he said he was going to escape the next morning. He told me how he was going. There was a very, very big hut which held about five or six hundred men. It was a riding school one time. The morning paper was secured in some way, and the O/C of the hut called all the men that were there down to one end of the hut, telling them he had the paper. Of course, everybody was anxious to hear the news. I was at the top part of the hut. I saw Joe Wilson walking in and he waved his hand to me. He climbed up on top of a platform where the guard was placed to keep an eye on the men. It was raised above the hut. The same man again, Bergin, was there waiting for him and gave him a uniform, into which Wilson changed. He walked on out and got away.

After an escape, to give the escapees time to get away, prisoners in the know did their best in concealing their absence so they would not be missed for as long as possible. Keys said:

> We were counted every night by officers. When they would have gone up one side of the hut, it was arranged that one or two fellows, after being counted, would get as quickly as possible over to the two empty beds on the other side. It was possible to keep the authorities in ignorance of the escape for a few days, and that gave the boys a chance of getting away.[15]

Johnny Grealy also spoke of a similar escape by Dan Sheehy, an officer in Kiltimagh Company, East Mayo Brigade: 'Bergin, the PA, gave Sheehy this uniform coat and Sheehy walked out before Bergin had made a head count, so he must have had everything planned. Bergin told Paddy Mullins [of Lurganboy, Co. Mayo] that he was going to be done in. Sheehy got back to his own area then, but Bergin was foully murdered by the Staters as he feared.'[16]

The escape of Malone, Wilson and Sheehy, and the belief that at least one individual was assisting Republican prisoners in the Curragh internment camps, led Military Intelligence to eventually focus on Joseph Bergin. A constant flow of information was also being smuggled in and out of the camps. John McCoy said, 'Joe Bergin would take anything out. He was talking too much about it. I was trying to put sense in him but he was mad as a hatter. His girl was working near the Curragh and they were taking it out on him …' McCoy added that Bergin wanted to get away to Dundalk and desert, but he could not help him 'as I knew no one alright and he seemed very upset by that. He was the only safe contact we had.'[17]

The 'girl' mentioned by McCoy was Peg Daly, from Claregate Street, Kildare Town. Donnach Ua Neill (Denis O'Neill) later gave a reference to the Military Pensions Board in respect of Peg Daly's pension application. He wrote:

> During my Civil War period she maintained dispatch service between Btn. about July 1922. She actively assisted in the establishment of a secret service connection with Free State Forces on the Curragh & which eventually culminated in the shooting of a Sergt. Bergin (Free State) near Milltown, Co. Kildare. Ammunition and some revolvers were got by her through this connection.[18]

Comdt Daniel McDonnell was the army provost marshal at the Curragh Camp and reported directly to Military Intelligence that there was an insider working with the Republican prisoners. McDonnell was no stranger to intelligence gathering. He had been an intelligence officer for GHQ during the War of Independence and had assisted Collins' assassination squad in identifying and eliminating British agents on Bloody Sunday. As a member of Headquarters Staff, McDonnell was involved in the takeover of the Curragh Camp from the evacuating British army. McDonnell had then been stationed at Oriel House as part of military intelligence before moving to the Curragh Camp as army provost marshal.[19] With the help of his intelligence officer, Lt Keane, McDonnell came to the conclusion that one of his men, Joseph Bergin, was a Republican agent. He relayed this information to the Army Director of Intelligence, Michael J. Costello. In late 1923, Col Costello summoned a young intelligence officer, Capt. James Murray, to his office and informed him that Pte Joseph Bergin was the Republican mole working inside the internment camps.

Murray, at Costello's request, visited the Curragh Camp on Tuesday, 11 December, where he met Comdt McDonnell, who he knew from his days in Dublin. Murray also was in contact with McDonnell's intelligence officer, Lt John Keane and his assistant Second Lieut George O'Hara.[20] Murray returned to Dublin, where he reported his findings to Col Costello. He was ordered to return to Kildare and to deal with the problem. McDonnell, Keane and O'Hara were in Kildare on the night of the murder and while they obviously knew something there was no evidence to connect them to Bergin's killing.[21]

To carry out that mission, Costello provided Murray with a car and driver, Cleary. Due to army regulations, only an accredited driver could drive a vehicle in and out of barracks,

Driver James Cleary was soon picked up for questioning and gave a statement to the police linking Costello and Murray to the touring car. He was put into protective custody while the police searched for Capt. Murray, but he had left the country. Murray travelled to Liverpool, where an intelligence agent, Thomas Deegan, gave him £50 and told him to proceed to Glasgow, where he met Michael O'Callaghan, another agent. He stayed in Glasgow until April 1924, hoping to bring his wife and children over, but Col Costello wanted Murray to go to America, to lay low for about a year. Instead, James Murray and his brother Michael, recently demobilised from the army, sailed for Buenos Aires, in Argentina. Michael returned home after to two weeks but James stayed there for seven months until Col Costello stopped paying Murray's wife an allowance. James Murray arrived back in Dublin on 18 December 1924 and did not hide the fact that he was home.[22]

Murray was arrested at his home in Dun Laoghaire on Christmas Eve by his old friend and comrade Col David Neligan and was brought to Mountjoy Jail.[23] Under the terms of the Defence Forces (Temporary Provisions) Act, 1923, as Murray had not been on active service – he was discharged from the army while absent – when the Bergin killing took place and he was outside the jurisdiction for more than three months, he could not be court-martialled. The army, obviously, accepted that Bergin was not 'officially' in military custody when he was killed. Murray was instead tried in a civil court with a jury.[24]

Dublin's Green Street Courthouse was jammed when Capt. Murray was put forward for trial before Judge Hanna on 8 June 1925 and charged with the murder of Joseph Bergin. The newspapers reported that the 'prisoner was quietly dressed and looked cool and unperturbed. He followed the proceedings attentively, and showed no sign of nervouseness'. Two witnesses for the prosecution, William O'Callaghan and his sister-in-law, Cecelia Brennan, were called. O'Callaghan did not appear as he had fled the country and was thought to be in London. Opening the case for the prosecution, Mr Carrigan (King's Counsel), K.C., said that Joseph Bergin had been murdered most foully, shot again and again and the only question was a verdict of guilty or not guilty. He outlined the circumstances of Bergin's murder and how and where the body was found.

The prosecution stated that the morning after the Bergin killing, around 7 a.m., Capt. Murray arrived at Col Costello's billet at Portobello Barracks. Costello was asleep and was woken by Murray, who told him he had met Bergin, interrogated him and found some documents on him. Costello ordered Murray to prepare a report and give it to him that evening, along with the confiscated documents. As he left, Murray said to Costello, 'You can find the car at the Telephone Exchange, Crown Alley.'

Costello asked, 'what is the meaning of that. Why did you not bring in the car?'

Murray replied, 'the people who were with me did not want to be seen coming back to barracks.'

According to Carrigan, the colonel never received his report or the captured documents and never saw Murray again until his arrest in December 1924. Carrigan continued by describing the car's condition when it was found at Crown Alley: 'it had blood stains on the inside and outside'. He referred to the 'impetuosity' of the driver, Cleary, who took the car away and washed it without making a report on its condition.

At the following day's proceedings, defence counsel Mr Gleeson stated that Col Costello essentially moved through events blindly, recognising that everyone admitted this, and was only aware of those he directly contacted. Gleeson said that Capt. Murray did not flee and was on a government assignment with Michael O'Callaghan in Scotland. O'Callaghan was not present, but his sister-in-law was in court. Comdt Michael Murray, brother of James Murray, was present and explained how he had travelled to Glasgow about ten times, delivering messages between his brother and Col Costello.

Capt. Murray was not a fugitive and returned from Argentina, Gleeson explained, to 'defend his name and his honour. He had been in communication with his brother in this country, and got thoroughly sick of the business, and came back and reported his presence here. Murray was a plain soldier who was unfortunate enough to have anything to do with this Department. He fought in the open field, and did not hide in the dark'. Gleeson claimed

Murray did not know his accomplices and told them he would not have anything to do with their business. He was not present when Bergin was tortured and killed, Gleeson said. Murray was innocent, Gleeson claimed, was a fall guy for others and should be found not guilty on the evidence presented.[25]

Both Col Costello and Capt. Murray entered the witness box, but gave conflicting evidence. According to Costello, Murray's accomplices were chosen by him. Letters read at Murray's trial suggested that Col Costello had assisted Murray after the killing. It was alleged that Costello had secured Murray's passage to Argentina and had agreed to pay money to his wife and children during his long disappearance. Murray, however, missed Ireland and returned prematurely. This was to prove an unwise decision. Costello alleged that Murray was a renegade and that he had merely instructed Murray to intercept Bergin, whom Military Intelligence suspected of being a Republican 'mole' and turn him into a Free State spy. As far as Costello was concerned, Capt. Murray was absent without leave until his arrest and discharge. Murray denied killing Bergin and claimed Costello had framed him. Michael Murray testified that senior officers had suggested to Capt. Murray that he take the blame for Noel Lemass' murder as well as Bergin's. 'Such things were not unusual in the army at the time,' he said, adding, 'unofficial executions were taken for granted.' He added that 'Jimmy [James Murray] knew too much about this man – the late Noel Lemass'. The mention of Lemass did not help Murray's case.[26]

The discovery of Noel Lemass' body was not made by accident, but rather as the result of a tip-off, which suggests that those involved in the killing also reported it. Gen. Eoin O'Duffy appeared at the Lemass inquest and was asked who had called the police to report the body. Before he could answer, the state solicitor claimed privilege over 'any communications that passed between the Government or any servant of the Government and any other person on the matter'.[27]

On 3 July 1923, Noel Lemass was abducted in broad daylight in Dublin by several men in plain clothes. At the time, the National forces had at least three secret service elements. One of them was the CID, operating from Oriel House in Westland Row, which had a reputation for ruthlessness and savagery. Its function was to investigate or interrogate suspected Republicans. This group had an established connection with Joe McGrath, who, from July 1922, was Director of Intelligence and head of the CID. Lemass was held in secret until the end of September or early October, when his body was dumped in the Dublin Mountains. It was discovered at Featherbed on 12 October. He had been badly beaten, his arm and jaw were broken, some fingers had been removed and he had been shot three times in the head: his clothing indicated his identity. While his body showed signs that he had possibly been tortured before his death, an inquest ended inconclusively.

The grotesqueness of his death caused outrage. All three organisations were disbanded by Kevin O'Higgins, despite McGrath's protestations, later that month, but nobody was ever convicted of the crime. Cyril Bretherton, a journalist for the Dublin-based *Morning Post*, wrote in his 1925 book *The Real Ireland* that 'Responsibility for the murder of Lemass was brought home with reasonable certainty to Joe McGrath.' He identified the motive as revenge for an ambush on intelligence officers near Leeson Street Bridge, Dublin, in which three were killed and a fourth wounded. Noel Lemass, Bretherton said, was known to have taken part. However, the Lemass family said this statement was without foundation and McGrath similarly denied any involvement in Lemass' death.[28]

Seán Lemass was released from jail for a week on compassionate grounds when his brother's body was found, but there was little compassion elsewhere. His mother was motivated to write to the press at one point to complain that the authorities had refused to return Noel's rosary beads, a gold tie-pin and 'one or two little things that could be of no value to anyone except his parents' and that they had sent only a formal acknowledgement of her letter.[29] Seán Lemass never mentioned his brother's death in public in the course of his political career.[30]

The inquest into Lemass' death found that the 'armed forces of the State' had been 'implicated in Lemass' removal and disappearance' on 3 July from a Dublin street. In his review, Justice Hardiman concluded that it remained a possibility that McGrath, in his status as head of the Free State's military secret service, ordered the killing of Lemass and that James Murray carried it out.[31] A verdict of murder was returned. Moreover, according to two witnesses, Capt. Murray had boasted about killing Lemass and dumping him in the Poulaphouca river. When the coroner requested that Capt. Murray attend the inquest and give evidence, the army refused to release him, saying that he was already in military custody for other crimes. The witnesses, Christopher Tuite and Richard Broderick, said they were told while in custody of Noel Lemass' killing and when they informed John Lemass of his son's demise that they were threatened with death by a group of National Army officers. A typewritten note was left at Tuite's home, which said, 'Owing to your lying statement, one of our men has been placed under arrest.' The note went on to say that if Tuite did not deny his statement, he would be killed. Tuite said Capt. James Murray threatened him with a revolver and brought him to Blessington, pointing to the Liffey river where Noel Lemass was 'done in', a fate he would share if he did not withdraw his statement. Richard Broderick received the same warning from Murray's brother, Michael, when the National Army raided his home.[32] Broderick was arrested at the Sinn Féin Club at Dorset Street. He was made to bring a carload of officers, driven by Capt. James Murray, to point out the home of Christopher Tuite in Stillorgan. Broderick said he was punched, kicked and beaten with revolvers several times by Murray and others. Murray also said he shot Harry McEntee. Broderick was brought to Portobello Barracks, where he received another beating from Col David Neligan. He was released the next day.[33]

After four days of evidence, a guilty verdict was announced, and James Murray was sentenced to death for the murder of Joseph Bergin. After a few moments of silence, broken only by the sound of his sister sobbing, Murray said, 'I only wish to declare my innocence and to state that I have been made the scapegoat in this crime, of which I am innocent. I only hope the officers who swore my life away will be prepared to meet their God when the time comes.' Joseph Mack was found not guilty of any part in the Bergin case and released from Mountjoy. All charges against John Dooley were dropped. William McAuliffe was identified by the driver, Cleary, as one of the suspects, but he was never charged.[34]

However, the Garda Commissioner W. R. E. Murphy said, 'The evidence at Murray's trail would appear to indicate that he was the most guilty of the three but the other two must have been present … It is possible these two men did not have desired to murder Bergin, but the fact remains that they did not restrain Murray and beyond question they were accessories after the fact.' Driver Cleary at first denied he could identify the two men with Murray, but later retracted this and said he could, naming Lt Joseph Mack and Sgt John Dooley. Col Neligan also said that Lt Mack and Sgt Dooley were with Murray on the night of the murder and that they had later gone to London, on Col Costello's orders.[35]

An appeal by James Murray was lodged and, on 1 July 1926, it was heard in the Court of Criminal Appeal. Included in the appeal were four letters which Murray claimed he had written to Col Costello while he was in Argentina, and a confession attributed to him concerning the death of Bergin. In the letters, Murray phrased his words to suggest he had been acting on orders, but he did not want to incriminate anyone else. Murray requested a settlement of the affair as he 'did not want to be a hunted man for the rest of his life'. Murray denied having written the 'confession' though he admitted the handwriting was like his. An Army handwriting expert swore that all five letters were by the same hand. According to Murray, Col Costello had ordered him to arrest and interrogate Bergin, so he maintained the arrest was lawful. Nevertheless, it was the opinion of the court that 'this appeal fails' and Murray was returned to Mountjoy Jail. Four days before he was due to be hanged for murder, his sentence was commuted to life imprisonment on the recommendation of the Executive Council under W. T. Cosgrave to the governor general. James Murray died of tuberculosis in the prison hospital in Portlaoise Jail on 13 July 1929. His wife and daughters emigrated to England, where they lived frugally.[36]

After Costello retired from the army in 1945 with the rank of major-general, he became managing director of the Irish Sugar Co., and twenty years later he was responsible for establishing Erin Foods, Ltd. When Michael J. Costello died in 1986, his obituary recorded that his death 'has closed a chapter of Titans of this State'. There is no doubt Costello was a towering figure in Irish business after the formation of the state, but his role in the Bergin murder was for a long time unspoken of and quietly ignored.[37]

12

HARE PARK, THE FINAL HURDLE

Peadar O'Donnell could not remember when he was sent to
Hare Park Camp, or even how he got there. He recalled that
it was after the end of the hunger strike and remembered leaving
Mountjoy Jail with a draft of prisoners destined for the Curragh
Camp. Along with Andy Cooney, O'Donnell was sent to the
'hospital until the doctor came round, when we were allotted
to a hut'. While in prison, Peadar O'Donnell had been elected
for Donegal in the 1923 general election. He had participated
in the mass hunger strike for forty-one days. O'Donnell noted
that 'the spirit in Harepark reminded me of the early days in
Tintown. There was a healthy vigour in the camp life and a
wild recklessness about its games ... We had a rather wonderful
social life in our hut, and remarkable discussions were developed
around the stoves each night'.[1]

Jack Feehan was held in Tintown No. 2 and was transferred
from there to Hare Park Camp on 1 January 1924. Feehan had
assumed he was being released but found himself in a different
site on the Curragh plains.[2] He said, 'This camp was well run
... Hare Park was turned into an educational camp and nearly
everyone was compelled to do some kind of work ... We had
everything in the world in the way of classes'. Carpentry classes
were conducted by Tom Bourke, engineering was taught by
Mick Sheehy, while Mick Roth (Kilkenny), an all-Ireland
dancer, was the dancing instructor.[3]

A secret smuggling operation supplied illegal alcohol, or
Poitín, in the camp. Feehan said, 'Poteen [*sic*] came in cakes of

jelly. The poteen was put into a pot and boiled. The jelly was then mixed in and allowed to cool and there was a nice cake of jelly ... I used to eat it as a stick.' Calves' food jelly was a delicacy for the sick and was sent to some prisoners, like Thomas 'Baby' Duggan (Galway), who was suffering from tuberculosis. Dr Jack Comer, the medical doctor, had requested the jelly for Duggan, who was unable to eat much of the prison food. Naturally, Duggan was not the only one to avail of the 'medicine'. There was so much drinking of illegal alcohol one night during a concert the military police had to be called in to get the men back to their huts.[4]

Matt Kilcawley (Kilglass, Co. Sligo) brewed his own alcohol in Tintown. 'We had a still in Hut 13,' he said, 'and we used treacle. I and another fellow who knew all about it [*Poitín* making] ... we had the treacle and the yeast. To make the brew, boil the hot water, put in the treacle, then put in the yeast to make it ferment. At least ten to fourteen days it takes. Then we would distil it. We had a worm of a type and a bit of copper piping.'[5]

'We had several Connemara and South Mayo lads there,' Paddy 'Con' MacMahon said, 'and they knew to a T how to make it. There were at least 30 to 40 fellows there [in the hut] and we made a good gallon of it. It tasted awful but it was a novelty.'[6]

Ted O'Sullivan (Castletownbere), OC of Cork No. 5 Brigade, had a bad experience on his arrival in Hare Park on 7 January 1924. 'Our beds and blankets in Hare Park Camp had been left out in the rain for the day inside the camp gate and so were very thoroughly wetted', O'Sullivan said. 'There was a fire in the middle of every hut. It was very frosty and the huts had been fairly well wrecked for asbestos sheeting had been once inside the galvanised sheeting and our blankets were stiff with frost.' He said there was much neglect by the camp medical staff and claimed, 'the doctors and dentists were no good'. O'Sullivan was released from captivity on 17 July 1924.[7]

Another prisoner, Mick Sheehan, a native of Newbridge, was moved from Newbridge Barracks to Hare Park. The move obviously came as a surprise. Sheehan wrote to his mother on 8 January, 'Just a few lines to let you know I received your parcel. I may tell you it was welcome as we left everything after us in Newbridge.' Paper was supplied by the camp authorities with the warning: 'N.B. – Writing must be on lines. Not more than one sheet, and one side of paper to be used for each letter.' The prisoner's name and camp number were also to be added.[8]

To pass the long hours, prisoners crafted a wide variety of handmade items, a tradition that dates back to the period after the 1916 Rising. The reorganisation of the IRA began inside the prison and camps and on the outside with those not willing to accept the Free State. Peadar O'Donnell wrote: 'The main theme of our lives in Hare Park became more and more reorganisation. Prisoners were formed into committees according to their old brigades and local reorganisation considered in detail … The schemes of reorganisation developed in the prisons were sent back to I.R.A. headquarters and the names of those in the camps who would set to work in their respective units were attached.'[9] While a hardcore of Republican activists were still jailed and were intent on continuing the fight for a Republic once freed, many who had been released were totally disillusioned.

Barney Mellows was a member of the camp council at Hare Park. He gave regular lectures in military tactics and took part in the hunger strike, enduring forty days of fasting. During the Battle of Dublin, Mellows was officer-in-charge of supplies in the 'The Block' area on O'Connell Street. He evaded capture after the general surrender in Dublin and went into hiding for several months while still directing Na Fianna Éireann activities. He was also associated with the staff of the Northern and Eastern Command of the IRA, but was arrested on 6 December 1922, two days before his brother Liam was executed. Imprisoned at

Wellington Barracks, Barney then spent time at Newbridge Barracks, Mountjoy Jail, Kilmainham Gaol and eventually Hare Park Camp. While imprisoned, he was elected in August 1923 to the Dáil for Galway (serving from 1923–27). He stood for the same seat for Sinn Féin in June 1927 but was not elected.[10]

One of the prisoners' lines of communication to the outside was through a man who collected the human waste from the camp. Jack Feehan and Billy Walsh collected letters from their comrades and put them in an airtight box, and when their contact came into the lavatory, they dropped the box into a bucket. The contents of the buckets were dumped in the sewer cart, and this in turn was dumped in a pit near the camp, where a contact collected it on the outside. Communications into the camp was accomplished using the same method. The lavatories were cleaned twice a week, and the lavatory smuggler was paid a small sum for his work. Incoming mail was more important as it would have orders from anti-Treaty GHQ and news on what was happening on the outside.[11]

Dispatches coming into the camp were numbered and those regarding orders and strategy from GHQ were read to the men. A communication destined for Kit Byrne, OC Tintown No. 1, intercepted by the camp authorities, revealed the officers recently elected, which included Byrne as camp commandant, P. J. McDonnell as vice-comdt, Éamon Lynch, adjutant, and Thomas Cogan, quartermaster. A previous letter going out from Byrne to his wife, Lillie, during the mass hunger strike, was also intercepted. In it Byrne complained that, 'There is about 60 on strike here still but they are not honest and the majority of them have dirtied their bibs & now they are trying to save their faces by staying on strike.' He then said he would not burden her with 'any more of my troubles' and reverted to family and personal matters.[12]

On 14 November 1923, Richard Mulcahy presented proposals

for the mass release of prisoners to the Executive Council. However, there was some unease in the government at the prospect of so many prisoner releases. Kevin O'Higgins said that he had been informed that 'Cork County has not been in a worse condition this three years and that there are other areas which are very little better'. Other ministers echoed his views.[13] A Republican meeting, which was to be held at Newbridge railway station on 4 November 1923, was proclaimed by the government, the instruction being that the police were to prevent any such assembly within 500 yards of the military barracks.[14]

During November, 3,304 internees were released country-wide, with another 3,574 freed the following month.[15] Pádraig O'Higgins, brother of Clare TD Brian O'Higgins, was released from Tintown No. 3 on 16 November and arrived at Newbridge Town Hall with several other prisoners, where they were attended by nursing staff. He had been on hunger strike up to the time of leaving the camp and was in a very weak condition. His sister-in-law, Mrs Brian O'Higgins, arrived during the evening by motor car from Dublin and brought Pádraig back to the capital. The *Leinster Leader* reported that his brother, Brian, was 'still in a very weak and serious condition at the Curragh'.

On being released from Tintown, twelve men walked to Kildare Town railway station only to find their train for the south had already left. They were invited back to the town by supporters and were given food and refreshments by the local committee of Cumann na mBan, who were looking after the interests of released prisoners. At the same time, 300 prisoners arrived at the Curragh Siding from Dundalk and were marched across the plains to Tintown. Another two special trains came from Kilkenny with prisoners also conveyed to the Curragh, while 387 prisoners from Limerick Jail arrived at Hare Park Camp.[16]

At 7.30 a.m. on 6 December 1923, J. Coughlan wrote

under the heading 'Daily Rumours', 'All prisoners except 200 hard cases to be released from camp within a week.'[17] Joseph Campbell made his final entry in his diary on 16 December 1923. It ended with a note, 'Release in the morning?'[18] The support group, the Women's Prisoners Defence League formed a Released Prisoners Committee (RPC), to welcome back those who were emerging from the jails and internment camps. They set up a rota of volunteers to meet the trains, while their headquarters in the old Sinn Féin offices in Harcourt Street became a meeting point for the prisoners and their families. Many were desperately grateful for the food and clothing distributed by the RPC in those harsh times. Most had no jobs and no prospect of finding employment in a state slowly recovering from a war that had cost an estimated £17 million.[19] On 20 December, 100 prisoners released from Tintown No. 3 Camp arrived at Dublin's Kingsbridge Station, where they were met by Charlotte Despard, who led many of them to 6 Harcourt Street for refreshments.[20]

Over 1,000 prisoners were released from the Curragh internment camps on 23 December 1923. They were treated to refreshments at the courthouse in Kildare by Miss McKenna and the Ladies' Committee before they left for their home destinations.[21] The newspapers stated that up to 2,000 prisoners were released – 2,304 were freed on 1 December alone. One of the reasons prisoners were released in such high numbers was the fear of an outbreak of an influenza epidemic amongst the weakened prison population. Many prisoners had died of pneumonia and chest ailments while incarcerated. By the end of the year, there were 1,852 prisoners left imprisoned, compared with 11,840 held in July. There were still 600 men in Newbridge Barracks at this stage and it was reported that Hare Park and Tintown still had high numbers of prisoners.[22]

Among those released from Newbridge and Tintown in the

third week of December were five TDs – Patrick Ryan, a Dáil member for Tipperary; Brian O'Higgins, Clare; Seán Buckley, West Cork; Dr Patrick McCarville, Monaghan; and Seán T. O'Kelly, formerly Dáil representative in Paris. Alderman Charles Murphy, who had been granted parole for family reasons, was also notified that he was officially released and did not have to return to his internment.[23]

Despite the continuing prisoner releases, authorities at the Curragh Camp received information that an escape tunnel was in progress. The tunnel was not located in any of the huts but was said to be in the middle of the compound, with its entrance concealed by a board with grass sods on top. At this late stage, Col M. J. Costello, Director of Intelligence, was even sceptical and said, 'on the face of it, this appears to be absolutely ridiculous, but I pass the information on, on the chance that there is more in it than appears on the surface.' Curragh Command Intelligence Officer, Capt. R. Kane replied within days saying '… a thorough search was carried out in all Internment Camps and I can definitely state that no tunnelling operations are being carried out at present in either of the Camps'.[24]

A further 166 prisoners were released on Christmas Eve and four freed on Christmas Day, leaving 1,866 still imprisoned.[25] Todd Andrews said he was called to the governor's office in Newbridge Barracks on Christmas Eve and told he could go home if he signed the form acknowledging his allegiance to the state. He told the governor how 'he could dispose of the form in a certain well know Dublin manner'. Needless to say, Andrews was not released. He returned to an almost deserted compound as most of his friends had been freed. The barrack blocks were cleared of prisoners and the remaining men concentrated in the huts. Andrews along with his friends George and Jack Plunkett spent 'rather a miserable Christmas [there]. All the life had gone out of the camp.'[26]

On New Year's night, a concert being held by the prisoners in the Hare Park hospital hut was stopped by the military police who claimed it was 'seditious'. Military policemen entered and cleared the audience out of the hall just as one of the artists finished P. H. Pearse's 'Oration at the Grave of O'Donovan Rossa'. The reason given was that the audience was inconveniencing the sick prisoners, but the hospital OC had already given his permission for the concert. The military governor had also permitted the huts to remain open until 10 p.m. so the concert could take place. *Éire. The Irish Nation* reported: 'The most prominent policeman in this affair was a Private Morrissey, said to be an ex-Guardsman, who was helped by Private Nolan and Murphy, all of the Military Police.'[27]

Although Kevin O'Higgins had given assurances that internment powers would not be needed after 1923, it was obvious most of the provisions for the Emergency Powers Bill, 1923, would have to be continued after the act expired on 1 February 1924. The Executive Council met in December 1923 and decided to continue the powers of internment.[28] Release of internees continued faster in the New Year, and the number of prisoners continued to fall; by 1 January 1924, only 1,852 were in custody.[29] On the evening of 3 January 1924, forty internees were released from Newbridge Barracks and treated to refreshments at the Hostel in the Town Hall by Miss Egan and her nursing staff before travelling to their home destinations. The remaining prisoners were transferred to the Curragh Camp and Mountjoy Jail and, on 30 January 1924, Newbridge Military Barracks was officially closed.[30]

Todd Andrews was among those who moved to the Curragh. He said, 'early in January we were herded together and marched to an internment centre on the Curragh – Tintown number 2 – where I became prisoner 876 although in fact it contained only five or six hundred prisoners in all, the residue from several internment camps which had been closed.' He had barely settled in when prisoner releases recommenced.[31] On 11 and 14 January, over 100 prisoners were released from Tintown No. 1 and Tintown No. 2 Camps.[32] The remaining prisoners in Kilmainham Gaol were removed to Tintown and Hare Park Camp, the Curragh. Among the last to leave was Ernie O'Malley, who was moved to Dublin's St Bricin's Military Hospital. He, too, would be destined for the Curragh.[33]

On 31 January 1924, the government had to reauthorise the provisions of the Public Safety (Emergency Powers) Act 1923 to remain in effect until January 1925. This was mainly designed to 'make provision for the arrest and detention of certain persons during a limited period'.[34]

The *Leinster Leader* (8 March 1924) reported that Tintown No. 1 Camp was empty of prisoners, resulting in the demobilisation of several military police. Sinn Féin's Publicity Department mentioned that out of the 782 prisoners in Hare Park Camp, 270 had been sentenced to imprisonment terms ranging from two to twenty years. Nineteen men had received sentences of twenty years, thirty of fifteen years, sixty-eight of ten years, sixteen of seven years, fifty-six of five years, forty-four of three years, sixteen of two years, twenty of two years' hard labour, and one of one year's hard labour.[35]

Among those remaining was Peadar O'Donnell, and he was developing 'itchy feet'. About 3 a.m. on 16 March, O'Donnell left his hut dressed in a topcoat and cap of a National Army officer, supplied by a near neighbour from the Rosses, and brown boots and leggings supplied by fellow prisoners. As he approached the prison gates, the searchlight in the guard tower suddenly pointed in a different direction. O'Donnell walked to the main gate, which was then 'flung open. There was some little delay before I got through the second wall of barbed wire, but a gate opened there also, eventually'.[36] O'Donnell ran towards the main road and made his way towards Dublin. He hid for several days before approaching a cottage, where he greeted the owner, saying, 'I'm Peadar O'Donnell. IRA Executive. I want to get in touch with the organisation here.' Luckily, for him, the owner knew who he was as he had been acquainted with Peadar's brother, Joe, who had been interned in Newbridge, and he put him in contact with the right people.[37] O'Donnell travelled from Dublin to Liverpool, from there to Belfast and then back to the comparative safety of his home county. Over the next few months, O'Donnell remained on the run until it was safe to surface with the granting a general amnesty and releasing the sentenced prisoners that autumn.[38]

On 2 April 1924, Pádraig Baxter, Farmers Party TD for Cavan, speaking in the Dáil asked Richard Mulcahy, Minister for Defence, that given the repeated reports and complaints of conditions under which the prisoners in Hare Park Camp were being detained, would he consider appointing a committee composed of the different parties to visit the camp and report back on the conditions of prisoner housing, sanitation, food and hospital accommodation.

The Minister for Defence replied that he was not aware of the reports and complaints suggested by Baxter and was satisfied that the conditions under which the prisoners in Hare Park Camp were detained were what they should be. He said arrangements were nearing completion for the appointment of an independent Visiting Committee to inspect Hare Park and other places of internment, and to visit the prisoners detained. The Visiting Committee was to report directly to him or Kevin O'Higgins (Minister for Home Affairs). In these circumstances, he did not see the necessity for the appointment of such a committee as suggested by Pádraig Baxter. In the meantime, Mulcahy said he already had reports from medical officers on the conditions in the camp, to which he was entirely satisfied.[39]

Todd Andrews spent his time talking about Irish history to his friends in Hare Park and mulling over the long days. One April day, an officer of the guard came to his hut, called his name and told Andrews he was being released. He took nothing with him except his shaving gear, leaving Jack Plunkett a five-pound note that Liam Lynch had given him over a year ago. Andrews was given a rail ticket to Kingsbridge Station in Dublin. From there he travelled by tram – the tram conductor let him travel free on learning he was a recently released prisoner – to Capel Street, where he walked into his father's jewellery shop. Andrews' father was 'emotionally overwhelmed by my unexpected arrival', he said. 'The Civil War was over for me. I had survived.'[40]

After two operations on his wounds at St Bricin's Hospital Ernie O'Malley was moved to the military hospital at the Curragh Camp. He was subsequently transferred to Hare Park Camp in April 1924. O'Malley described his new accommodation:

The huts were of wood and each contained about thirty-six men. The beds were in rows against the wall, with a passage down the centre. Our hut was reasonably respectable; very few windows had any glass; its place was supplied by strands of barbed wire. There were gaps in the floor, all superfluous woodwork having been removed for firewood … In the morning the doors were opened at seven o'clock. Men went outside for [physical] 'jerks' in the open and washed from running water behind a street of huts. Orderlies carried in breakfast or men prepared their own, using a tin can in which holes had been punched as a brazier; cardboard and paper supplied the fuel. Inspection of huts occurred about 10 a.m.; huts were expected to be cleaned and tidied, beds made up and all men indoors. The men stood at ease at the foot of their beds; at the command of the hut leader they sprang to attention and numbered off, while Free State officers checked the count. Each hut supplied orderlies for drawing food, for the cookhouse, for fatigue work, and for the sanitary squad.

Rows of huts faced each other throughout the camp, backed by the playing fields. The camp was surrounded with heavy rows of barbed wire, with sentry posts on platforms at intervals. At night powerful lamps lighted [*sic*] up the limits of the camp and military police prowled around. Even in daytime, we could not walk within a certain distance of the barbed wire entanglements, which were placed at considerable distance from the nearest huts, so as to lengthen the tunnels which prisoners were expected to dig.[41]

On 3 May 1924, the *Leinster Leader* reported that twelve prisoners had been released from Hare Park Camp at the end of the week. According to the following week's paper, a further twenty were released from 'the Curragh' during the week.[42]

A public meeting called by Kildare Co. Council at Market Square, Newbridge, on 4 May, demanded the release of all political prisoners held in England and Ireland. On the platform were many local politicians from opposing sides, all united in their demand for the prisoners' release. The speakers addressed the meeting from a lorry drawn up beside the Town Hall, and attendance increased as the meeting progressed. Easter Week 1916 veteran Domhnall Ua Buachalla, chaired the meeting and amongst those present were William Colohan, Labour TD, and a dozen county councillors. Cllr Michael Smyth (Labour), another IRA veteran arrested and jailed on several occasions between 1916–21, but neutral during the Civil War, proposed the following resolution: 'That we protest against the continued detention of political prisoners in Ireland and Great Britain, and we demand the immediate and unconditional release of all Irish political prisoners whether sentenced or unsentenced.' All members of Kildare County Council, regardless of their political party, unanimously approved the resolution.[43]

Demands for the prisoners' release continued unabated. There were 618 prisoners still held on 21 May, which included men who had been sentenced to death and others who were under investigation by the garda síochána for offences not linked to the Civil War. All correspondence for prisoners at Hare Park was halted that week, while the men were kept in their huts from 5 p.m. each evening. No parcels or food supplies were delivered either, although when questioned by local news reporters, no reason for these measures was provided.[44]

However, the reason was not political and was possibly a row between the camp authorities and the Curragh Camp postmaster. The acting military governor of Hare Park Camp complained about the 'manner in which parcels and letters are being delivered at this Camp. Today we had a bag of 10 Parcels and some letters, one at least registered, delivered here by representatives from Tintown. Naturally we refused to take delivery of same as they had been opened and censored, and … in their hands for some time past. This sort of business cannot be allowed to go on, and if the same thing occurs again I will take the matter up direct with the Postmaster General, Dublin, to have it righted. The items mentioned have been returned to Tintown and I may mention are in a very broken condition.'[45] In the meantime, prisoners suffered needlessly.

Michael Kilroy, who had commanded the recent hunger strike and had been moved to Hare Park from Mountjoy Jail, was on friendly terms with a military policeman named Paddy McGlory, from Donegal. In the early hours of Sunday, 11 May, Kilroy made a sensational escape from Hare Park. Paddy McGlory walked Kilroy to the gate and turned his back as Kilroy went out unnoticed. Kilroy was housed in Tom Derrig's hut and a prisoner of similar build and looks was sent from another hut to replace him. He slept in Kilroy's bed that night to add to the confusion and as Kilroy wore glasses, his 'double' also wore glasses. Kilroy was not missed because his 'double' was being examined by the prisoners' medical doctor, Jack Comer, during the headcount. It was only when it was reported from the outside that a search for Kilroy began some hours after he had succeeded in getting away. His comrades were locked in their hut for the day while the military police made a count and a recount until it was confirmed Kilroy was gone. He was not recaptured. Three years later, Paddy McGlory married Michael Kilroy's sister.[46]

On 7 June, the *Kildare Observer* reported that Tintown 1 and Tintown 3 Camps were closed. Six sentenced prisoners – Paddy Mullaney, Mick O'Neill, Jack O'Connor, Tom Cardwell, Jim Dempsey and Tim Tyrell – all members of the North Kildare Mullaney Column, were unconditionally released from Hare Park Camp on 7 June. The six men had been court-martialled and sentenced to death, but had their sentences commuted to seven years' imprisonment. Before their release, the men were paraded in the camp and informed that the governor-general had exercised his clemency powers to remit the full sentences.[47]

A further sixteen prisoners were released on Saturday, 14 June, leaving 275 prisoners remaining at Hare Park Camp. One of the prisoners released was James Whelan, of Clifden, Co. Galway, brother of Thomas Whelan, who had been hanged on 13 March 1921 for his alleged part in the Bloody Sunday assassinations in Dublin.[48]

Five sentenced prisoners were released from Hare Park Camp during the week ending 21 June. Four of them – Frank and Tom Dunne, Hugh Cunningham and Thomas Deevy – had been sentenced to ten years imprisonment. A comrade of the Dunne brothers, Thomas Gibson, had been executed in Maryborough Jail on a charge of having left his barracks and handing over five rifles and a grenade to the anti-Treaty side.[49] With sentenced prisoners who had been recommended for release but against whom charges were pending, it was decided sensibly that 'as a general rule prosecutions for these charges should not be gone with'. At that stage, there were 237 'political prisoners in military custody'.[50]

Impatient to wait for their release, the internees in Hare Park began digging an escape tunnel. Jack Feehan said it came out from Dr Comer's hospital hut towards the trench. He said that men of small stature were picked for tunnelling. Feehan was picked along with George Staunton, from Lettercallow,

Co. Galway; he did not know any other tunnellers. Soil from the tunnel was packed under the hospital hut and brought up by means of a double rope. The soil was sand and digging was accomplished with an iron bar. Feehan said they were constantly told to keep the tunnel like a burrow. 'I was about a fortnight [working] on it, but it was going on before I came to the camp because you went down a twelve-foot shaft to be down under the trench. They had boards cut in the floor so you just lifted them up and the bottom of the press was taken out and then it was covered with a box of medicine. It was very hard work and your eyes got very sore from the sand in them … Underground it was close and hot but there was no foul air in the sand. You had to take off your clothes before you went down and there was a suit below for each man to put on. Three men could stand in the shaft and there was a [peg] for hanging your clothes up on and togs which went to your knees for working in and as well there was a bit of an old jacket to wear at work. You'd get a while to clean yourself … Working with the bar a shift lasted an hour and a half; in all that time you'd go about a yard.'

Feehan said one of the tunnellers who was released let it slip in a local pub that a tunnel was in progress and the information was relayed back to the Curragh Camp. He had been appointed OC of the prisoners, and the commandant of Hare Park came to him and said, 'Feehan, you're making a tunnel, and if I have to bring in a steam roller, I'll get it. The men were confined to their huts and parcels stopped, but then the general release of prisoners began. Feehan said, '… the Staters never got the tunnel. We were exactly outside the trench and that was inside the barbed wire. There was about a week's work on the tunnel and only another ten yards to go.'[51]

Most of the camps and jails were cleared by now, and on 1 July 1924, only 209 men were in custody throughout the country.[52] On 17 July, Ernie O'Malley was released with some of the last

IRA officers from the Curragh Camp. He said, 'The enemy could not be gracious, even after two years of imprisonment, and we cursed them heartily as we waited. They wanted to avoid an organised welcome to the prisoners; that could mean they were losing ground.' O'Malley and Seán Russell made their way to Kildare railway station, some miles away, where they found Gerry Boland, TD (Roscommon), Liam Pilkington (Sligo), Matt O'Kelly (brother of Seán T. O'Kelly), James Donovan, Humphrey Murphy, Tom Derrig, Peter Glynn (Sligo), Michael Robin and Stan Barry (Cork) waiting on a train to Dublin. 'We laughed as we eyed our clothes,' O'Malley wrote, 'it was easy to pick out our men on the platform. People looked at us timorously. A few came to shake our hands. At last the train puffed in to the shout of "Here she is".'[53]

O'Malley was exhausted; he was still suffering from the many bullet wounds he received when he was captured nearly two years earlier and the torture he had endured as a prisoner in Dublin Castle during the War of Independence. He had also endured forty-one days on hunger strike. Ernie O'Malley went home to his parents after his release, where his younger brother Kevin said, 'he just walked in and went to his seat in the corner and had tea and bread and butter … [Our] parents were there. He didn't say very much. Behaved as though he was always coming home.' O'Malley's parents were Redmonite Home-Rulers and his conservative father, Luke, had refused to support the IRA in the War of Independence or the anti-Treaty forces in the Civil War. Luke O'Malley could not understand how die-hards like his son had held out for an Irish Republic rather than helping to build the new Irish Free State. After three months, with little money and fewer prospects of employment, Ernie O'Malley decided to make a lengthy journey to Europe to restore his mental and physical health. He financed his travels through monetary gifts and loans.[54] Many other veterans were not as fortunate.

With these final releases, only a handful of men were left in Hare Park Camp. Nine men were taken from Hare Park to Mountjoy Jail to be put on trial for alleged 'criminal offences'.[55] Frank Henderson, former OC Dublin Brigade, and a young prisoner, Daniel Healy (20), from Kanturk, Co. Cork, were moved to the Glasshouse Military Prison. Healy, who was earlier being released with the last batch of prisoners, had refused to leave Henderson alone and insisted on remaining with him until the order for his release came. On 25 July, the necessary order for Henderson's release was received and he left the Glasshouse with Daniel Healy. These were the last prisoners freed from the Curragh internment camps, fourteen months after hostilities had ended.[56]

On 7 November 1924, the Executive Council agreed to an amnesty, abandoning prosecutions for all acts committed by either side between signing the Treaty on 6 December 1921 and 12 May 1923. All convicted Republican prisoners, around 200, still in custody, were to be released. Those on the run could also return home without fear of arrest. Though this might be seen as a conciliatory gesture towards Republicans, criminal acts committed by Free State forces in the suppression of these 'disturbances' were also covered. Cosgrave said that the government's decision was induced by a 'belief that the highest interests of the state and the protection of law and order would best be served by the generous course it is now taking'.[57]

13

WE HAVE KEPT THE FAITH

For many internees, the end of hostilities in 1923 and their subsequent release marked the conclusion of a decade of war, which had involved violence, imprisonment and death at the hands of two entirely different governments. Some men and women had been interned or jailed in three different campaigns – the 1916 Rising, the War of Independence and the subsequent Civil War. The trauma of constant imprisonment is an experience rarely acknowledged.

Not all events were adverse. Curragh internee Francis Stuart described his internment days as 'the worst of my life, the most vicious. Nothing is worse'. However, he gained much from reading Dostoevsky and participating in discussions with steadfast Republican revolutionary Peadar O'Donnell, as well as writer Joseph Campbell and fellow rank-and-file activists like Jim Phelan. His prison experience became, in Kevin Kiely's words, 'the young man's university of real life'. Stuart was proud of his connection with these men and of sharing his youth with them during fifteen months of captivity. He later wrote two Civil War novels, *Pigeon Irish* (1931) and *The Coloured Dome* (1932), with some deeds and characters inspired by real people and events.[1] Irish writer Seosamh Mac Grianna, from Ranafast, Co. Donegal, and his three brothers Séamus, Hiúdaí, and Domhnall, were captured by National troops during the summer of 1922 and interned in Newbridge Barracks. Both Seosamh and Hiúdaí were among the internees who went on hunger strike in October-November 1923. Mac Grianna's difficulty in finding a permanent post may have been due to his

Republicanism, but it may also have been related to his ability as a teacher. He disliked teaching, particularly teaching Irish. It is believed that he suffered a nervous breakdown in Co. Leitrim because of stress brought on by teaching. Apart from taking part in summer schools in Omeath, Co. Louth, and Ranafast, he never returned to the profession.[2] His long-term partner, Peigí Green, contended that he had 'become ill since the Civil War' and his writing was a sort of coping strategy. Mac Grianna was treated in Grangegorman Mental Asylum in 1935–6 and he spent much of his later life in St Conal's Psychiatric Hospital, in Letterkenny, where he died in 1990.[3]

Síobhra Aiken, the great-granddaughter of Frank Aiken, wrote in her seminal monograph *Spiritual Wounds* that Peadar O'Donnell's writings, both in memoir and fiction, reflect his urge to document and perhaps process his experience. They were motivated to set the record straight on internment and to speak up on behalf of his fellow prisoners – those whose 'minds that were bruised in the prisons …'

John McCoy was upbeat about his imprisonment. He said, 'I was not finally released until June, 1924. My internment in prisons and prison camps during the Civil War period, which lasted for almost two years, provided some of the most interesting experiences of my life. I met men from all parts of Ireland and from all walks of life and with those men experienced all the disabilities that a military defeat can entail for prisoners belonging to the defeated side.'[4]

Thomas J. McElligott had a most varied career, but was highly disillusioned with the aftermath of the Revolution. He was a member of the RIC, but resigned, when the British government introduced recruits from Britain who had no police experience – they became known as 'Black and Tans'. McElligott then formulated a scheme by which he hoped to place the whole RIC force under the control of the Republican government, but it did not materialise. He became associated with Austin Stack, in the Ministry for Home Affairs, and after Dáil Éireann accepted the articles of agreement for the Anglo-Irish Treaty, he continued his connection with the ministry until the breaking of the National Pact. He then left and sided with the anti-Treaty Republicans. McElligott never joined the IRA, but as an anti-Treaty Republican, he was arrested in Dublin in 1922 and was imprisoned in Mountjoy and Tintown No 3 Camp. He took part in the mass hunger strike, remaining on the fast until it was called off.[5]

After his release, McElligott became active in the post-Civil War Sinn Féin organisation. He resumed his police pensions campaign and worked in support of families still in distress since the early 1920s. McElligott was frustrated by the police pensions legislation of 1923–4, which barely improved the plight of his ex-colleagues, and by the reluctance of Commissioner Eoin O'Duffy, to recruit former RIC personnel into An Garda Síochána.[6]

Many released prisoners with no jobs came home to find emigration the only alternative to destitution. Former dockworker Tom Leahy was released from the Curragh Camp on 6 August 1923 and went to Dublin Dockyards to seek his old job back. His place as a riveter had long been filled, but he was told that he would be sent a message if anything turned up. No message ever came, and Leahy went to Glasgow where he rose to senior shop steward in the Clydeside shipyards. He secured far better pay and conditions than he would have if he remained in Dublin, but he never forgot 'the men or events in those stirring glorious years'.[7]

John Higgins, the father of the president of Ireland Michael D. Higgins, was arrested in January 1923 and interned in Tintown. He was released from custody in December 1923. Higgins was active in the War of Independence and the Civil War on the anti-Treaty side as an intelligence officer with Charleville

Company, 3rd Cork Battalion. Before the Civil War, John Higgins had a decent job as a grocer at Owen Binchy and Sons in Charleville, with a salary of £130 a year and £50 in travel expenses. His former employer, Mr Binchy, who was believed to be a nationalist, refused to take him back, even after a deputation from his old Republican comrades pleaded on his behalf.

Con Cummins of Cummins' public house on Newbridge Main Street said that Michael D. Higgins had told him that his father had spent some six months in Newbridge after being interned and that he had rented a room in Cummins'. The Cummins family were active Republicans and involved in the local Sinn Féin courts. Newbridge Sinn Féin had been founded there and it was for a time the headquarters of the local branch. It may have been a natural place for John Higgins to seek assistance as the premises also operated as boarding house.[8]

John Higgins wrote in his submission for a pension to the military services pensions board in 1935 regarding his previous employer accepting him back: 'I was idle until the 1st Aug 1924, when I got a position as a junior grocer's assistant from Michael Nolan, Eyre Street, Newbridge, Co. Kildare, at a salary of £50 per year indoor. At the time, very few people would employ an ex-internee.' At thirty, Higgins had to start again on a salary less than a third of what he was earning before the Civil War. The Nolans were a local Republican family and may have employed Higgins on that basis when other employers were turning their back on those who had been anti-Treaty. In recent years, a member of the Cummins family sent the president a photograph with the window of the room he stayed in marked with an X.

Michael D. Higgins recalled: 'My father did say one thing that affected me very much. When he came out, the names of the ex-internees were given in [to the authorities] for any trouble that was going on. That affected him.' As a result of his participation in the Civil War, John and his brother Peter were divided. 'My father and my uncle were not antagonistic to each other but I just felt that a bond had been broken and I don't think my father was ever able to fully recover it,' Michael D. Higgins said. 'It makes me sad to think of the division. My uncle and my father never discussed it very much with us as children.'

President Higgins is convinced his father's long struggle to get a military pension was due to his anti-Treaty activities. 'No hesitation at all in that. People who went on to have property and defined addresses were able to assemble all their evidence easier. I think you will see, my father sends all the stuff [application forms] and it gets lost. It was of the nature of the side they were on, they were more scattered. Isn't it extraordinary the difference there was about what side you were on? If you were dealt with on the Free State side, you were dealt with quite early,' he said.[9] (However, this later changed when Fianna Fáil came to power.)

Republicans found themselves boycotted when they looked for work and as they refused to take the oath of allegiance, employment in the state sector was out of the question. Many were unable to return to their profession. The government's attitude was to reward its supporters with employment, housing and in some cases land. Applicants for civil service examinations were required to give an undertaking that they had not taken part in, or helped, 'the forces in revolt' and they had to promise 'to be faithful to that government and to give no aid or support of any kind to those who are or may in future be engaged in conflict against the government'.[10]

There are many reasons why the Civil War caused more division in, and ultimately more success against, the IRA, which was crushed as British General 'Bloody' Maxwell observed. 'by means far more drastic than any which the British Government dare to impose during the worst period of the rebellion'.[11]

Internment under British rule was used by the crown not

only as a form of preventive detention but also in an attempt to gather intelligence, despite having no specific power to interrogate internees. Accusations of brutality were common, and in view of the British army's comments in relation to such claims, were probably at least partly justified. As to the question of effectiveness, internment did not seem to impede the War of Independence IRA greatly. Significantly, British army sources were not uniform in the endorsement of the efficacy of internment. Some claimed the internments of early 1920 had a considerable effect on the IRA. Still, another hinted at counter-productive effects in that the mass arrests at the end of the year prompted organisational improvements in the Republican Army, forced more men to go 'on the run,' with the result that they formed more active service units.[12]

Unlike the British who vacillated for much of the War of Independence about whether to impose martial law, the Provisional Government simply declared a state of war at the outset and empowered the army and the CID to arrest whomsoever they thought best. The results, unmediated by legality, were often highly arbitrary.[13]

Internment in the Civil War was far more effective. The National Army had a huge advantage in knowing who their enemy was – mainly their former comrades – who knew all their trusted haunts and were therefore able to capture more and more prisoners. There were 13,000 Republicans subsequently interned during the Civil War, although not all of them would have been actively involved in military operations. During the Civil War, internment powers were first resorted to out of strategic military necessity, and later as a counter-insurgency tool primarily designed to take Republican activists out of circulation. Eventually, these powers were used on a scale roughly three times greater than that used by the British under the ROIA.[14]

Complaints about overcrowding in prisons and the behaviour of prison guards became a regular feature of Republican propaganda in the course of and after the Civil War. A major riot by Republican prisoners in Mountjoy in July 1922 caused the jail to be put under the control of the military, with Diarmuid O'Hegarty appointed governor of the prison. He announced that prisoners would be treated as 'military captives … and that any resistance to their guards or any attempt to assist their own forces, revolt, mutiny, conspiracy, insubordination, attempt to escape or cell wrecking will render them liable to be shot down …'[15] Referring to such appointments, Gearóid O'Sullivan, adjutant-general of the National Army, later commented: 'You had to … get men whom you could trust, not because they had any particular ability'.[16] The result was that the camps and prisons under the control of the Provisional Government saw much bloodletting. During the period when the British controlled the Curragh internment camps (1921), there were no fatalities among the Republican prisoners. However, during 1922–24, seventeen Republican prisoners died – seven were executed by firing squad; four died of 'ill-treatment' or 'neglect'; three died on hunger strike, two were shot 'trying to escape', while another, Joseph Bergin, was deliberately murdered.

Another serious mark against pro-Treaty conduct, and a significant blow to Republican morale, was the campaign of executions. Under martial law, British military courts imposed sentences of death by hanging, death by shooting, penal servitude for between three years to life and imprisonment for up to two years. There were twenty-four executions for political offences carried out in 1920–1.[17] The military courts of the Provisional Government had a conviction rate of eighty-five per cent in cases in which a finding was reached. A wide variety of sentencing options were used. Death sentences were imposed and confirmed in twenty-nine per cent of the total number of cases tried. Seventy-seven executions were carried out between December 1922 and April 1923, compared to twenty-four by the British.[18] The December 1922 executions of seven men from Kildare, in the Curragh Camp, were the largest single executions conducted between 1919–23.

Whether lawful or not, the Free State government persisted with the execution policy to break the morale of the anti-Treaty Republicans. The government believed that execution was a necessary evil to persuade republicans to cease their actions against the newly formed state. The execution policy certainly put fear into many on the anti-Treaty side, especially their supporters and family members, bringing pressure on the IRA to end the conflict. It was a draconian measure that shortened the war.[19] Exclusion from absolution and the last sacraments to volunteers who were killed in action or were executed was also devastating for Republicans and their families.

With the death of Michael Collins, the spirit of compromise vanished from the leaders of the Provisional Government and was replaced by a ruthless intransigence. Inside the Curragh Camp, the harsh prison regime was responsible for brutality, medical neglect, the shootings of would-be escapees, executions of those arrested under arms, the brutal murder of at least one Republican and the stoppage of vital food parcels. When hostilities had long ceased and their release was not forthcoming, the prisoners began a hunger strike. This protest failed in its aim due to government intransigence and resulted in the death of several internees. The failure of the hunger strike and the continued incarceration of prisoners caused further demoralisation among the Curragh prisoners, most of whom, as internees, had no release date in sight. The discipline that had kept them united started to erode. Prisoner releases were indiscriminate. In more moves to break morale and organisation, individual officers would be released, then the rank and file and then officers would be rereleased. All cohesion began to be lost, and as Ernie O'Malley said, 'The majority of us were aimless and loafing'.[20] Outside, the prisoners' families and dependents were impoverished, and the government's repressive conditions continued as long as resistance lasted. All these conditions contributed to the demoralisation of the internees in the Curragh who went from a stage of defiance to defeat.

In the end, the policy of the Free State government won out. Internment, the executions and the mass hunger strike for most prisoners were too much. The government's unwavering stance emphasised its power and authority, highlighting the futility of resuming armed resistance and the ongoing political ineffectiveness of the Republican movement. The men who remained active supporters of armed struggle after 1923 were a minority and the IRA shrank progressively in size and power. Militant Republicans were met with imprisonment, denial of employment and economic security. The vast majority of former prisoners, however embittered by their prison experiences, had had enough and accepted they had been defeated militarily. Many subsequently took their lead from their leader Éamonn de Valera on the journey towards constitutional politics.[21] The Civil War left a profound legacy throughout the country and, for decades after, caused lasting division in families and communities.

Appendix I

Escapees from Newbridge Barracks 14–15 October 1922

Armagh
Hannaway, Frank. Castle Street, Armagh
Loughran, Eugene. Ballycranny, Ballyrath
McGlennan (McGlanan/McGlennon), Charles. Ballybrodden

Carlow
Brennan, Eugene. Nurney
Dowling, Patrick. Killeshin
Lennon, James. Borris
Maher, Michael. Leighhlinbridge
Malone, Thomas. Killeshin
Murphy, John. Ballingrane
O'Brien, Seamus. Knockgarry
O'Ryan, Michael. Carlow
Pender, John. Ballickmoyler
Ryan, Michael. Butlersgrange
Sutton, Patrick. Milford
Woods, Patrick. Leighlinbridge

Cork
Leary, Con. Kilindish
McGrath, John. Mallow
Reynolds, William. Ballinhassig
Sullivan, William. Ballinaclashet, Kinsale

Derry
Burke, Leo.

Heaney, Michael. Dungiven

McCallion, Alfred. 11 Barry Street, Derry

McCann, Seamus. 5 Waterloo Street, Derry

Donegal

Gallagher, Charles. Milltown

McGee, Dan. Killult, Falcarragh

McMenamin, Hugh. Castlefin

O'Brien, John. Ramelton

O'Boyle, Neil Plunkett. Leac Eineach, Burtonport

O'Donnell, Frank. Meenmore, Dungloe

O'Flaherty, Manus. Carrick, Castelfin

Quinn, John. Magheracorran

Dublin

Cooney, Patrick. Balbriggan

Jordan, Patrick. 90 Allingham Buildings, Dublin

Hetherington, John. 3 Bellmount Terrace, Dublin

Hyland, Seán. 58 Mulgrave Street, Dun Laoighaire

Kenny, James. Mountain View House, Co. Dublin

O'Brien, Thomas.

Spain, James. 9 Geraldine Street, Dublin

Stoneham, Daniel. 29 Sackville Avenue, Dublin

Walsh, Joseph. 8 Castlewood Terrace, Dublin

Whelan, James. Flemington, Balbriggan

Whelan, Peter. Flemington, Balbriggan

Kerry

Allman, Patrick. Rockfield

Hussey, William. High Street, Killarney

O'Connor, Seamus. Castleisland

O'Sullivan, William. 28 Dean's Lane, Tralee

Kildare

Bagnall, Patrick. Kildare Town

Birchall, John. Grangebeg

Brennan, Patrick. Lughill, Monasterevin

Breslin, Michael. Abbey View, Kildare

Breslin, James John. Abbey View, Kildare

Byrne, Denis. Fassaugh, Monasterevin

Byrne, Michael. Bride Street, Kildare

Byrne, William 'Liam. Ballysax

Connolly, Laurence. Simonstown, Celbridge

Conroy, Andy. Ballyneagh, Monasterevan

Dempsey, James. Castletown (Major Connolly) Lodge, Kilgowan

Dooley, Jeremiah. Rathangan

Dowling, John. Kilcullen

Dunne, Peter. Harbour View, Kildare

Gannon, William. Cross Keys, Kildare

Harris, Thomas. Caragh, Naas

Horgan, Seán. Harristown, Kildare

Houlihan, James. Claregate Street, Kildare.

Hughes, Joseph. Cherryville

Kelly, Michael. Castledermot

Lambe, Maurice. Main Street, Kilcullen

Melia, Bernard. Ballygreany

Moore, Peter. Skireen

Murphy, Michael. Maynooth

Myers, Henry. Kilcullen

Neligan, Pat. Monasterevin

O'Connor, Bernard. Main Street, Kildare

O'Keefe, Pat. Kilcock

O'Keefe, James. Kilcock

Rafferty, John. Naas

Smith, John. Grangebeg

Smyth, Joseph. Monasterevan

Walsh, James. Fairview, Kildare

Whyte, James 'Jimmy'. 18 South Main St, Naas

Williams, Thomas J. 7 Main Street, Naas

Limerick

Nash, Joseph. 79 O'Connell Street, Limerick

Stubbins, Seán. Ballincolly, Kilmallock

Mayo

Forde, Liam. Lisacul, Ballaghaderreen

Meath

Connell, Nicholas. Duleek

Cooney, Peter. Gormanstown

Offaly

Byrne, James. Town Hall, Edenderry

Dempsey, Patrick. Edenderry

Lynam, Christopher 'Kitt'. Ballyfore

Roscommon

O'Donovan, James L. 'Seamus'. Castleview

Tipperary

Flood, T. Ballinure

Tyrone

Kelly, Tom. 56 Irish Street, Dungannon

McDonald, Archie. Dungannon

McGurk, James. Carrickmore

Ogle, John. Dungannon

Slane, Robert. Sixmilecross

Westmeath

Hynes, Ned. Ash Road, Mullingar

Lynch, John. Castlepollard

Wicklow

Byrne, Denis. Dunlavin

Coogan, Patrick. Carrigeen

Glynn, Patrick. Chapel Hill, Baltinglass

Hall, James. Brittas

Harris, Michael. Dunlavin

Kelly, Joseph. Dunlavin

Kearns, ? Dunlavin

Neary, Michael. 93 Main Street, Bray

Wexford

Allen, Charley. Rathgreene

Allen, Denis. Ratheenagurren, Gorey

Dwyer, Patrick. Gorey

Dwyer, Thomas. Enniscorthy

Whitty, Patrick. 17 William Street, Wexford

Appendix II

Escapees from Tintown 1, 21 April 1923

Armagh
McCoy, John. Mullaghbawn
O'Hanlon, Mick. Mullaghbawn

Cork
Buckley, G. 48 Shears Street, Cork
O'Callaghan, Liam. Cork
O'Sullivan, Billy. Glengariff Road, Bantry
McAuliffe, Patrick. Killerin, Kanturk

Dublin
Bird, John. 3 Erne Terrace, Brunswick Street
Reid, Nicky/Mickey. Howth
Mordaunt, Edward P. 54 Lower Mount Street

Galway
Burke, John. Glenbricken, Clifden
Connely, Thomas. Spiddal
Corbett, Joseph. Clifden
Kennedy, John J. Lecarrow, Athenry
King, John. Clifden

Kerry
Clifford, Patsy
Connor, John. Green Lane, Tralee
Curnane, Paddy. Tarbet
Lyons, Daniel. Derry, Listowel

Quinn, Thomas. Strand Street, Tralee

Watters, P. J. Ballincourt, Tralee

Kildare

Brennan, Patrick. Brownstown, Kilcullen

Wallace, Edward 'Dixie'. Newbridge

Kilkenny

Delaney, Michael. Coolagh, Callan

Downey, Joseph. Friary Street, Kilkenny

Dunphy, Patrick. Ballincur, Mooncoin

Fitzpatrick, Edward. Kilmanagh

Limerick

Colbert, James. Athea

Dargan, John. 15 Rutland Street, Limerick

Egan, Dan. Ballyneety

Healy, Tim. Bank Place, Rathkeale

Johnston, Maurice. 31 Frederick Place, Limerick

Kiely, Maurice. Coolaboy, Drumcollagher

O'Brien, Michael. 53 Back Clare Street, Limerick

O'Farrell, John. Church Street, Rathkeale

Reidy, Séan. Lower Main Street, Rathkeale

Roche, James. Bank Place, Rathkeale

Saunders, Joseph. 75 Carey Road, Limerick

Mayo

Boyle, Jim. Foxford

Browne, James. Kilmeena

Cannon, Patrick. Ballyhein, Castlebar

Cannon, Patrick J. Cornacushlan, Islandeady

Carabine, Patrick. Main Street, Belmullet

Cryan, Battie. Bridge Street, Westport

Flannigan, Barney. Laherdane

Fordham, Martin. Auden Street, Kiltimagh

Gallagher, John. Faghey, Westport

Hegarty, Paddy. Crossmolina

Heneghan, M. 8 Mannion Street, St Helena, Lancashire

Hughes, James 'Gus'. New Antrim Road, Castlebar

Kilroy, Jimmy. Westport

Malone, Willie. Westport

Ó Maoláin, Tomás. Roemore

Reidy, Tommy. Derrynaraw

Rushe, Jim. Kiltimagh

Tracey, ? Ballygar

Waters, William. Castlehill, Crossmolina

Roscommon

Kelly, Paddy. Ballinaboy, Beechwood

Sligo

Kelly, John. Colloney

Scanlon, Tom. Sligo Town

Waterford

Mackey, Patrick. Ballygunner

ENDNOTES

Emergency Powers

1 Hopkinson, Michael. 'From treaty to civil war 1921–2', in *A new history of Ireland. VII. Ireland 1921–84* (ed. Hill, J. R.), pp. 2–3, 5; *Irish Independent,* 7 December 1921. The Government of Ireland Act was passed in November 1920 and was intended to partition Ireland into two territories, Southern Ireland andNorthern Ireland, each to be self-governing.Northern Ireland was created by the Anglo-Irish Treaty.

2 *Sunday Independent,* 8 January 1922. This interim government would operate until a new parliament, elected by the people, enacted the Constitution of the Irish Free State, set to come into official existence on 6 December 1922.

3 *Evening Herald,* 16 January 1922.

4 Anne-Marie McInerney, 'Hidden away: the treatment of Civil War internees', RTÉ.ie/history, 17 January 2023. Max Green was the son-in-law of John Redmond, MP.

5 Yeates, Pádraic. *A City in Civil War. Dublin 1921–4* (Dublin, 2015), p. 64.

6 Ferriter, Diarmaid, *A nation not a rabble. The Irish Revolution 1913–1923* (London, 2015), p. 262.

7 Fewer, Michael. *The Battle of the Four Courts. The first three days of the Irish Civil War* (London, 2018), p. 87; https://www.dib.ie/biography/lynch-william-fanaghan-liam-a4949. There were still 5,000 British troops in Dublin awaiting evacuation.

8 *Ibid.,* pp. 88, 95, 112.

9 Fewer, *The Battle of the Four Courts,* p. 143; Yeates, *A City in Civil War,* p. 82.

10 Dorney, John. *The Civil War in Dublin. The fight for the Irish capital 1922–1924* (Newbridge, 2017), p. 112.

11 *Freeman's Journal,* 17 May 1922. The camp took its name from the former Hare Park located nearby by the Kildare Hunt Club before construction of the military camp in the 1850s.

12 Cummins, Seamus A. *'Mullaney's Men': The rise and fall of the anti-Treaty forces in North Kildare, Grangewilliam, 1922* (Naas, 2022), pp. 12–14.

13 Durney, James. *Stand you now for Ireland's cause. A biographical dictionary of Co. Kildare republican activists 1913–1923* (Naas, 2023), p. 267.

14 Ó Longaigh, Seosamh. *Emergency Law in Independent Ireland,*

1922–1948 (Dublin, 2006), p. 17.

15 Dorney, John, *The Civil War in Dublin*, pp. 112, 119; Harrington, Niall C. *Kerry Landing, 1922. An episode of the Civil War* (Dublin, 1992), p. 168.

16 Dorney, John, *The Civil War in Dublin*, p. 196. A particularly sad occurrence took place on 20 August 1922 in Newbridge when Mrs Mary Blakely (50), who had just returned from a visit to a relative who was a prisoner at the Curragh Camp suddenly took ill and died of a heart attack just as she reached her home at Market Square in the town.

17 Yeates, *A City in Civil War*, pp. 99–100.

18 *Leinster Leader*, 16 September 1922.

19 Enright, Seán, *The Irish Civil War. Law, execution and atrocity* (Newbridge, 2019), p. 10.

20 The writ of *habeas corpus* primarily acts as a writ of inquiry, issued to test the reasons or grounds for detention. Thus, the writ stands as a safeguard against imprisonment of those held in violation of the law, by ordering the responsible enforcement authorities to provide valid reasons for the detention.

21 *Cork Examiner*, 4 August 1922. Crowley was appointed as a circuit court judge in the revolutionary courts on 1 August 1920. He invited confrontation from crown forces and was arrested at his court at Ballina, after he defied the RIC when they called on the court to disperse. Stripped of his British civil service pension – he had been an excise officer – Crowley was sentenced to two years' hard labour and served eighteen months.

22 Diarmaid Ó Cruadhlaoich. *Step by step. From the Republic back into the Empire* (Dublin, 1935), p. 6. George Gavan Duffy resigned in protest, objecting that the government had abolished the Dáil supreme court rather than meet an application for *habeas corpus* in open court. The conduct of the Civil War further disillusioned him, and he was one of the courageous voices in the Dáil who objected to the execution of anti-Treaty prisoners held by the Free State government.

23 *Ibid.*, p. 7; Enright, *The Irish Civil War*, p. 10.

24 Mathews, Arthur. *Walled in by Hate. Kevin O'Higgins, his friends and enemies* (Newbridge, 2024) pp. 97–8.

25 *Dundalk Democrat*, 16 September 1922.

26 Ó Cruadhlaoich, *Step by step*, p. 7.

27 *Freeman's Journal*, 28 November 1922.

28 *Evening Herald*, 5 September 1922. Seán Beaumont, a native of Co. Mayo, was Inspector of Irish at the Department of Agriculture and Technical Instruction, Dublin. He was later Gaelic editor of the *Irish Press* newspaper.

29 *Irish Independent,* 16 September 1922.

30 *Southern Star,* 23 September 1922. Beaumont's application for release was refused, but he was by then at liberty.

31 *Cork Examiner,* 11 September 1922; *Meath Chronicle,* 16 September 1922.

32 https://www.mna100.ie/centenary-moments/women-prisoners-dfence-league/ Ward, Margaret. *Maud Gonne. Ireland's Joan of Arc* (London, 1990), p. 135; Cardozo, Nancy. *Maud Gonne* (New York, 1990), p. 353. Maud Gonne MacBride was the widow of John MacBride, executed in 1916 for his part in the Easter Rising. Charlotte Despard was a suffragist, nationalist, socialist and writer, and brother of Lord John French, viceroy of Ireland (1918–21).

33 Linklater, Andro. *An unhusbanded life. Charlotte Despard. Suffragette, Socialist and Sinn Féiner* (London, 1980), pp. 224–5; Mathews, *Wallea in by Hate,* p. 47.

34 Linklater, *An unhusbanded life,* p. 225.

The Former Jailed

1 Ferriter, *A nation not a rabble,* p. 273.

2 Ó Longaigh, *Emergency Law in Independent Ireland,* p. 18.

3 McNamara, Conor. *Liam Mellows. Soldier of the Irish Republic. Selected writings 1914–1922* (Newbridge, 2019), p. 26. General Richard Mulcahy, Minister for Defence, was appointed commander-in-chief of the National Army on 1 July 1922.

4 Yeates, *A City in Civil War,* pp. 152–3.

5 Ferriter, *Between Two Hells,* p. 76.

6 *Freeman's Journal,* 9 September; *Westmeath Independent,* 28 October 1922.

7 Ferriter, *Between Two Hells,* p. 76.

8 *Kildare Observer,* 12 August 1922.

9 Bord na Móna. Peat Research Centre. *From boot and saddle to biotechnology. On the Newbridge Barrack site* (Naas, 1998), p. 34.

10 *Ibid.,* p. 34. A cupola is a relatively small, dome-like, tall structure on top of a building. It is often used to provide a lookout or to admit light and air.

11 Report from Rodolphe A. Haccius, Commission of International Red Cross, regarding inspection of internment camp at Newbridge, County Kildare, 18 April 1923, National Library Ireland, Dublin.

12 *Leinster Leader,* 26 August 1922

13 *Ibid.,* 9 September 1922.

14 Ó Duibhir, Liam. *Donegal and the Civil War. The untold story*

(Cork, 2011), p. 206.

15 *Leinster Leader,* 9 September 1922.

16 *Ibid.,* 16 September 1922.

17 Ferriter, *Between Two Hells,* p. 77; Seán Hayes Papers are held in Cork City and County Archives.

18 Share, *Bernard. In time of Civil War. The conflict on the Irish railways 1922–23* (Cork, 2006), p. 49.

19 Yeates, *A City in Civil War,* pp. 226–7.

20 Patrick O'Keefe, 'My reminiscences of 1914–1923,' *Oughterany. Journal of the Donadea Local History Group,* Vol. I, No. 1, 1993, pp. 48–9.

21 Durney, James. *Stand you now for Ireland's cause. A biographical dictionary of Co. Kildare republican activists 1913–1923* (Naas, 2023), p. 175.

22 O'Connor, Séamus. *Tomorrow was another day* (Tralee, 1970), pp. 66–7; 'Memories of freedom fight recalled in new Anvil book', *Corkman,* 1 August 1970. Seamus O'Connor did not live to see his book published, having died in November 1969 of a heart attack.

23 Dodd, Conor. *Casualties of Conflict. Fatalities of the War of Independence and Civil War in Glasnevin Cemetery* (Cork, 2023), pp. 230–1. Denis O'Dea later starred in movies by John Ford (*The Informer*) and Alfred Hitchcock, as well as Disney productions such as *Treasure Island* and *Darby O'Gill and the little people.* He died in 1978.

24 Ó Duibhir, *Donegal and the Civil War,* p. 206.

25 *Leinster Leader,* 30 September 1922.

26 Durney, James, *Stand You Now for Ireland's Cause,* pp. 135, 349–50.

27 *Leinster Leader,* 14 October 1922.

28 MS 42,236, Newbridge Barracks autograph book, courtesy of National Library of Ireland, Dublin. https://catalogue. nli.ie/Record/vtls000640075 Most of the entries are dated between 5–19 December 1923, shortly after the ending of the hunger-strike.

29 *Leinster Leader,* 14 October 1922.

30 *Northern Standard,* 25 August 1922.

31 *Leinster Leader,* 14 October 1922.

32 Durney. *Stand you now for Ireland's cause,* p. 159. Squires Gannon was a winner of two All-Ireland medals (1927 and 1928) and played his last game for the county in the 1929 All-Ireland Final, having played in five finals (1926 was a replay).

33 Family letter of Charlie O'Neill, courtesy of Dr Gerri O'Neill, Dublin City University, 2 February 2023. The letter was dated 6

March 1923.

34 O'Malley, Cormac K. H. & Horgan, Tim. *The men will talk to me. Kerry interviews by Ernie O'Malley* (Cork, 2012), p. 46. Con Casey's brother-in-law, Charlie Daly, was executed by firing squad on 14 March 1923 at Drumboe, Co. Donegal, as a reprisal for a fatal attack on National Army troops.

35 Barry, Denis. *The unknown Commandant. The life and times of Denis Barry 1883–1927* (Cork, 2010), p. 87.

36 *Belfast Newsletter* 4 October 1922.

Down and out in Newbridge Barracks

1 O'Keefe, Patrick. 'My reminiscences of 191–1923', p. 49.

2 Nellie Kearns Military Pension application MSP34REF17238, www.military archives.ie

3 Ó Duibhir, *Donegal and the Civil War*, p. 207.

4 'The Escape from Newbridge Barracks', *Leinster Leader*, 31 December 1927.

5 O'Connor, *Tomorrow was another day*, pp. 67–8.

6 'The Escape from Newbridge Barracks', *Leinster Leader*, 31 December 1927

7 O'Keefe, 'My reminiscences of 1914–1923'.

8 A count of escapees made by me from Civil War Prison Registers, Military Archives, Dublin.

9 Ó Duibhir, *Donegal and the Civil War*, p. 208.

10 *Poblacht na h-Éireann, War News No. 84*, 4 November 1922.

11 *Nationalist and Leinster Times*, 21 October 1922.

12 O'Connor, *Tomorrow was another day*, pp. 67–8.

13 Ó Duibhir, *Donegal and the Civil War*, pp. 207–8; McCann was a captain with Derry Brigade, active since the War of Independence.

14 O'Connor, *Tomorrow was another day*, pp. 68–72.

15 'Memories of freedom fight recalled in new Anvil book', *Corkman*, 1 August 1970. Jimmy Kenny later served as a garda detective and was assigned as a bodyguard to Eamon de Valera when he was Taoiseach. He died on 26 January 1981.

16 'The Escape from Newbridge Barracks', *Leinster Leader*, 31 December 1927.

17 *Nationalist and Leinster Times*, 21 October 1922. This prisoner is possibly John Horgan, a railway stationmaster at Harristown, Co. Kildare. He had been arrested on 4 September 1922 and interned at Newbridge.

18 'Passing of distinguished doctor', *Leinster Leader*, 29 October 1960.

19 O'Connor, *Tomorrow was another day*, pp. 72–3. Half a crown was worth two shillings and six pence.

20 Durney, James. 'The Greatest Escape. Newbridge Barracks 14–15 October 1922', https://kildare.ie/ehistory/

21 William Byrne, MSP34REF22534, Military Service Pensions Collection, Military Archives, Dublin.

22 https://www.dib.ie/biography/odonovan-james-laurence-jim-seamus-a6715; Richard Harris, MSP34REF15109 and James L. O'Donovan, MSP34REF 1590, Military Service Pensions Collection, Military Archives, Dublin. In 1939, O'Donovan travelled to Germany to discuss cooperation between Germany and the IRA. He was interned in the Curragh Camp from 1941–43.

23 *New Ross Standard*, 20 October 1922.

24 Aaron Ó Maonaigh, 'The men will talk to me: Ernie O'Malley's interviews with Wexford veterans of the Irish Revolution', *The Past: Organ of the Uí Cinsealaigh Historical Society*, 35 (2021), pp. 46–59.

25 Conversation with Tony McCarthy, 19 July 2024; *Evening Echo*, 25 October 1977.

26 Knipe, Gregory, *The Fourth Northerners and the Irish Revolution* (Wexford, 2020), pp. 179–80.

27 *Derry Journal*, 29 November 1922; Durney, *Stand you now for Ireland's cause*, p. 350.

28 *Kildare Observer*, 2 December 1922.

29 *Ibid.*, 19 May 1923. A street in Letterkenny, Co. Donegal, is named 'Plunkett O'Boyle Terrace' in his honour.

30 Autograph book, 'Newbridge Detention Camp, 1923', copy held in County Kildare Archives & Local Studies, donated by Mick and Pat Sheehan, Newbridge, 2007. While the owner of the autograph book is not known, it is possibly that of Mick Sheehan, who had been interned in Newbridge in 1922–23.

31 *Leinster Leader*, 20 January 1923.

Back in the Curragh again

1 *Cork Examiner*, 30 November 1922.

2 Letter Hare Park Camp, 3 August 1923, CW/P/09/03, Military Archives, Dublin.

3 *Irish Independent*, 20 December 1922.

4 *Freeman's Journal*, 20 December 1922. At the beginning of the conflict the Provisional Government had decided to call Republican forces 'Irregulars' and ordered the press that they were not to be referred to as 'Executive forces' or be described as 'forces' or 'troops'.

5 Letter from Irish Republican Prisoners Dependents Fund, 6 Harcourt Street, Dublin, 5 February 1923, CW/P/09/03, Military Archives, Dublin.

6 Letter from Hare Park Camp, 7 February 1923, CW/P/09/03, Military Archives, Dublin.

7 Letters dated 20 June and 26 June 1923, CW/P/09/03, Military Archives, Dublin.

8 *Irish Independent*, 31 August 1922; *Poblacht na hÉireann, War News, No. 56*, 12 September 1922; *Kildare Observer*, 9 September 1922.

9 Patrick Mulrennan, Military Pension Application, DP7961. His mother, Mary Mulrennan, subsequently made an application for a military pension.

10 O'Malley, Cormac and Horgan, Tim. *The men will talk to me. Kerry interviews by Ernie O'Malley*, p. 129.

11 Horgan, John. *Seán Lemass. The enigmatic patriot* (Dublin, 1997), p. 26; Evans, Bryce. *Seán Lemass. Democratic Dictator* (Cork, 2011), p. 24.

12 Farrell, Brian. *Seán Lemass* (Dublin, 1991), pp. 8–9. Seán Lemass is the subject of at least four biographies.

13 Lawlor, Chris. *Robert Barton. A remarkable revolutionary* (Gloucestershire, 2024), pp. 133–4, 141.

14 Ring, Jim. *Erskine Childers* (London, 1996), p. 285.

15 *Ibid.*, pp. 85, 191, 207; Lawlor, *Robert Barton*, pp. 28, 35, 43.

16 'Hidden away: the treatment of Civil War internees', RTÉ News, 17 Janu- ary 2023.

17 Letter, dated 10 January 1923, CW/P/08/08, Military Archives, Dublin.

18 Military Archives Pension Application, DP3596. Foley's date of birth was not recorded on his file but his age at time of death was given as twenty, while his father stated that he was seventeen when he died. According to family information he was born on 29 August 1905.

19 Information supplied by Liam Canny, 21 June 2024.

20 *Leinster Leader*, 17 February 1923.

21 *Ibid.*, 10 March 1923.

22 Hugh Crawford, 'The internment camps' in *The Curragh Revisited* (Curragh Local History Group, 2002), p. 11.

23 O'Malley, Cormac and Ó Comhraí, Cormac, *The men will talk to me. Galway interviews by Ernie O'Malley*, p. 261.

24 *Freeman's Journal*, 27 April 1923. Lt-Comdt Seán Kavanagh was appointed OC Hare Park Camp, with the rank of Comdt, and was replaced by Capt. Waters as second-in-command of Newbridge Barracks.

25 Aiken, *et al, The men will talk to me. Ernie O'Malley's interviews*

with the Northern Divisions, p. 144.

26 File AW/889. Court of Inquiry re Escape of Internees from Tintown Internment Camp, 1 May 1923. Military Archives, Cathal Brugha Barracks, Dublin.

27 Ciara Lacey, 'Living conditions in the Curragh Internment Camp, in the post civil war years, 1923–1926, including evidence from Joe Keane.' https://kildarelibraries.ie/ehistory/living conditions-in-the-curragh -internment-camp-1923-26/

28 Report from Rodolphe A. Haccius, Commission of International Red Cross, regarding inspection of the internment camp at Tintown, 20 April 1923, National Library of Ireland, Dublin.

29 *Ibid.*

30 https://www.oireachtas.ie/en/debates/debate/dail/1923-06-22/11/

31 Letter from Tintown No. 2 Camp, dated 12 March 1923, CW/P/10/02, Military Archives, Dublin.

32 O'Hanlon, Paddy. *End of Term report* (Armagh, 2011), pp. 7–9.

33 'Mayo men feature in famous I.R.A. escape from the Curragh Camp', *The Mayo News,* 24 January 1959.

34 *Freeman's Journal,* 7 July 1923; Patrick Gallagher, Military Service Pension Application, DP314. His mother, Agnes Gallagher, subsequently applied for a military pension.

The Executioner's Song

1 Annie Moore's son, John O'Reilly, in a letter to me (9 April 2010) claims the 'dug-out' was in fact an unfinished tunnel, which was to lead out to the nearby railway line.

2 *Freeman's Journal,* 20 December 1922.

3 Interview with Pat Sheehan, Henry Street, Newbridge, 2 February 2001; interview with John O'Reilly, Thorpe-Bay, Southend on Sea, Essex, 12 January 2010.

4 Durney, James. *The Civil War in Kildare* (Cork, 2011), p. 123.

5 Corrigan, Mario. *Nine Lives. Mooresbridge, December 1922* (Kildare, 2022), p. 17.

6 *Freeman's Journal,* 20 December 1922. Men's overcoats, trench coats, boots and pants, ladies' hats, knitting wool, large quantities of groceries, bacon and three sacks of flour, were also found at the dug-out, taken from goods trains and grocery stores.

7 Yeates, *A City in Civil War,* pp. 222–3.

8 *Evening Echo,* 4 October 1922. On the following day the Executive Council of the Free State Government decided to seek the support of the Catholic hierarchy in putting down the IRA. The bishops agreed and on 10 October, issued a joint pastoral letter condemning Republicans and warning them that

they would not be absolved in confession and would be denied the sacraments.

9 Mathews, *Walled in by Hate*, p. 105.
10 Curran, Joseph M. *The birth of the Irish Free State 1921–1923* (Alabama, 1980), pp. 256–7, 265.
11 Corrigan, *Nine Lives,* p. 5.
12 *Cork Examiner,* 11 December 1922.
13 Ferriter, *Between Two Hells*, p. 94.
14 *Leinster Leader,* 23 December 1922; *Kildare Observer,* 23 December 1922.
15 Durney, *The Civil War in Kildare*, p. 127.
16 *Éire. The Irish Nation,* 7 April 1923.
17 *Sinn Féin,* 22 December 1923.
18 *Éire. The Irish Nation,* 7 April 1923.
19 Corrigan, *Nine Lives.* p. 30. The term 'go west' or 'go to America' was a euphemism for being killed in action. Usually at that time when a person emigrated west to America they were never seen again.
20 Ferriter, *A nation not a rabble*, pp. 286–7.
21 Durney, *The Civil War in Kildare*, p. 128.
22 Corrigan, *Nine Lives* pp. 148, 150. According to Mario Corrigan one of the executed, James O'Connor, was born in Co. Kildare, but later moved to Tipperary when his father was given the post of railway gate keeper. He is the maternal great-uncle of Sinn Féin president, Mary Lou McDonald.

Tintown tunnels
1 McGuffin, John, *Internment* (Tralee, 1973), p. 41.
2 O'Malley & Ó Comhraí, *The men will talk to me. Galway interviews by Ernie O'Malley*, p. 267.
3 www.dib.ie/biography/odonnell-peadar-a6700.
4 O'Donnell, Peadar, *The gates flew open* (London, 1932), pp. 96–8; Aiken, S., Macbhloscaidh, F., Ó Duibhir, L., Ó Tuama, D., *The men will talk to me. Ernie O'Malley's interviews with the Northern Divisions*, p. 141.
5 O'Malley, Ernie, *The Singing Flame* (Dublin, 1978), pp. 272–3.
6 Durney, James, *Interned. The Curragh internment camps in the War of Inde- pendence* (Cork, 2020), p. 278. A national schoolteacher, Ó Maoláin had been active since 1916 and was held as a prisoner in Athlone Barracks before being transferred to Tintown with Tommy Reidy. Ó Maoláin later became a Fianna Fáil TD for Co. Dublin (1938–43).
7 O'Malley, Cormac K. H. & Keane, Vincent, *The men will talk to me. Mayo interviews by Ernie O'Malley* (Cork, 2014), p. 73. Paddy

Cannon said the tunnel was begun on 19 January 1923.

8 'Mayo men feature in famous I.R.A. escape from the Curragh Camp', *The Mayo News,* 31 January 1959.

9 Durney, *Stand You Now for Ireland's Cause*, p. 368.

10 O'Donnell, *The Gates Flew Open*, p. 103.

11 Sinead Brennan,'Dr Francis Ferran TD', *Western People,* 16 November 1922.

12 O'Donnell, *The Gates flew open*, pp 102–3.

13 *Ibid.*, pp. 105–6.

14 Aiken, *et al.*, *The men will talk to me. Ernie O'Malley's interviews with the Northern Divisions*, pp. 144, 219.

15 *Leinster Leader,* 7 April 1923; St Lawrence Cemetery Burial Register; Éire, 9 June 1923; *Limerick Leader*, 19 August 2017. His family petitioned President Michael D. Higgins to posthumously recognise his services and the O'Brien family were awarded Owen's IRA Service Medal in 2017.

16 'Mayo men feature in famous I.R.A. escapes from the Curragh Camp', *The Mayo News,* 31 January 1959.

17 Aiken, *et al.*, *The men will talk to me. Ernie O'Malley's interviews with the Northern Divisions*, pp. 127–8; interview with Dr Rory O'Hanlon, Carrickmacross, Co. Monaghan, 9 October 2024. Mick O'Hanlon, from Mullaghbawn, Co. Armagh, was Intelligence Officer, 4th Northern Division, and was an organiser in Cavan. He had been arrested in Virginia, Co. Cavan, in November in possession of a revolver and taken to the Curragh.

18 'Mayo men feature in famous I.R.A. escapes from the Curragh Camp'; *The Mayo News*, 31 January 1959; O'Malley, & Keane, *The men will talk to me. Mayo interviews by Ernie O'Malley*, pp. 94–5.

19 *Ibid.*, p. 149. Other reports record the tunnel shaft was ten feet deep.

20 Aiken, *et al.*, *The men will talk to me. Ernie O'Malley's interviews with the Northern Divisions*, pp. 142–3.

21 O'Malley & Keane, *The men will talk to me. Mayo interviews by Ernie O'Malley*, pp. 149-–50.

22 O'Donnell, *The gates flew open*, pp. 108–9.

23 Aiken, *et al.*, *The men will talk to me. Ernie O'Malley's interviews with the Northern Divisions*, pp. 142–3.

24 *Ibid.*, p. 143; O'Malley & Keane, *The men will talk to me. Mayo interviews by Ernie O'Malley*, p. 150.

25 O'Donnell, *The Gates flew open*, pp. 109–10.

26 'Mayo men feature in famous I.R.A. escapes from the Curragh Camp', *The Mayo News,* 31 January 1959.

27 *Ibid.*

28 Aiken, *et al., The men will talk to me. Ernie O'Malley's interviews with the Northern Divisions,* p. 143; 'Mayo men feature in famous I.R.A. escapes from the Curragh Camp', *The Mayo News,* 24 & 31 January 1959.

Zero Hour

1 Aiken, *et al., The men will talk to me. Ernie O'Malley's interviews with the Northern Divisions,* p. 144; O'Malley & Keane, *The men will talk to me. Mayo interviews by Ernie O'Malley,* p. 151; 'Mayo men feature in famous I.R.A. escapes from the Curragh Camp', *The Mayo News,* 24 & 31 January 1959.

2 Aiken, *et al. The men will talk to me. Ernie O'Malley's interviews with the Northern Divisions,* p. 144. Jim Boyle was not recaptured and returned to Mayo to re-organise his battalion.

3 Joyce, P. W. *The Geography of the Counties of Ireland* (London, 1883), pp. 113–6. Four pages of the book contained a general description of County Kildare.

4 File AW/889, MA, Court of Inquiry re Escape of Internees from Tintown Internment Camp.

5 O'Malley & Keane, *The men will talk to me. Mayo interviews by Ernie O'Malley,* p. 151; Bielenberg, Andy, Borgonovo, John & Ó Ruairc, Pádraig Óg. *The men will talk to me. West Cork interviews by Ernie O'Malley* (Cork, 2015), p. 66.

6 Thomas Reidy, MSP34REF17580. Reidy was captured following an engagement with National Army forces at Lecanvey, near Croagh Patrick, in August 1922. Recaptured in Mayo in September 1923, Reidy was interned in Castlebar and the Curragh until his release in March 1924. Reidy later emigrated to Detroit, USA. According to his death certificate, Tommy Reidy had been missing for two months before his body was found on 31 March 1937 in Wayne, Michigan.

7 'Mayo men feature in famous I.R.A. escapes from the Curragh Camp', *The Mayo News,* 31 January 1959.

8 O'Malley & Keane, *The men will talk to me. Mayo interviews by Ernie O'Malley,* pp. 151–4. Heavey stayed with the Plunkett O'Boyle Column for several weeks until he was re-captured on 13 May 1923.

9 Bielenberg, *et al., The men will talk to me. West Cork interviews by Ernie O'Malley,* pp. 66–8.

10 Military Pension Applications, John Bird, DP1049; Willie Malone, MSP34REF349.

11 Aiken, *et al. The men will talk to me. Ernie O'Malley's interviews with the Northern Divisions,* p. 145.

12 My conversation with Dr Rory O'Hanlon, 16 July 2024.

13 Aiken, *et al. The men will talk to me. Ernie O'Malley's interviews with the Northern Divisions,* p. 145.

14 File AW/889, MA, 'Court of Inquiry re Escape of Internees from Tintown Internment Camp.'

15 *Ibid.*

16 O'Malley & Ó Comhraí, *The men will talk to me. Galway interviews by Ernie O'Malley,* p. 264.

17 O'Malley & Keane, *The men will talk to me. Mayo interviews by Ernie O'Malley,* pp. 91–2; 'Mayo men feature in famous I.R.A. escapes from the Curragh Camp', *The Mayo News,* 31 January 1959.

18 Durney, *Stand you now for Ireland's Cause,* p. 129. Paddy Hegarty was recaptured and was not released until December 1923.

19 O'Malley & Keane, *The men will talk to me. Mayo interviews by Ernie O'Malley,* p. 93.

20 James Dunne, Witness Statement 1571, Bureau of Military History, Dublin. Jim Dunne and John McCoy later became friends when McCoy moved his family from Armagh to Kill.

21 *Liberator,* 1 September 1923; *Nationalist and Munster Advertiser,* 7 Feb- ruary 1970.

22 Kiely, Karel. *Rebel Hearts. A biographical list of republican women activists in Co. Kildare 1913–1923* (Naas, 2023), p. 33.

23 Durney, *Stand you now for Ireland's cause,* pp. 38, 64.

24 *Kildare Observer,* 28 April 1923.

25 Leonard Cardwell, Military Pension Application DP595. In his application Cardwell said it was Newbridge the prisoners had escaped from and that it was March 1923.

26 *Freeman's Journal,* 26 April 1923.

27 O'Malley & Keane, *The men will talk to me. Mayo interviews by Ernie O'Malley,* p. 93. Paddy Cannon was interned in Gormanstown and Newbridge until his release in December 1923.

28 *Kildare Observer,* 28 April 1923.

29 Aiken, *et al, The men will talk to me. Ernie O'Malley's interviews with the Northern Divisions,* pp. 145–6; *Drogheda Independent,* 5 May 1923. The newspaper report gave McCoy's comrade as John Scanlon of Sarsfield Street, Dublin

30 John McCoy, Witness Statement 492, Bureau of Military History; Dublin; Aiken, *et al, The men will talk to me. Ernie O'Malley's interviews with the Northern Divisions,* pp. 171–2.

31 My interview with Dr Rory O'Hanlon, Carrickmacross, Co. Monaghan, 9 October 2024.

32 Brennan 'Dr Francis Ferran TD', *Western People,* 16 November 2022.

33 Durney, *Stand You Now for Ireland's Cause,* p. 368.
34 O'Malley & Ó Comhraí, *The men will talk to me. Galway interviews by Ernie O'Malley,* pp. 267–8.
35 Letter from Tintown No. 2 Camp, 30 April 1923, CW/P/09/03, Military Archives, Dublin.
36 Questions on treatment of prisoners by Ailfrid Ó Brion. *Dáil Éireann deb., Vol. iv,* 31 October 1923. Sourced online 8 April 2010. www.oireachtas.ie

An esteemed visitation

1 *Irish Independent,* 27 December 1922.
2 *Nationalist & Leinster Times,* 22 September 1923.
3 Family letter of Charlie O'Neill, courtesy of Dr Gerri O'Neill, DCU, 2 February 2023. The letter was dated 6 March 1923.
4 Letter from Hare Park Camp, 21 September 1923, CW/P/08/08, Military Archives, Dublin.
5 *Freeman's Journal,* 23 February 1923.
6 Campbell, *Emergency law in Ireland,* p. 229; *Leitrim Observer* 3 March 1923.
7 Cardozo, Nancy. *Maud Gonne* (New York, 1990), p. 359; Ward, Margaret. *Maud Gonne. Ireland's Joan of Arc* (London, 1990), p. 140.
8 https://www.icrc.org/en/our-history
9 Lia Brazil 'Irish Civil War imprisonment, humanitarianism and the Red Cross', in O Keeffe, H., Crowley, J., Ó Drisceoil, D., Borgonovo, J., & Murphy, M., *Atlas of the Irish Civil War. New Perspectives* (Cork, 2024), p. 301.
10 *Irish Independent,* 8 June 1923.
11 Commission of International Red Cross, regarding inspection of internment camp at Newbridge, 18 April 1923.
12 Campbell, *Emergency law in Ireland,* pp. 230–1; Typescript report from Rodolphe A. Haccius, Commission of International Red Cross, regarding inspection of internment camp at Tintown, 20 April 1923, National Library Ireland, Dublin.
13 *Ibid.*
14 www.oireachtas.ie/en/debates/debate/dail/1923-07-03/28/
15 *Irish Independent,* 8 June 1923.
16 *Freeman's Journal,* 4 July 1923.
17 Lia Brazil, 'Irish Civil War imprisonment, humanitarianism and the Red Cross,' in O'Keeffe, *et al, Atlas of the Irish Civil War. New Perspectives,* p. 301.
18 Hegarty Thorne, Kathleen. *Echoes of their footsteps. The Irish Civil War 1922–1924* (Oregon, 2016), p. 211.
19 Ferriter, *Between Two Hells,* p. 111.

20 *Irish Independent*, 11 July 1923.
21 Brazil, 'Irish Civil War imprisonment, humanitarianism and the Red Cross' in O'Keeffe, *et al. Atlas of the Irish Civil War. New Perspectives*, p. 303.
22 Ní Chuilleanáin, Eiléan (ed). *'As I was among the captives', Joseph Campbell's Prison Diary 1922–1923* (Cork, 2001), p. 72.
23 *Irish Independent*, 13 June 1923.
24 *Ibid.*, 11 July 1922.
25 Owen Boyle, Military Pension Application, DP1131.
26 *Nationalist and Munster Advertiser*, 21 July 1923.
27 *Leinster Leader*, 2 August 1924; Noonan, Gerard. *The IRA in Britain, 1919–1923*. 'In the heart of enemy lines' (Liverpool, 2014), pp. 152–3.
28 *Drogheda Independent*, 26 September 1975. The Matthew Ginnity Perpetual Trophy was presented to the Meath GAA Board by former government minister, Michael Hilliard in 1975.
29 Peter Maher, Military Pension Application DP2920.
30 Daniel Downey, Military Pension Application DP1323. A application was made by his mother Rose Downey and his aunt Kate McGeeney.

Tintown Times
1 O'Malley & Ó Comhraí, *The men will talk to me. Galway interviews by Ernie O'Malley*, pp. 221, 243.
2 *Ibid.*, pp. 244, 250–1.
3 CW/P/11/01, Military Archives, Dublin.
4 O'Malley & Ó Comhraí, *The men will talk to me. Galway interviews by Ernie O'Malley*, pp. 185–6.
5 *Ibid.*, pp. 258–9.
6 Ní Chuilleanáin, *'As I was among the captives'*, pp. 1–5.
7 *Ibid.*, pp. 53–4.
8 *Ibid.*, p. 56; Irishgenealogy.ie.
9 MSP34REF21426 Pension Application, Military Archives, Dublin.
10 Deasy, Liam. *Brother against Brother* (Cork, 1982), p. 114; https://www.dib.ie/biography/deasy-liam-a2497 In 1924, Liam Deasy was court-martialled and expelled by the IRA for launching the appeal.
11 Ní Chuilleanáin, *'As I was among the captives'*, p. 62.
12 Shannon, Gerard. *Liam Lynch. To declare a Republic* (Newbridge, 2023), p. 277.
13 Andrews. C. S. *Dublin made me* (Cork, 1979), pp. 285, 294.
14 *Ibid.*, pp. 295–8.
15 *Freeman's Journal*, 16 April 1923.

16 *Cork Examiner,* 29 May 1923.

17 *Nationalist & Munster Advertiser,* 9 May 1923; *Freeman's Journal,* 19 May 1923. Michael McGrath had served in France with the Australian Army during the First World War.

18 *Leinster Leader,* 16 June 1923.

19 Letter from Tintown No. 1 Camp, 15 March 1924, CW/P/10/02, Military Archives, Dublin.

20 *Leinster Leader,* 4 August 1923.

21 *Freeman's Journal,* 3 August 1923. The Royal Assent was given because the position of the governor general, which represented the British crown in the Free State, was vacant at the time.

22 Campbell, Colm. *Emergency Law in Ireland 1918–1925* (Oxford, 1994), pp. 171–2.

23 www.irishstatutebook.ie

24 *Leinster Leader,* 4 August 1923.

25 *Ibid.,* 16 June 1923.

26 Military Pension Application DP6058.

27 *An Phoblacht,* 2 August 2023; Flynn, Barry. *Pawns in the game. Irish hunger strikes 1912–1981* (Cork, 2011), p.70.

28 *Freeman's Journal,* 28 October 1922; *Irish Independent,* 10 August 1923; irishgenealgy.ie. On his death certificate Whitty is recorded as being a 'released political prisoner'.

29 *The Nationalist* (Tipperary), 4 August 1923; https://civilrecords. irish genealogy.

30 'The Song of the Legion of the Rearguard. The Rallying-song of the Republic', The Emton Press, Dublin, 1924, copy in Kildare County Archive and Local Studies. The song was first sung in public on 9 December 1923 at the Four Martyrs' Anniversary Concert, Theatre Royal, Dublin, by Miss Molly Foley's Concert Party. It was published in print one year later and by 1927 it was adopted by the newly-formed Fianna Fáil party as their anthem.

31 *The Liberator,* 16 August 1923.

32 *Irish Independent,* 14 August 1923. Robert Barton was narrowly defeated, polling 4,218 votes, against Richard Wilson, Farmer's Party who received 4, 281.

33 Ó Beachain, Donnacha. *Destiny of the Soldiers. Fianna Fáil, Irish Republicanism and the IRA, 1926–1973* (Dublin, 2010), p. 25; Ferriter, *A nation not a rabble,* p. 292.

34 Yeates, *A City in Civil War,* pp. 263–4.

35 Ó Beachain, *Destiny of the Soldiers,* p. 25. A new Sinn Féin party had been only inaugurated in the Mansion House on 11 June 1923.

36 *Kilkenny People,* 1 September 2023; Tipperary Live, 30 August 2023.

37 *Tipperary Live*, 6 October 2023.

Hunger for Release
1 O'Halpin, Eunan. *Defending Ireland. The Irish State and its enemies since 1922* (Oxford, 1999), pp. 42–3.
2 Ó Longaigh, *Emergency law in independent Ireland*, p. 39. Nora Connolly-O'Brien was a daughter of executed 1916 leader James Connolly. She was subsequently released in August 1923 on a writ of *habeas corpus* on grounds that her arrest had been unlawful.
3 *Irish Times*, 21 November 1923. This was more than double the amount interned by the British in the War of Independence. Seosamh Ó Longaigh in *Emergency Law in independent Ireland* has a figure of 11,480 prisoners.
4 'Hidden away: the treatment of Civil War internees', by Anne-Marie McInerney. *RTÉ History*, 17 January 2023. In general, most counties saw an upsurge in violence and prisoners detained during the Civil War.
5 Ó Longaigh, *Emergency Law in independent Ireland*, p. 50. The Protective Corps was formed in Dublin to protect the houses and persons of ministers, deputies and government officials.
6 Yeates, *A City in Civil War*, p. 264.
7 O'Halpin, *Defending Ireland*, p. 43.
8 https://catalogue.nli.ie/Record/vtls000614159 Officers report from Tintown No. 2, 16 September 1923.
9 McCabe, M. P. *For God and Ireland. The fight for moral superiority in Ireland 1922–1932* (Dublin, 2013), p. 170.
10 *Sinn Féin*, 17 November 1923.
11 Hugh Kennedy was appointed as the first attorney-general for the Irish Free State in March 1923; *Evening Herald*, 21 August 1923; *Southern Star*, 25 August 1923; *Galway Advertiser*, 1 September 1923.
12 Letter from Dan Hurley to his mother, 23 September 1923, courtesy Cork Public Museum.
13 Yeates, *A City in Civil War*, p. 275.
14 McCabe, *For God and Ireland*, pp. 170–1.
15 Garvin, Tom. *1922: Birth of Irish Democracy*, pp. 135–6. Dan O'Donovan was a brother of escapee James L. Donovan, and later became secretary of the Department of Social Welfare.
16 *Ulster Herald*, 22 September 1923.
17 Ó Longaigh, *Emergency law in Independent Ireland*, p. 292.
18 O'Malley, *The Singing Flame*, p. 251. O'Malley had been severely wounded in a dramatic shoot-out at his Dublin hiding place in November 1922. Because of his wounds he was exempt from

the protest, but O'Malley refused this concession and joined the hunger strike.

19 Hopkinson, Michael. *The Irish War of Independence Dublin* (2004), p. 134.
20 Flynn, *Pawns in the game*, p. 72.
21 *Irish Times*, 17 October 1923.
22 'Civil War Hunger Strike', Joe Connell, https://www. kilmainhamtales.ie/civil-war-hunger-strike.php
23 Flynn, *Pawns in the game*, p. 73.
24 *Belfast Newsletter*, 22 October 1923.
25 *Sinn Féin*, 29 October 1923.
26 O'Malley & Horgan, *The men will talk to me. Kerry interviews by Ernie O'Malley*, p. 128. Comdt Patrick Paul Fitzgerald was from Tralee.
27 MSP34REF4061, Military Archives, Dublin.
28 Andrews, *Dublin made me*, p. 301.
29 Cullen, Seamus. *Kildare. The Irish revolution 1912–23* (Dublin, 2022), p. 133.
30 O'Malley & Ó Comhraí, *The men will talk to me. Galway interviews by Ernie O'Malley*, p. 184; Peter Joseph 'Petie' McDonnell, from Leennane, Co. Galway, was OC First Western Division.
31 Ferriter, *A nation not a rabble*, p. 286.
32 *Ibid*., p. 269. Chris 'Kit' Byrne (Dublin) was OC Tintown No. 1 Camp.
33 *Éire. The Irish Nation*, 3 & 5 November 1923.
34 *Irish Times*, 20 October 1923. Two days later the same committee announced that another 1,000 prisoners at Hare Park Camp had also joined the strike.
35 *Western People*, 3 November 1923.
36 *Ibid*.
37 *Éire. The Irish Nation*, 3 November 1923.
38 Stephen Keys, Witness Statement 1209, Bureau of Military History, Dublin. Keys was released at the end of spring 1924.
39 *Ballina Herald*, 21 June 1952.
40 Andrews, *Dublin made me*, p. 301. Jack Plunkett's brother, Joseph, had been executed in 1916 for his part in the Easter Rising.
41 McCabe, *For God and Ireland*, p. 184. 800 prisoners were released in the week ending 13 October.
42 *Belfast Newsletter*, 22 October 1923.
43 McCabe, *For God and Ireland*, p. 184.
44 Flynn, *Pawns in the game*, p. 74; *Sinn Féin*, 3 November 1923.
45 *Sinn Féin*, 26 October 1923. The source of these figures was from released prisoners according to the news sheet.

46 McCabe, *For God and Ireland*, p. 184.

47 Andrews, *Dublin made me*, p. 302.

48 Wayne Sugg, 'Post civil war hunger-strikes', *An Phoblacht/ Republican News*, 15 October 1998.

49 Hopkinson, *Green against Green*, p. 269.

50 *Ballina Herald*, 21, June 1952.

51 O'Shea, Owen. *No middle path. The Civil War in Kerry* (Newbridge, 2022), p. 155.

52 Ferriter, *Between Two Hells*, p. 115.

53 Kiely, Kevin. *Francis Stuart. Artist and outcast* (Dublin, 2007), pp. 53–4. Francis Stuart was born in Townsville, Australia, son of Ulster Protestants who had married in Ireland. Stuart's father committed suicide in a psychiatric institution when he was four months old, forcing the family to return to Ireland. While studying in Dublin Stuart met Iseult Gonne, daughter of Maud Gonne MacBride, which brought him into Dublin's literary and nationalist circles. Stuart subsequently eloped to London with Iseult in January 1920, when he was seventeen years old and she twenty-five. He converted to Catholicism for their marriage.

54 Stuart, Francis. *Things to live for. Notes for an Autobiography* (London, 1934), pp. 44–6.

55 *Ibid.*, pp. 47–9.

56 Ní Chuilleanáin, 'As I was among the captives', pp. 88–9.

57 Flynn, *Pawns in the game*, p. 75.

58 McCabe, *For God and Ireland*, p. 184.

59 Ní Chuilleanáin, 'As I was among the captives', pp. 103–4.

60 Stuart, *Things to live for*, p. 49.

61 *Freeman's Journal*, 31 October 1923.

62 *Irish Times*, 31 October 1923.

63 *Cork Examiner*, 29 October 1923.

64 Hopkinson, *Green against Green*, p. 269.

65 McCabe, *For God and Ireland*, p. 182.

66 Ní Chuilleanáin, 'As I was among the captives', p. 108.

67 *Kildare Observer*, 10 November 1923.

68 McCabe, *For God and Ireland*, p. 182.

69 O'Malley & Horgan, *The men will talk to me. Kerry interviews by Ernie O'Malley*, p. 231.

70 *Irish Independent*, 9 November 1923.

71 *Sinn Féin*, 17 November 1923.

72 Joseph Considine, Military Pension Application MSP34REF14702.

73 Flynn, *Pawns in the game*, p. 76.

74 Barry, *The Unknown Commandant*, p. 92.

75 *Evening Telegraph*, 20 November 1923.

76 *Freeman's Journal*, 23 November 1923.

77 *Nationalist and Leinster Times*, 24 November 1923.

78 McCabe, *For God and Ireland*, p. 182; *Nationalist and Leinster Times*, 24 November 1923.

79 *Cork Examiner*, 29 November 1923.

80 Hegarty, *Echoes of their footsteps*, p. 248.

81 *Sinn Féin*, 24 November 1923; Flynn, *Pawns in the game*, p. 77.

82 Flynn, *Pawns in the game*, pp. 83–4. The George V Military Hospital at Arbour Hill was renamed in 1922 in honour of St Bricin of Tomregan, because of his skill as a surgeon in seventh century Ireland.

83 https://www.dib.ie/biography/logue-michael-a4875; Ferriter, *Between Two Hells*, p. 116.

84 Héléne O'Keefe 'Freedom or the Grave: The mass hunger strike of October-November 1923,' in O'Keefe, *et al, Atlas of the Irish Civil War. New Perspectives,* p. 313; Archbishop Logue died the following year, aged eighty-four.

85 MacEvilly, Michael. *A splendid resistance. The life of I.R.A. Chief of Staff, D. Andy Cooney* (Dublin, 2011), p. 123. Cooney was born in Ballyphilip, Nenagh, Co. Tipperary, and joined the Irish Volunteers while studying medicine in University College Dublin. He was captured at the Four Courts, Dublin, in July 1922.

86 *Irish News,* 24 November 2023

87 *Irish Independent,* 23 November 1923.

88 *Ballina Herald,* 21 June 1952. Denis Sheerin recovered from his ordeal and was released from Tintown on 13 December 1923.

89 *Sinn Féin,* 1 December 1923.

90 Flynn, *Pawns in the game*, p. 84.

91 Ní Chuilleanáin, *As I was among the captives'*, pp. 111–2; Derrig and Robinson were members of the IRA Executive. Derrig was captured at Raglan Road, Dublin, in April 1923, and lost his left eye in an incident when fired on in Mountjoy Jail. He was later interned at the Curragh, where he conducted classes in Irish, commerce and economics for his fellow inmates. David L. Robinson was a former British army officer and cousin to Erskine Childers. He had been editing *An t-Óglách* along with Childers. In his diary Joseph Campbell mistakenly refers to David Robinson as Séamus Robinson.

92 McCabe, *For God and Ireland*, p. 184.

93 O'Malley, *The Singing Flame*, p. 262.

94 O'Donnell, *The Gates flew open*, p. 226.

95 McCabe, *For God and Ireland*, p. 184.

96 Andrews, *Dublin made me*, p. 296.

97 *Éire. The Irish Nation*, 22 December 1923.

98 Yeates, *A City in Civil War*, p. 265.

99 Hopkinson, *Green against Green*, pp. 271–2.

100 *Sinn Féin*, 15 December 1923.

101 Durney, *On the one road*, p. 138.

102 *Éire. The Irish Nation*, 26 January 1924.

103 *Cork Examiner*, 13 November 1924. Further information supplied by Mick Healy (Newbridge), 17 May 2016.

104 *Leinster Leader*, 1 December 1923 & 2 August 1924.

105 *The Liberator*, 17 November 1923.

106 *Freeman's Journal*, 3 December 1923. His death certificate recorded that he died from cardiac failure. https://civilrecords. irishgenealogy.ie/church records/images/deaths_returns/ deaths_1923/05046/4381372.pdf

107 https://www.irishgenealogy.ie/files/civil/deaths_returns/ deaths_1923/ 05046/4381372.pdf

108 *Leinster Leader*, 1 December 1923.

Murder Most Foul

1 *Wolfe Tone Annual*, 1962, 'Salute to the Soldiers of 1922,' p. 52.

2 Bolton, Albert D. (ed.) 'Attorney-General of the Irish Free State v. Murray', in *The Irish Reports* (Dublin, 1926), p. 270. Michael J. Costello, was the son of Republican activist Denis Costello of Kilmihill, Co. Clare, and Teresa Costello, who were both schoolteachers. His godfather was Thomas MacDonagh, whom his father succeeded in his teaching post. In 1920 when Denis Costello was arrested by the Black and Tans, Michael J., although only sixteen, immediately joined the IRA and became an intelligence officer for the North Tipperary Battalion. In 1922, he joined the National Army with the rank of lieutenant and in October 1923 was appointed director of army intelligence at GHQ, Parkgate Street, Dublin.

3 *Leinster Leader*, 10 & 17 January 1925; 25 July 1925; 29 July 1929.

4 *Ibid.*, p. 271; McLoughlin, Mark A. *Strength of Comradeship. The Milltown Murder. Private Joseph Bergin, December 1922* (Naas, 2022), p. 25.

5 *Ibid.*, pp. 26–7.

6 *Ibid.*, pp. 12, 30, 39.

7 *Ibid.*, pp. 26, 31.

8 *Ibid.*, pp. 16–8.

9 O'Malley & Ó Comhraí, *The men will talk to me. Galway interviews by Ernie O'Malley*, p. 241. Jack Twomey was friendly with Tomás Malone before the split in the Republican movement.

10 *Ibid.*, p. 247

11 Malone, Tom. *Alias Seán Forde. The story of Commandant Tomás Malone, Vice O.C East Limerick Flying Column, Irish Republican Army* (Dublin, 2000), p. 97.

12 *Evening Echo*, 30 August 1922.

13 Malone, *Alias Seán Forde,* p. 97.

14 Stephen Keys, Witness Statement 1209, Bureau of Military History, Dublin. Military Police were also called Póilíní Airm or PA, being the Irish for military police.

15 *Ibid.*

16 O'Malley & Keane, *The men will talk to me. Mayo interviews by Ernie O'Malley,* p. 301. Dan Sheehy later emigrated to NYC.

17 Aiken, *et. al, The men will talk to me. Ernie O'Malley's interviews with the Northern Divisions,* p. 173.

18 MSP34REF18912 Margaret Mary Daly, reference letter from Denis O'Neill, formerly of Kildare Town Company, IRA.

19 Obituary. Lt-Col Daniel McDonnell, *Irish Press,* 31 May 1972.

20 McLoughlin, *Strength of Comradeship,* pp. 35–6.

21 21 July 1925 letter, Bergin File_NAI_JUS_2007_15pdf.

22 *Ibid.*, 41, 64, 67, 70.

23 *Ibid.*, p. 71. David Neligan was Michael Collins 'Spy in the Castle' during the War of Independence. In the Civil War he was notoriously brutal to captured Republicans. Murray would have known Neligan from his time as an intelligence operative in Dublin.

24 Costello, Con. 'Justice or injustice? Looking Back, Series 726, *Leinster Leader,* 29 August 1996.

25 *Kildare Observer,* 13 June 1925.

26 *Evening Herald*, 12 June 1925. James Murray was a suspect in five killings, two during the War of Independence and three in the Civil War era.

27 Evans, *Seán Lemass*, pp. 27–8.

28 *Evening Herald*, 22 February 1927; 'Woe to his enemies: Joe McGrath and the scramble for power in a New Ireland, 1921–4', Daniel Murry, 1 September 2022. https://erinascendantwordpress.wordpress.com/. In February 1927 Joseph McGrath won £3,700 damages against Cyril H. Bretherton and his publishers, who withdrew the imputations unreservedly. This sum of money, according to some of his detractors, allowed McGrath to set up the hospital sweepstakes and become one of the new state's first original millionaires.

29 Horan, *Seán Lemass*, p. 27.

30 Ferriter, *A nation not a rabble,* p. 287.

31 Ronan McCreevey, 'Who killed Noel Lemass, the brother of former taoiseach Seán Lemass, in 1923?' *Irish Times,* 2 May

2023.

32 Evans, *Seán Lemass*, p. 26; *Belfast Newsletter*, 24 October 1923. However, at the inquest there was nothing to indicate that the body had been ever in the water.

33 *Nenagh Guardian*, 27 October 1923.

34 McLoughlin, *Strength of Comradeship*, pp, 75, 84, 86.

35 16 July 1925 letter, Bergin File_NAI_JUS_2007_15pdf.

36 Costello, 'Justice or injustice?'; McLoughlin, *Strength of Comradeship*, p. 76.

37 'Closing a Chapter,' *Irish Press*, 21 October 1986.

Hare Park. The Final Hurdle

1 O'Donnell, *The Gates flew open*, pp. 230–2. Donal Ó Driscoll records O'Donnell's arrival as December 1923.

2 O'Malley & Ó Comhraí, *The men will talk to me. Galway interviews by Ernie O'Malley*, pp. 99–100, 175.

3 *Ibid.*, p. 183.

4 *Ibid.*, pp. 178-80. Thomas 'Baby' Duggan was quartermaster of the Mid-Galway Brigade during the War of Independence and had been captured at Claregalway in October 1922; John Joseph 'Jack' Comer, Williamstown, Co. Galway, was the medical officer of the 3rd Southern Division when he was arrested in February 1923.

5 O'Malley & Keane, *The men will talk to me. Mayo interviews by Ernie O'Malley*, p. 262.

6 Ó Ruairc, Pádraig Óg. *The men will talk to me. Clare interviews by Ernie O'Malley* (Cork, 2016), p. 133. Paddy MacMahon was a former British soldier and First World War veteran and commandant 1st Battalion, Mid-Clare Brigade.

7 Bielenberg, *et. al. The men will talk to me. West Cork interviews by Ernie O'Malley*, pp. 145–7.

8 Copy of letter from Mick Sheehan, Hut 22, Hare Park Camp, 8 January 1924, held in County Kildare Archives & Local Studies, Naas.

9 O'Donnell, *The Gates flew open*, p. 236.

10 https://www.dib.ie/biography/mellows-herbert-charles-barney-a9951

11 O'Malley & Ó Comhraí, T*he men will talk to me. Galway interviews by Ernie O'Malley*, pp. 180–1.

12 Typed copies of intercepted letters, Kit Byrne, File: T2/13, Military Governor's Office, Tintown A Internment Camp, Correspondence Civil War Collection, Military Archives, Dublin.

13 Ó Longaigh, *Emergency Law in Independent Ireland*, p. 51.

14 *Belfast Newsletter,* 5 November 1923.

15 Ó Longaigh, *Emergency Law in Independent Ireland*, p. 51.

16 *Leinster Leader,* 17 November 1924; CW/P/0808, Military Archives, Dublin.

17 MS 42,236, Newbridge Barracks autograph book, courtesy of National Library of Ireland.

18 Ní Chuilleanáin, '*As I was among the captives*', p. 120.

19 Ward, *Maud Gonne,* p. 142.

20 *Irish Times,* 31 December 1923.

21 *Leinster Leader,* 12 January 1924. There were 5,494 prisoners still in cap- tivity on 1 December 1923.

22 *Ibid.,* 29 December 1923; Ó Longaigh, *Emergency Law in Independent Ireland,* p. 292.

23 *Fermanagh Herald,* 22 December 1923.

24 Letters to and from Curragh Command, 17 December 1923 & 1 January 1924, Civil War Collection ?

25 *Freeman's Journal,* 28 December 1923.

26 Andrews, *Dublin made me,* p. 303. The Plunkett brothers had been interned since the summer of 1922.

27 *Éire. The Irish Nation,* 26 January 1924.

28 Ó Longaigh, *Emergency Law in Independent Ireland*, p. 45.

29 *Ibid.,* p. 51.

30 *Leinster Leader,* 5 January 1924; *The Belfast Newsletter,* 31 January 1924.

31 Andrews, *Dublin made me,* p. 303.

32 *Leinster Leader,* 19 January 1924.

33 *Freeman's Journal,* 15 January 1924. At that time there were between 800–900 prisoners in Hare Park Camp.

34 www.irishstatutebook.ie

35 *Cork Examiner,* 24 March 1924.

36 O'Donnell, *The gates flew open,* p. 238.

37 Thorne, *Echoes of their footsteps,* p. 260.

38 Ó Drisceoil, Donal. *Peadar O'Donnell* (Cork, 2001), p. 36. The neighbour from the Rosses was a camp guard, and he willingly provided O'Donnell with the National Army topcoat and cap. O'Donnell never revealed the identity of his sympathetic guard. Following his escape, O'Donnell became editor of *An Phoblacht*, but later moved away from the Republican Movement, which he felt was too conservative. O'Donnell was involved in organising an Irish Brigade on the anti-fascist side in the Spanish Civil War. He was later editor of *The Bell,* the most significant literary magazine in Ireland from 1946 to 1954.

39 https://www.oireachtas.ie. After the collapse of the Farmers Party, Baxter ran for Cumann na Gaedheal, then the National

Centre Party, then Fine Gael and finally the National Agricultural Party.

40 Andrews, *Dublin made me*, p. 304.

41 O'Malley, *The Singing Flame*, pp. 272–3.

42 *Leinster Leader*, 3 & 10 May 1924.

43 *Kildare Observer*, 10 May 1924.

44 *Ibid.*, 10 May 1924; Yeates, *A City in Civil War*, pp. 264–5.

45 Letter from Hare Park Camp, dated 15 May 1923, CW/P/10/02, Military Archives, Dublin.

46 *Derry Journal*, 21 May 1924; O'Malley & Ó Comhraí, *The men will talk to me. Galway interviews by Ernie O'Malley*, pp. 180, 246, 249. After the formation of the first Fianna Fáil government in 1932 Michael Kilroy proposed Éamon de Valera as its president.

47 *Leinster Leader*, 14 June 1924.

48 *Ibid.*, 21 June 1924.

49 Philip McConway, 'The Civil War in Offaly', *The Midland Tribune*, 2 January 2008. The Free State was merciless with its own troops. Cpl Thomas Gibson, Bogtown Lane, Co. Offaly, was arrested with Frank and Tom Dunne on 10 January 1923. Court-martialled for desertion and treachery, Gibson was executed on 26 February 1923 at Maryborough Jail.

50 Ferriter, *Between Two Hells*, p. 117

51 O'Malley & Ó Comhraí, *The men will talk to me. Galway interviews by Ernie O'Malley*, pp .176–8. Feehan was OC of Hare Park Camp for the last month having replaced Seán MacGuill of Dundalk when he was released.

52 Ó Longaigh, *Emergency Law in Independent Ireland*, p. 52.

53 *Ibid.*, p. 290.

54 Martin, Harry F., & O'Malley, Cormac K. H. *Ernie O'Malley. A life.* (Newbridge, 2021), pp. 116–17, 120. O'Malley travelled throughout Europe, America and Mexico, mixing with people like Jack B. Yeats, Samuel Beckett and John Ford. He later wrote two biographical works on his revolutionary life, *On Another Man's Wound* and *The Singing Flame*.

55 *Derry Journal*, 18 July 1924.

56 *Leinster Leader*, 26 July 1924; Evening Herald, 15 August 1924.

57 Yeates, *A City in Civil War*, p. 314.

We have Kept the Faith

1 Kiely, *Stuart*, pp. 55–6.

2 https://www.dib.ie/biography/mac-grianna-seosamh-a5052

3 Aiken, *Spiritual Wounds*, p. 25.

4 John McCoy, Witness Statement 492, Bureau of Military History, Dublin.

5 *Kerry Reporter,* 18 October 1924.
6 https://www.dib.ie/biography/mcelligott-thomas-j-a5655;
    O'Duffy was appointed commissioner in September 1922 and
    intended that the new Irish police force would conform to his
    own national ideals in contrast to the semi-military RIC which
    it replaced and whose former members he was reluctant to
    recruit.
7 *Ibid.*, p. 318.
8 Research conducted on behalf of President Michael D. Higgins,
    Sep- tember 2015, by Karel Kiely, Mario Corrigan and James
    Durney, Kildare Co. Archives and Local Studies.
9 Ronan McCreevey, 'Stories of the Revolution: President relives
    painful struggle', *Irish Times,* 11 December 2015.
10 McCullagh, David. *De Valera, Vol. I, Rise 1882–1932*, p. 340.
11 Durney, *On the one road*, p. 135.
12 Campbell, *Emergency Law in Ireland*, pp. 110–1.
13 Dorney, *The Civil War in Dublin*, p. 194;
14 *Ibid.*, p. 243.
15 Neeson, *The civil war in Ireland*, p. 187.
16 Hopkinson, *Green against Green*, pp. 138–9.
17 Campbell, *Emergency law in Ireland,* p. 97.
18 *Ibid.*, p. 209.
19 Prendergast, Gareth. *Clear, Hold, Build. How the Free State won
    the Irish Civil War* (Dublin, 2025), p. 141.
20 O'Malley, *The Singing Flame*, p. 289.
21 O'Halpin, *Defending Ireland,* p. 44.

Sources/Bibliography

Primary

Autograph book from 'Newbridge Detention Camp, 1923', copy held in County Kildare Archives & Local Studies, donated by Mick and Pat Sheehan, Newbridge, 2007.

Family letters of Charlie O'Neill, courtesy of Dr Gerri O'Neill, Dublin City University, sourced 2 February 2023.

My interview with Dr Rory O'Hanlon, Carrickmacross, Co. Monaghan, 9 October 2024.

Civil War Collection: Files, CW/P/08/03; CW/P/08/08; CW/P/09/03; CW/P/10/01; CW/P/10/02; T2/13, Military Governor's Office, Tintown A Internment Camp, Correspondence; File AW/889. Court of Inquiry re Escape of Internees from Tintown Internment Camp, 1 May 1923, Military Archives, Cathal Brugha Barracks, Dublin.

MS 42,236, Newbridge Barracks autograph book, courtesy of National Library of Ireland, Dublin.

Military Pension Applications: John Bird, DP1049; Jim Boyle, MSP34REF7496; Daniel Downey, DP1323; Peter Maher, DP2920; Willie Malone, MSP34REF349; Thomas Reidy, MSP34REF17580, Military Archives, Cathal Brugha Barracks, Dublin.

Stephen Keys, Witness Statement 1209, John McCoy, Witness Statement 492, Bureau of Military History, Dublin.

Report from Rodolphe A. Haccius, Commission of the International Red Cross, regarding inspection of internment camp at Newbridge, County Kildare, 18 April 1923, National Library Ireland, Dublin.

Report from Rodolphe A. Haccius, Commission of International Red Cross, regarding inspection of internment camp at Tintown, 20 April 1923, National Library Ireland, Dublin.

Books

Aiken, Síobhra. *Spiritual Wounds. Trauma, testimony and the Irish Civil War.* Newbridge, 2022.

Aiken, Síobhra, Macbhloscaidh, Fearghal, Ó Duibhir, Liam, Ó Tuama, Diarmuid. *The men will talk to me. Ernie O'Malley's interviews with the Northern Divisions.* Newbridge, 2018.

Andrews. C. S. 'Todd'. *Dublin made me* (Cork, 1979)

Barry, Denis. *The Unknown Commandant. The life and times of Denis Barry 1883–1927.* Cork, 2010.

Bielenberg, Andy, Borgonovo, John & Ó Ruairc, Pádraig Óg. *The men will talk to me. West Cork interviews by Ernie O'Malley.* Cork, 2015.

Bord na Móna. *Peat Research Centre. From boot and saddle to biotechnology. On the Newbridge Barrack site.* Naas, 1998.

Campbell, Colm. *Emergency Law in Ireland 1918–1925.* Oxford, 1994.

Cardozo, Nancy. *Maud Gonne.* New York, 1990.

Corrigan, Mario. *Nine Lives Mooresbridge, December 1922.* Kildare, 2022.

Cullen, Seamus. *Kildare. The Irish Revolution 1912–23.* Dublin, 2022.

Cummins, Seamus A. *'Mullaney's Men.' The rise and fall of the anti-Treaty forces in North Kildare, Grangewilliam, 1922.* Naas, 2022.

Deasy, Liam. *Brother against Brother.* Cork, 1982.

Dorney, John. *The Civil War in Dublin. The fight for the Irish capital 1922–1924.* Newbridge, 2017.

Durney, James. *The Civil War in Kildare.* Cork, 2011.

—— *Stand you now for Ireland's cause. A biographical dictionary of Co. Kildare republican activists 1913–1923.* Naas, 2023.

Enright, Seán. *The Irish Civil War. Law, execution and atrocity.* Newbridge, 2019.

Evans, Bryce. *Seán Lemass. Democratic Dictator.* Cork, 2011.

Farrell, Brian. *Seán Lemass.* Dublin, 1991.

Ferriter, Diarmaid, *A nation not a rabble. The Irish Revolution 1913–1923.* London, 2015.

—— *Between Two Hells. The Irish Civil War.* London, 2021.

Fewer, Michael. *The Battle of the Four Courts. The first three days of the Irish Civil War.* London, 2018.

Flynn, Barry. *Pawns in the game. Irish hunger strikes 1912–1981.* Cork, 2011.

Garvin, Tom. *1922: Birth of Irish Democracy.* Dublin, 1996.

Thorne, Kathleen Hegarty. *Echoes of Their Footsteps, The Irish Civil War 1922–1924.* Newberg, Oregon, 2014.

—— *They put the Flag a-flyin'. The Roscommon Volunteers 1916-1923.* Newberg, Oregan, 2007.

Hopkinson, Michael. *The Irish War of Independence.* Dublin, 2004.

—— *Green against green. The Irish Civil War.* Dublin, 2004.

Horgan, John. *Seán Lemass. The enigmatic patriot.* Dublin, 1997.

Joyce, P. W. *The Geography of the Counties of Ireland.* London, 1883.

Kiely, Karel. *Rebel Hearts. A biographical list of republican women activists in Co. Kildare 1913–1923.* Naas, 2023.

Kiely, Kevin. *Francis Stuart. Artist and outcast.* Dublin, 2007.

Knipe, Gregory. *The Fourth Northerners and the Irish Revolution.* Wexford, 2020.

Lawlor, Chris. *Robert Barton. A remarkable revolutionary.* Gloucestershire, 2024.

Linklater, Andro. *An unhusbanded life. Charlotte Despard. Suffragette, Socialist and Sinn Féiner.* London, 1980.

MacEvilly, Michael. *A splendid resistance. The life of I.R.A. Chief of Staff, Dr. Andy Cooney.* Dublin, 2011.

Malone, Tom. *Alias Seán Forde. The story of Commandant Tomás Malone, Vice O.C. East Limerick Flying Column, Irish Republican Army.* Dublin, 2000.

Martin, Harry F, & O'Malley, Cormac K. H. *Ernie O'Malley. A life.* Newbridge, 2021.

Mathews, Arthur. *Walled in by Hate. Kevin O'Higgins, his friends and enemies.* Newbridge, 2024.

McCabe, M. P. *For God and Ireland. The fight for moral superiority in Ireland 1922–1932.* Dublin, 2013.

McCullagh, David. *De Valera, Vol. I, Rise 1882–1932.* Dublin, 2017.

McLaughlin, Mark A. *Strength of comradeship – The Milltown murder. Private Joseph Bergin – 14 December 1923.* Naas, 2023.

Ní Chuilleanáin, Eiléan (ed). *'As I was among the captives.' Joseph Campbell's Prison Diary 1922–1923.* Cork, 2001.

Noonan, Gerard. *The IRA in Britain, 1919–1923. 'In the heart of enemy lines.'* Liverpool, 2014.

Ó Beachain, Donnacha. *Destiny of the Soldiers. Fianna Fáil, Irish Republicanism and the IRA, 1926–1973.* Dublin, 2010.

O'Donnell, Peadar. *And the gates flew open.* London, 1932.

Ó Drisceoil, Donal. *Peadar O'Donnell.* Cork, 2001.

Ó Duibhir, Liam. *Donegal and the Civil War. The untold story.* Cork, 2011.

O'Halpin, Eunan. *Defending Ireland. The Irish State and its enemies since 1922.* Oxford, 1999.

O'Hanlon, Paddy. *End of Term Report.* Armagh, 2011.

O'Keefe, Hélène, Crowley, John, Ó Drisceoil Donal, Borgonovo, John & Murphy, Mike (eds.) *Atlas of the Irish Civil War. New Perspectives.* Cork, 2024.

Ó Longaigh, Seosamh. *Emergency Law in Independent Ireland, 1922–1948.* Dublin, 2006.

O'Malley, Cormac K. H. & Ó Comhraí, Cormac. *The men will talk to me. Galway interviews by Ernie O'Malley.* Cork, 2013.

O'Malley, Cormac K. H. & Horgan, Tim. *The men will talk to me. Kerry interviews by Ernie O'Malley.* Cork, 2012.

O'Malley, Cormac K. H. & Keane, Vincent. *The men will talk to me. Mayo interviews by Ernie O'Malley.* Cork, 2014.

O'Malley, Ernie. *The Singing Flame.* Dublin, 1978.

Ó Ruairc, Pádraig Óg. *The men will talk to me. Clare interviews by Ernie*

O'Malley. Cork, 2016.

O'Shea, Owen. *No middle path. The Civil War in Kerry.* Newbridge, 2022.

Prendergast, Gareth. *Clear, Hold, Build. How the Free State won the Irish Civil War.* Dublin, 2025.

Ring, Jim. *Erskine Childers.* London, 1996.

Share, Bernard. *In time of Civil War. The conflict on the Irish railways 1922–23.* Cork, 2006.

Ward, Margaret. *Maud Gonne. Ireland's Joan of Arc.* London, 1990.

Yeates, Pádraic. *A City in Civil War. Dublin 1921–4.* Dublin, 2015.

Essays, articles

Albert D. Bolton, 'Attorney-General of the Irish Free State v. Murray', in *The Irish Reports.* Dublin, 1926.

Lia Brazil, 'Irish Civil War imprisonment, humanitarianism and the Red Cross', in O'Keeffe, H., Crowley, J., Ó Drisceoil, D., Borgonovo, J. & Murphy, M., (eds.) *Atlas of the Irish Civil War, New Perspectives.* Cork, 2024.

Hugh Crawford, 'The internment camps' in *The Curragh Revisited.* Curragh Local History Group, 2002.

John Dorney, 'The Irish Story. Executions during the Civil War'. https://www.theirishstory.com/2022/11/17/executions-during-the-irish-civil-war/

'Mayo men feature in famous I.R.A. escape from the Curragh Camp', *The Mayo News,* 24 & 31 January 1959.

Mattie Lennon, 'How a Donegal Rebel Died in Wicklow' https://www.facebook.com/Lifford1916committee

See some more Mercier Press Civil War Books at

https://www.mercierpress.ie/shop

INDEX

Derry 40, 72, 75, 109, 114, 201,
    202
Despard, Charlotte 21, 105, 106,
    180
de Valera, Éamon 23, 56, 118,
    123, 200
Dodd, Justice William Huston
    129
Doherty, Pte Michael James 114
Donegal 36, 39, 72, 110, 114,
    175, 187, 192, 202
Donnelly, Fr 69
Donnelly, Jimmy 77
Donovan, James 190
Dooley, Jeremiah 32, 206
Dooley, John 173
Douglas, James 93
Dowling, John 203
Dowling, Patrick 201
Down 29, 165
Downey, Daniel 111, 120
Downey, Joseph 207
Doyle, Dr 146
Doyle, Fr P. 150
Doyle, Joseph 86
Driver, Frank 31
Drogheda 15, 28
Dublin 11, 12, 13, 14, 15, 16, 17,
    18, 22, 23, 25, 26, 27, 28,
    29, 30, 32, 33, 37, 39, 41,
    42, 43, 45, 46, 47, 51, 52,
    54, 57, 58, 60, 66, 68, 69,
    72, 73, 76, 85, 89, 92, 93,
    96, 98, 100, 105, 106, 108,
    109, 113, 117, 123, 124,
    126, 129, 138, 141, 149,
    160, 161, 162, 164, 167,
    168, 171, 172, 177, 179,
    180, 181, 183, 184, 185,
    187, 188, 190, 191, 194,
    202, 206, 209
Dublin Castle 11, 190
Duffy, George Gavan 17, 104
Duggan, Thomas 'Baby' 176

Dunboyne 89
Dundalk 28, 32, 46, 48, 63, 70,
    87, 89, 111, 127, 131, 153,
    166, 179
Dundalk Jail 28, 32, 46, 48, 70,
    87, 89, 131, 153
Dunne, Fr 113
Dunne, Frank 188
Dunne, Peter 203
Dunne, Reginald 13
Dunne, Tom 188
Dunphy, Patrick 207
Dwyer, Patrick 205
Dwyer, Thomas 205

E

Easter 1916 Rising 28, 30, 42,
    177, 192
Eastern Division, 1st 15, 34
East Limerick Brigade 76, 115,
    163
East Mayo Brigade 55, 165
Egan, Dan 207
Ellison, Capt. C. 88
Emergency Act 57
Emergency Powers Act 121
Emergency Powers Bill 24, 182
Enniscorthy 47
Enright, Éamon 95
Escapes 19, 27, 33, 36, 37, 38,
    39, 40, 41, 42, 44, 45, 46,
    49, 54, 55, 64, 65, 66, 70,
    72, 74, 75, 76, 78, 80, 83,
    85, 86, 90, 91, 95, 116,
    153, 156, 163, 164, 165,
    166, 181, 187, 188, 198
Executions 9, 15, 24, 49, 50, 56,
    57, 67, 68, 69, 70, 71, 87,
    115, 124, 125, 133, 151,
    170, 177, 188, 198, 199,
    200

F

G

H

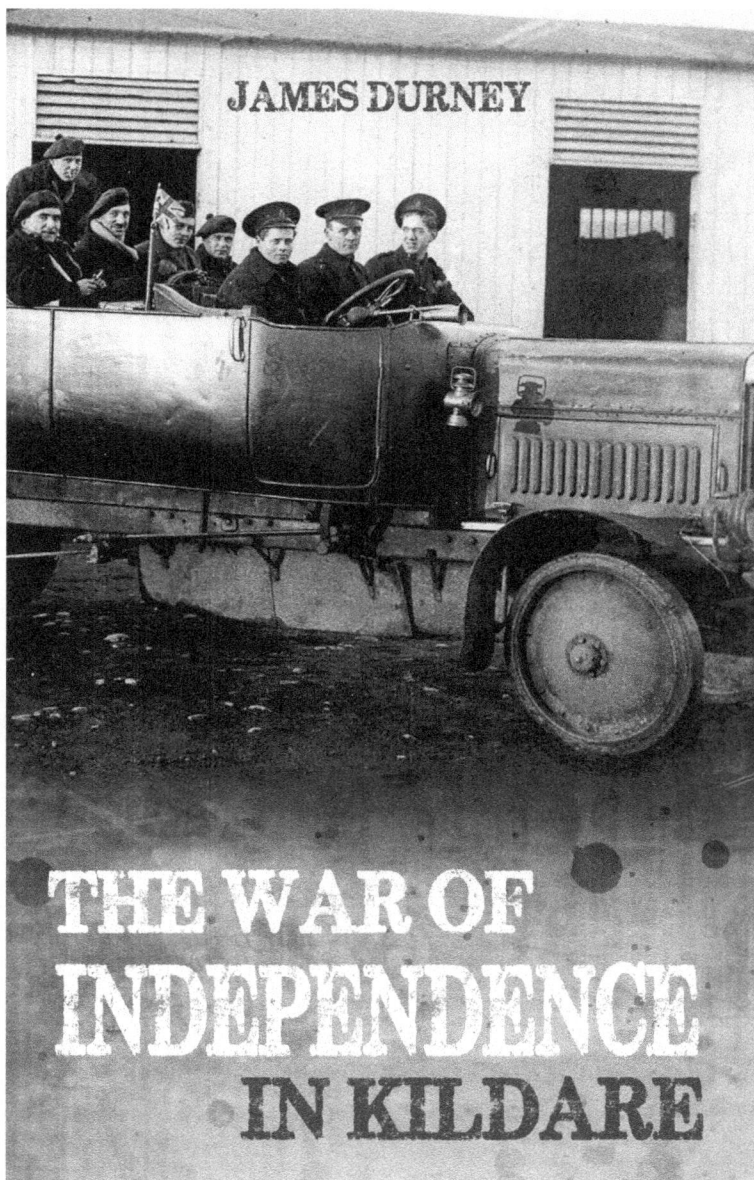

JAMES DURNEY

THE WAR OF
INDEPENDENCE
IN KILDARE

INTERNED

The Curragh Internment Camps in the War of Independence

James Durney

THE
JAMES DURNEY
CIVIL WAR
IN KILDARE

www.ingramcontent.com/pod-product-compliance
Lightning Source LLC
Chambersburg PA
CBHW021221090426
42740CB00006B/325